新概念研究生英语读写教程

（财经类非英语专业）

主　审　梁为祥

主　编　肖　辉

副主编　孙勇彬　　叶卫华

参　编　陈芙蓉　　邵　怡　　王海盟
　　　　刘婷婷　　左　敏

东南大学出版社

·南京·

内 容 提 要

　　本书是紧扣"硕士研究生英语教学大纲",贴近财经类各专业而设计编写,实用性较强。

　　练习设计充分体现培养学生理解能力的理念,其内容有:回答问题、释义、根据课文中的信息选词或短语、句子、选短语或词组完成句子、翻译、写作及阅读等。通过练习的训练,不仅可以更好地消化课文,而且还可以学到更多的专业知识,从而更好地提高实际运用能力。

图书在版编目(C I P)数据

新概念研究生英语读写教程 / 肖辉主编. —南京:
东南大学出版社,2011.6
ISBN 978 - 7 - 5641 - 2812 - 8

Ⅰ.①新…　Ⅱ.①肖…　Ⅲ.①英语－阅读教学－研究
生－教材②英语－写作－研究生－教材　Ⅳ.①H31

中国版本图书馆 CIP 数据核字(2011)第 107450 号

东南大学出版社出版发行
(南京四牌楼2号　邮编210096)
出版人:江建中
江苏省新华书店经销　南京雄州印刷有限公司印刷
开本:787 mm×1092 mm　1/16　印张:11.5　字数:280 千字
2011 年 6 月第 1 版　2011 年 6 月第 1 次印刷
ISBN　978 - 7 - 5641 - 2812 - 8
定价:28.00 元

前　　言

1978 年我国恢复研究生招生制度,1983 年,教育部颁发了《研究生外国语学习考试规定》(试行),统一了研究生入学考试标准及教学大纲。规定中指出"着重培养学生以阅读为主,正确理解、熟练运用外国语的实际能力"。研究生英语课程设置体系初步建立。1992年,国家教委颁布了《研究生英语教学大纲》,提出"硕士生英语教学的目的是培养学生具有较熟练的阅读能力,一定的写、译能力和基本的听、说能力,能够以英语为工具进行本专业的学习和研究"。研究生课程设置体系至此比较完整地形成。随着我国经济的发展、用人单位对非英语专业研究生英语应用能力提出越来越高的要求。

英语教育与国家的对外政策和经济建设息息相关。不同时期、不同背景下的英语教育目的和宗旨是不一样的。在新中国成立后的很长一段时期内,英语教育的目的是培养具有外语"听、说、读、写、译"语言技能的工具型人才。改革开放以来,随着对外交往的增多,特别是对外经贸的发展,培养"财经类非英语专业研究生英语应用型人才"成了财经类院校非英语专业研究生英语教育的一个重要任务。

我们应当看到,新世纪为我国财经类院校非英语专业研究生英语教育带来机遇的同时也提出了挑战,有改革才有出路,有改革才有进步,只有打破那种培养"纯英语人才"的传统的教学模式,更新教育观念,把英语知识与所学专业知识紧密结合起来,才能培养出适应社会需求的复合型英语人才,才能培养出受社会欢迎,有特色,高素质的创新型、实用型英语人才。只有这样,我们才能紧跟时代。作为财经类非英语专业研究生英语课程改革与建设的一部分,我们编写了这本《新概念研究生英语读写教程》。

本书共分 10 个单元,每一单元包括与财经类知识密切相关的课文,课文后附有词汇学习和表达。围绕课文,在老师的引导下进行各种形式的练习以便充分巩固课堂所学的知识。课文练习包括根据课文回答下列问题、解释难句和语言点、运用课文中的信息选择最佳词或词组来解释课文句子中下划线的意思、从下列课文单词中选择最佳词组或表达填空,必要时可改变词形、将下列句子翻译成英文、将下列段落翻译成中文。另外还介绍了不同类型的写作,之后还配有一篇阅读材料,学生们可根据阅读材料回答问题以检测自己的阅读理解能力。

本教材可以作为财经类高校非英语专业研究生读、写教材,也可以作为非财经类高校非英语专业研究生为了拓展知识的补充性读物。各学校也可以根据情况选择一部分内容作为学期或阶段目标强化使用。

本教材由东南大学外国语学院梁为祥教授担任主审、南京财经大学外国语学院肖辉教授担任主编、孙勇彬教授担任副主编。参编的有陈芙蓉、邵怡、王海盟、刘婷婷、左敏。在编写过程中还得到李俊儒、胡美珠同志的关心和支持,在此表示感谢。

由于编者水平有限,疏漏之处在所难免。敬请批评指正。

Contents

Think Big to Save the Bigger Banks

One thing we have learnt in the past year is that some banks are definitely too big to fail. We may yet discover something even more disturbing: that some are too big to save.

Tim Geithner, the US Treasury Secretary, who has staged something of a reputational recovery this week—helped by the fickle stock market—will this morning testify to Congress on his plans for reforming regulation and gaining more power to wind up insolvent financial institutions.

Mr Geithner has intelligent things to say about how the Treasury and the Federal Reserve could have done a better job of letting Lehman Brothers go down gracefully, and saving American International Group without having to stick to bonus contracts. He wants the US government to be able to seize control of such institutions when spending public money.

The fact that it could not—that it had to lend $85bn to AIG to keep it afloat last September rather than take over the insurance group, and was unable to deal properly with Lehman Brothers—is one reason why he has been in trouble with Congress.

But here is a disconcerting thought. What if the US government, with its balance sheet and its reserve-currency dollar, gained the powers that Mr Geithner and Ben Bernanke, chairman of the Federal Reserve, seek? Would that be enough to guarantee that it could resolve the next AIG-style crisis? Unfortunately not.

This crisis, with its discoveries that the UK arm of Lehman Brothers was beyond the reach of the Fed, and that AIG booked many credit derivatives trades through a London-based French banking subsidiary, showed that such institutions have outgrown the US. They not only have many foreign subsidiaries; they have woven a global web of financial contracts.

That makes it very hard to take control of them, even if American taxpayers were sanguine about their money being used to pay off foreign counterparties, which their politicians are not. Nationalisation may not be enough to corral them; it would require internationalisation.

The fact that there is, in this sense, no such notion as internationalisation is the problem. No cross-border body exists with the authority or resources to take over a global financial institution, wind it down safely and divide the bill fairly among taxpayers of many countries.

The "resolution authority" Mr Geithner and Mr Bernanke have teamed up to obtain is modelled on the Federal Deposit Insurance Corporation, the agency that winds up insolvent banks in the US. The FDIC has extensive powers to seize banks, turf out their managers, hand over the assets and liabilities to other banks and absorb any losses.

It did that last week, for example, with Colorado National Bank of Colorado Springs, whose $83m in deposits and four branches were forcibly handed over to Herring Bank of Amarillo, Texas. The FDIC will pay 80 per cent of losses—some $9m—out of its insurance fund, to which US banks all pay levies.

This kind of approach would be a great deal better than the desperate improvisation we witnessed last autumn. Investment banks could be prevented from going into Chapter 11 bankruptcy without having to accept all of their liabilities.

As Mr Bernanke pointed out to a House committee on Tuesday, it would allow the government to rip up obnoxious contracts, such as AIG's guaranteed retention bonuses, and impose some losses on creditors and counterparties, such as holders of AIG's credit default swaps.

But resolution authority may not be sufficient. The Colorado National Banks of the world are conveniently small and self-contained, with a ready buyer to hand once losses are solved. Lehman and AIG, however, were not tiny domestic outfits Take Lehman. On September 15, when its holding company went into Chapter 11 bankruptcy, the New York Fed, under Mr Geithner, tried to keep its investment banking arm going so that it could be wound down in an orderly way. The Fed failed, for reasons that are instructive.

Although the Fed propped up the US broker-dealer operations, it found that it could not effectively fund the UK arm, which had depended on the bankrupt holding company for cash. It also faced obstacles in dealing with the German banking subsidiary, Lehman Bankhaus.

Resolution authority would have helped, since the government could have—and presumably would in any future case of a Wall Street collapse—stood behind the holding company and backed the foreign subsidiaries through it. That would not, however, guarantee that it could catch all of the overseas entities through which such institutions trade.

Even if it could, there is a political problem. Congressional unrest is growing over the fact that the US government paid off Lehman's CDS counterparties, including foreign banks led by Société Générale and Deutsche Bank, at par. It was being a good global citizen, but that does not earn you points on Capitol Hill.

If you seek to limit global financial risk, it is sensible not to make any distinction between counterparties on the grounds of nationality. Try telling that, however, to taxpayers who must contribute billions of dollars.

A theoretical solution would be to have a global financial authority, with powers akin to the International Monetary Fund, that could salvage a global institution and apportion the costs appropriately. That, however, is not politically achievable, even if it would work in practice.

Perhaps another way can be found to split the bill when one country pays to prop up another's banks. I am not holding my breath but without it no government can be sure, however enormous its domestic powers, of solving the next AIG.

Nationalisation Is Not a Panacea

In mid-September, as the credit crisis swirled around Wall Street, I wrote a column recommending that Hank Paulson, the former US Treasury secretary, refrain from bailing out Lehman Brothers. He did indeed let the investment bank go under, and the rest is history.

Looking back, I still think Lehman should have been allowed to fail, but I was wrong not to grasp that it had to be done in an orderly way. Once the chances of a private sector takeover were exhausted, intervention was required to prevent chaos. Now we are back where we started, this time with large commercial banks instead of Wall Street brokers.

Both the UK and US governments face pressure not merely to bail out these banks, which they have already attempted, but to nationalise them. This episode of nerves broke out after investors were told by Royal Bank of Scotland on Monday that it faces a £28bn ($ 40bn) loss for 2008.

Share prices in UK high street banks have fallen so sharply—leaving RBS with a market capitalisation of about £4bn and Barclays worth £6bn—that some financiers and politicians are calling for the UK government to end the uncertainty and take them into public ownership.

There have been similar calls in the US, after Citigroup and Bank of America disclosed big write-downs and large banks including State Street appeared not to have enough equity to ride out a big recession. It is now extremely hard for such institutions to raise common equity, which is what they need, on stock markets or by private placement.

Unlike in the Lehman case, I do not think governments should allow big banks that are cornerstones of their economies to go under. If the UK government has to follow the example of the Irish government in the case of Anglo Irish Bank and take over at least one big bank, so be it.

But I do not believe any country should be eager to nationalise its banks, except *in extremis.*

My argument for letting Lehman go was that the US government, if it kept stepping into rescue investment banks, would strain its finances and could face currency weakness.

In fact, those problems struck home most painfully in the UK. Gordon Brown, the prime minister, won plaudits from the world in October for intervening more radically and expensively than the US to bail out banks. Three months later, Mr Brown faces the triple threat of a banking, currency and fiscal crisis.

The lesson is that, while dramatic interventions are satisfying at the time, they do not necessarily solve matters. Nationalisation could be needed, but it is not a panacea.

There are arguments for it, beyond the moral hazard point that it hurts shareholders for allowing dangerous risk-taking. Some were advanced by Willem Buiter on his FT.com blog last week and by John McFall and Jon Moulton on this page on Tuesday.

Probably the best is that it provides clear backing for financial institutions that struggling economies depend on to keep lending. There is a danger that privately owned banks with weak balance sheets "have enough capital to stay on their feet and stumble around a bit" but are afraid of doing the job, as Professor Buiter put it.

Furthermore, if a government thinks it will eventually have to nationalise, there are merits in getting on with it. Japan took until 1998 to inject public funds into its banks during its 1990s crisis, while Sweden achieved more by briskly insisting on banks writing off their equity and recapitalising them.

The fact remains that governments are bad owners for banks, as anyone who has followed the history of Germany's regional state-owned banks can attest. They are heavily conflicted because, although politicians like to castigate bankers for risk-taking, they also push them to lend freely in order to make the voters happy.

More specifically, the costs of a full public recapitalisation of banks in the US or UK, in addition to the public ring-fencing of their troubled assets into state-controlled "bad banks", would be enormous.

This is particularly true of the US, which cannot just acquire a few large banks, like the UK or Sweden, and be satisfied that it has dealt with most of the banking market.

New Words and Expressions

fickle [ˈfikl] **adj.** (of moods, the weather, etc) often changing; not constant(指心情,天气等)常变的;多变的

testify [ˈtestifai] **vi.** give evidence 作证;提供证据

insolvent [inˈsɔlvənt] **adj.** unable to pay debts; bankrupt 无力还债的;破产的

derivative [diˈrivətiv] **n.** (thing, word, substance) derived from another; not original or primitive 由他物而来的物质或物件;衍生物

sanguine [ˈsæŋgwin] **adj.** hopeful; optimistic 有望的;乐天的

counterparty [ˈkauntəˌpɑːti] **n.** person or thing exactly like, or closely corresponding to, another 互相对立的人或物

corral [kɔːˈrɑːl] **vt.** control 控制

notion [ˈnəuʃən] **n.** idea; opinion 观念;意见

liabilities [ˌlaiəˈbilitis] **n.** (pl) debts; sums of money that must be paid (contrasted with assets) (复)债务;负债 (与 assets 相对)

improvisation [ˌimprəvaiˈzeiʃən] **n.** act of doing sth quickly, in time of need 临时准备

obnoxious [ɔbˈnɔkʃəs] **adj.** nasty; very disagreeable 可憎的;非常讨厌的

retention [riˈtenʃən] **n.** act of keeping or continuing to have or hold 保持;保留

outfit [ˈautfit] **n.** agency 机构

salvage [ˈsælvidʒ] **vt.** save from loss, fire, wreck, etc. 抢救;救援

apportion [əˈpɔːʃən] **vt.** divide; distribute; give as a share 分;分配

swirl [swəːl] **vi.** (of water, air, etc) (cause to) move or flow at varying speeds, with twists and turns (指水、空气等)(使)起漩流;(使)涡旋而动

intervention [ˌintəˈvenʃən] **n.** act of interference so as to prevent sth or change the result 干涉;阻挠;调停

episode [ˈepisəud] **n.** (description of) one event in a chain of events 一连串事件中的一个事件;插曲

recession [riˈseʃən] **n.** slackening of business and industrial activity 工商业之衰退;不景气

equity [ˈekwəti] **n.** (often pl) ordinary stocks and shares not bearing fixed interest (常用复数)无固定利息的股票

plaudit [ˈplɔːdit] **n.** (usu pl) cry, clapping or other sign of approval (通常用复数) 喝彩;鼓掌;称赞

attest [əˈtest] **vt.**, **vi.** be or give clear proof of 证明;是……的明证

castigate [ˈkæstigeit] **vt.** punish severely with blows or by criticizing 严惩;苛评

Exercises

Ⅰ. **Answer the following questions.**

1. Why Mr. Geithner has been in trouble with Congress?

2. What is the sensible way to limit global financial risk?

3. What was the author's argument for letting Lehman go?

4. What is the theoretical solution to limit global financial risk?

5. What is the lesson that the author has learned from nationalisation?

Ⅱ. **Paraphrase the difficult sentences or language points.**

1. One thing we have learnt in the past year is that some banks are definitely too big to fail.

2. That makes it very hard to take control of them, even if American taxpayers were sanguine about their money being used to pay off foreign counterparties, which their politicians are not.

3. If you seek to limit global financial risk, it is sensible not to make any distinction between counterparties on the grounds of nationality.

4. Nationalisation is not a panacea.

5. Once the chances of a private sector takeover were exhausted, intervention was required to prevent chaos.

Ⅲ. **Choose the word or phrase that best explains the meaning of the underlined part from the text.**

1. One thing we have learnt in the past year is that some banks are definitely <u>too big to fail.</u>

   A. The banks are very big and they will fail.

   B. The banks are very big but they can't fail.

   C. The banks are so big that they will fail.

2. The fact that it could not—that it had to lend $85bn to AIG to <u>keep it afloat</u> last September rather than take over the insurance group…

   A. …to let AIG floating

   B. …to let AIG awash

   C. …to let AIG start business

3. Nationalisation may not be enough to <u>corral</u> them; it would require internationalisation.

   A. to control   B. to confine   C. to count

4. …<u>it is sensible not to</u> make any distinction between counterparties on the grounds of nationality.

   A. …it is sensitive to not…

   B. …it is wise not to…

   C. …it is not sensory to…

5. Nationalisation is not a <u>panacea</u>.

   A. method   B. remedy for all troubles   C. panache

6. The fact remains that governments are bad owners for banks, as anyone who has followed the history of Germany's regional state-owned banks can <u>attest</u>.

   A. to give proof   B. to arrest   C. to test

7. That makes it very hard to take control of them, even if American taxpayers <u>were sanguine about</u> their money being used to …

　　A. …, even if American taxpayers were worried about …

　　B. …, even if American taxpayers were optimistic about …

　　C. …, even if American taxpayers were fearful about …

8. This crisis, with its discoveries that the UK arm of Lehman Brothers <u>was beyond the reach of</u> the Fed, …

　　A. This crisis, with its discoveries that the UK arm of Lehman Brothers was beside the Fed, …

　　B. This crisis, with its discoveries that the UK arm of Lehman Brothers was out of control of the Fed, …

　　C. This crisis, with its discoveries that the UK arm of Lehman Brothers was with in the reach of the Fed, …

9. Once the chances of a private sector takeover <u>were exhausted</u>, intervention was required to prevent chaos.

　　A. Once there were chances of a private sector take over, …

　　B. Once there would be chances of a private sector take over, …

　　C. Once there was no chance of a private sector take over, …

10. Both the UK and US governments face pressure not merely to <u>bail out</u> these banks, …

　　A. … to help these banks out of difficulties, …

　　B. … to bush out these banks, …

　　C. … to watch out these banks, …

Ⅳ. Choose the best phrase or expression in the text from the following list to fit in each of the following blanks. Change the word form where necessary.

---

wind up, take over, impose on, akin to, bail out, go under, write off, come up with, all in all, complete with

---

1. _____ , this is a well-scheduled party.

2. The man has _____ a debt recently.

3. Big industries, the cornerstones of the country's economy, should not be allowed to _____ in the financial crisis.

4. The company has been asked to _____ its insolvent financial accounts by the bank.

5. The author recommended the US Treasury secretary refrain from _____ Lehman Brothers.

6. The local insurance company _____ by the foreign counterpart three months ago.

7. Don't _____ yourself _____ people who don't want to work with you.

8. That would be true if the entire global banking system, _____ all stocks and securities, were nationalised.

9. Pity is often _____ love.

10. The committee _____ a satisfactory solution to the complex situation.

Ⅴ. Translate the following into English.

1. 这加大了控制它们的难度，即便美国纳税人对于他们的钱正被用于偿还外国人的债务持乐观态度——但他们的政府并不这么认为。国有化可能不足以控制它们；我们需要国际化。

2. 如果你试图控制全球金融风险，那么明智的做法就是，不要按国别来区分对手方。不过，你要试着告诉那些必须贡献数十亿美元的纳税人这点。

3. 我们得到的教训是，尽管引人瞩目的干预在当时是令人满意的，但它们不一定能解决问题。国有化可能是需要的，但它不是万能药。

4. 拥有权力或财力，能够接管一家全球性金融机构，让其安全破产，并且在诸多国家的纳税人中间公平分配账单的跨境机构，并不存在。

5. 联邦存款保险公司拥有广泛的权力来接管银行，驱逐它们的管理者，把资产和债务移交给其他银行并承担任何亏损。

6. 美国联邦存款保险公司将会动用其保险基金，偿还 Colorado National Bank 80% 的亏损——约 900 万美元。美国所有的银行都会向这只基金缴纳保费。

7. 尽管纽约联邦储备银行为这家美国经纪公司的业务提供了支持，但它却发现事实上自己无法向这家公司的英国分公司提供融资。

8. 美国政府扮演了全球良好公民的角色，但这不会为它在国会加分。

9. 当某个国家掏钱援助另一个国家的银行时，或许可以找到另一种方法来分担这笔账单。

10. 美英政府现在所面临的压力都不仅仅是纾困这些银行（它们已经尝试过），而是对它们实施国有化。

Ⅵ. Translate the following into Chinese.

1. Mr Geithner has intelligent things to say about how the Treasury and the Federal Reserve could have done a better job of letting Lehman Brothers go down gracefully, and saving American International Group without having to stick to bonus contracts. He wants the US government to be able to seize control of such institutions when spending public money.

2. This crisis, with its discoveries that the UK arm of Lehman Brothers was beyond the reach of the Fed, and that AIG booked many credit derivatives trades through a London-based French banking subsidary, showed that such institutions have outgrown the US. They not only have many foreign subsidiaries; they have woven a global web of financial contracts.

Writing

Business Letter

Directions: A business letter is a formal means of communication between two people, a person and a corporation, or two corporations.

THE 7 C's OF BUSINESS WRITING

The seven C's are:

Clear

Concise

Correct

Courteous

Conversational

Convincing

Complete

COMMON TYPES OF BUSINESS LETTERS

The different types of letters are: acknowledgement, adjustment, complaint, inquiry, order, and response letter.

Acknowledgement letter = This letter is meant to thank the reader for something they did for you in the office.

Adjustment Letter = This letter should be used in response to a written complaint against someone or something.

Complaint Letter = The complaint letter is much like the adjustment letter except no wrong doing as taken place. Instead, this letter is just to let the reader know that an error has been found and needs to be corrected as soon as possible.

Inquiry Letter = An inquiry letter is written as a request for a certain something or in response to a request made by someone.

Order Letter = Order letters are exactly as they sound, they are used to order material that is running low and will be needed soon.

Response Letter = A response letter is also exactly how it sounds. It is a letter written in response to another letter received by someone.

Parts of a Business Letter

Date

Write out the month, day and year two inches from the top of the page. Depending which format you are using for your letter, either left justify the date or tab to the center point and type the date.

Sender's Address

Do not write the sender's name or title, as it is included in the letter's closing. Include only the street address, city and zip code.

Inside Address

The inside address is the recipient's address. It is always best to write to a specific individual at the firm to which you are writing. Include a personal title such as Ms. , Mrs. , Mr. , or Dr. To write the address, use the U. S. Post Office Format. For international addresses, type the name of the country in all-capital letters on the last line.

The inside address begins one line below the sender's address or one inch below the date.

Salutation

Use the same name as the inside address, including the personal title.

It is also acceptable to use the full name in a salutation if you cannot determine gender.

Body

For block and modified block formats, single space and left justify each paragraph within the body of the letter. Leave a blank line between each paragraph. When writing a business letter, be careful to remember that conciseness is very important. In the first paragraph, consider a friendly opening and then a statement of the main point. The next paragraph should begin justifying the importance of the main point. In the next few paragraphs, continue justification with background information and supporting details. The closing paragraph should restate the purpose of the letter and, in some cases, request some type of action.

Closing

The closing begins at the same horizontal point as your date and one line after the last body paragraph. Capitalize the first word only (for example: Thank you) and leave four lines between the closing and the sender's name for a signature.

Enclosures

If you have enclosed any documents along with the letter, such as a resume, you indicate this simply by typing Enclosures one line below the closing.

Sample:

Your Company Logo and Contact Information

January 11,2005

Brian Eno,Chief Engineer

Ecology Systems,Inc.

8458 Obstructed View Lane

Durham, NC 27708

Dear Mr. Eno:

Enclosed is the report estimating our power consumption for the year as requested by John Brenan, Vice President, on September 4.

The report is the result of several meetings with Jamie Anson, Manager of Plant Operations, and her staff and an extensive survey of all our employees. The survey was delayed by the transfer of key staff in Building A. We believe, however, that the report will provide the information you need to furnish us with a cost estimate for the installation of your Mark II Energy Saving System.

We would like to thank Billy Budd of ESI for his assistance in preparing the survey. If you need more information, please let me know.

Sincerely,

Nora Cassidy

New Projects Office

ncassidy@company. com

Enclosure: Report

Writing task: write a business letter for one of the following occasions:

1. To establish business relationship with ABC Iron and Steel Import and Export Company;

2. To complain the low quality of Pearl company's product.

Reading Practice

Passage

Budgeting

Budgeting plays a crucial role in planning and control. Plans identify objectives and the actions needed to achieve them. Budgets are the quantitative expressions of these plans, stated in either physical or financial terms or both. When used for planning, a budgeting is a method for translating the goals and strategies of an organization into operational terms. Budgets can also be used in control. Control is the process of setting standards, receiving feedback on actual performance, and taking corrective action whenever actual performance deviates significantly from planned performance. Thus, budgets can be used to compare actual outcomes with planned outcomes, and they can steer operations back on course, if necessary.

Budgets are usually prepared for areas within an organization and for activities (sales, production, research, and so on). This system of budgets serves as the comprehensive financial plan for the organization as a whole and gives an organization several advantages.

1. It forces managers to plan.

2. It provides resource information that can be used to improve decision making.

3. It aids in the use of resources and employees by setting a benchmark that can be used for the subsequent evaluation of performance.

4. It improves communication and coordination.

Budgeting forces management to plan for the future—to develop an overall direction for the organization, foresee problems, and develop future policies. When managers spend time planning, they grow to understand the capabilities of their businesses and where the resources of the business should be used.

Budgets convey significant information about the resource capabilities of an organization, making better decisions possible. For example, a cash budget points out potential excesses and deficiencies of cash. If the company has extra cash, managers can invest it in short-term investments, rather than leaving it idle. A cash deficiency, on the other hand, may suggest the importance of improved accounts receivable collection.

Budgets also set standards that can control the use of a company's resources and control and motivate employees.

Budgets also serve to communicate the plans of the organization to each employee and to coordinate their efforts. Accordingly, all employees can be aware of their role in achieving those objectives. This is why explicitly linking the budget to the long-run plans of the organization is so important.

The Budgeting process can range from the fairly informal process undergone by a small firm, to an elaborately detailed, several-month procedure employed by large firms. Key features of the process include directing and coordinating the compilation of the budget.

Directing and coordinating

Every organization must have someone responsible for directing and coordinating the overall budgeting process. This budget director is usually the controller or someone who reports to the controller. The budget director works under the direction of the budget committee. The budget committee has the responsibility to review the budget, provide policy guidelines and budgetary goals, resolve differences that may arise as the budget is prepared, approve the final budget, and monitor the actual performance of the organization as the year unfolds. The budget committee also has the responsibility to ensure that the budget is linked to the strategic plan of the organization. Large companies with multiple divisions must have budgets for each division. Within a division, a budget is prepared for each subdivision.

Types of budgets

When we refer to the company's budget for the year, we are talking about the master budget. The master budget is a comprehensive financial plan made up of various individual departmental and activity budgets. A master budget can be divided into operating and financial budgets. Operating budgets are concerned with the income-generating activities of a firm: sales, production, and finished goods inventories. The ultimate outcome of the operating budgets is a pro forma or budgeted income statement. Note that "pro forma" is synonymous with "budgeted" and "estimated". In effect, the pro forma income statement is done "according to form"but with estimated, not historical, data. Financial budgets are concerned with the inflows and outflows of cash and with financial position. Planned cash inflows and outflows are detailed in a cash budget, and expected financial position at the end of the budget period is shown in a budgeted, or pro forma, balance sheet.

The master budget is usually prepared for a one-year period corresponding to the company's fiscal year. The yearly budgets are broken down into quarterly and monthly budgets.

Most organizations prepare the budget for the coming year during the last four or five months of the current year. However, some organizations have developed a continuous budgeting philosophy. A continuous budget is a moving twelve-month budget. As a month expires in the budget, an additional month in the future is added so that the company always has a twelve-month plan on hand.

Similar to a continuous budget is a continuously updated budget. The objective of this budget is not to have twelve months of budgeted information at all times, but instead to update the master budget each month as new information becomes available.

Ⅶ. Answer the following questions:

1. What is budget, master budget or operating budget?
2. What are the functions of budgeting?
3. What is a budget director?
4. What are the key features of the process of the budget?

We Should Change Tack On Climate
After Copenhagen

After 12 days of protests, posturing and seemingly endless palaver, the elephantine gathering that was the Copenhagen climate summit has laboured mightily and brought forth…a mouse. As vague as it is toothless, the accord on curbing greenhouse gas emissions that emerged from the Bella Centre this weekend imposes no real obligations, sets no binding emissions targets and requires no specific actions by anyone.

So should we be disappointed? Well, actually, no. It is not that man-made global warming isn't real or that we don't need to take meaningful action to combat it. It is and we do.

Nonetheless, the dismal outcome of the 15th United Nations Climate Change Conference should make us hopeful. Why? Because its failure may be just the wake-up call the world has needed—the splash of cold water that may finally get us to face the facts about what works and what does not work to cure climate change.

For 17 years now, ever since the Rio "Earth Summit" back in 1992, the effort to combat global warming has been dominated by a single idea—the notion that the only solution is to drastically cut carbon emissions. Anyone incautious enough to suggest that there might be more effective ways of controlling climate change, or that it is simply not politically or economically feasible to try to force a world that gets 80 per cent of its energy from carbon-emitting fossil fuels to suddenly change its ways, was dismissed as a crackpot or, worse, a secret global-warming denier. The fact that the Rio-Kyoto-Copenhagen approach to global warming was clearly getting us nowhere was apparently one of those inconvenient truths that people prefer to ignore.

Well, call me a cock-eyed optimist, but Copenhagen's failure strikes me as being too abject to ignore. For all of President Barack Obama's talk of an "unprecedented breakthrough", all the world leaders really did was try to paper over their differences with a three-page communiqué that basically asks us to cross our fingers and hope for the best. They would have done better to have acknowledged their impotence and gone home empty-handed. Never has the fundamental bankruptcy of the carbon-cutting strategy seemed more obvious.

So I am hopeful that political leaders may finally be ready to face the truth about global warming—namely, that if we are serious about wanting to solve it, we need to adopt a new approach. Promising to cut carbon emissions may make us feel virtuous, but that is all it does. If we actually want to cool down the planet, we need policies that are technologically smarter, politically more feasible and economically more efficient.

The stark lesson of Copenhagen is that the world is neither willing nor able to go cold turkey when it comes to ending its addiction to fossil fuels. The problem, particularly for China, India, and the rest of the developing world, is that there simply are not any affordable alternatives.

Keep in mind that global energy demand is expected to double by 2050. What this means is that if we want to reduce (if not actually eliminate) our use of fossil fuels without totally crippling the world economy, we are going to have to increase our reliance on green energy technologies by several orders of magnitude.

In a paper for the Copenhagen Consensus Centre in July 2009, Isabel Galiana and Professor Chris Green of McGill University examined the state of non-carbon based energy today—including nuclear, wind, solar and geothermal energy—and came to some disconcerting conclusions. Based on present rates of progress, they found that, taken together, alternative energy sources could, if hugely scaled up, get us less than halfway towards a path of stable carbon emissions by 2050, and only a fraction of the way towards stabilisation by 2100. The technology will simply not be ready in terms of scalability or stability. In many cases, the most basic research and development is still required. We are not even close to getting the needed technological revolution started.

The Copenhagen accord attempts to deal with this reality by offering a vague promise that developed nations will eventually contribute as much as $100bn a year to help poor countries cope with climate change. If this money were to be spent on helping developing countries adapt to climate change, the pledge might make sense, since it would be likely to make a real and immediate difference in people's quality of life. But that is not where the money is supposed to go. The text of the agreement specifies that most if not all of the funds are to be spent "in the context of meaningful mitigation." In other words, the money would be used to subsidise carbon cuts, a pointless exercise that would do nothing to ameliorate current miseries—and at best might reduce temperatures slightly a century from now.

But what if we put these funds to better use? What if, instead of condemning billions of people around the world to continued poverty by trying to make carbon-emitting fuels more expensive, we devoted ourselves to making green energy cheaper? As solutions go, it is quicker, more efficient and far less painful.

Right now, solar panels cost so much that only well-heeled, well-meaning westerners can afford to install them. But if we could make them or other green energy technologies cheaper than fossil fuels over the next 20 to 40 years—and there is no reason to think that we cannot—we would not have to force (or subsidise) anyone to stop burning carbon-emitting fuels. Everyone, including the Chinese and the Indians, would shift to the cheaper and cleaner alternatives— solving global warming.

So how do we get to this happy place? We need to increase spending on green-energy R&D by a factor of 50. For 0.2 per cent of global gross domestic product, or $100bn a year, we could bring about the technological breakthroughs it will take to make green energy cheaper and fuel our carbon-free future. For both developed and developing world governments, it would be a lot more politically palatable than carbon cuts.

The millions of concerned people around the world who put their hopes in Copenhagen may have been bitterly disappointed by the paltry outcome. But the summit's failure could be a blessing in disguise. For the last 17 years, we have been putting the cart before the horse, pretending we could cut carbon emissions now and solve the technology problem later. Perhaps now, as they limp home from Copenhagen, our leaders will recognise the deep flaws in their current approach and chart a smarter course.

Why Copenhagen Must Be the End of the Beginning

The Copenhagen summit on climate change is going to fall short. Does this matter? Yes and no: yes, because the case for action is so strong; no, because the likely agreement would be inadequate.

My view that decisive action is justified is contentious. Sceptics offer two counter-arguments: first, that the science underlying climate change is highly uncertain; second, that costs exceed benefits.

Yet it is not enough to argue that the science is uncertain. Given the risks, we have to be quite sure the science is wrong before following the sceptics. By the time we know it is not, it is likely to be too late to act effectively. We cannot repeat experiments with just one planet.

The case for changing these trends soon is that the costs of curbing large rises in temperature would otherwise become extremely high or, at worst, prohibitive. The IEA argues that if the aim is to limit greenhouse gas concentrations to 450 parts per million, every year of delay in moving towards the required trajectory adds an extra $500bn of costs to the estimated global cost of $10,500bn. These costs result from the extremely long life of the capital assets used in power generation and the even longer life of CO_2 in the atmosphere.

The alternative scenario is quite different: instead of the 40.2 Gt of energy-related emissions in 2030, we would have just 26.4 Gt. The gap is huge. A briefing paper from the European Climate Foundation shows that the pledges made in advance of Copenhagen would not close it. Even on the most optimistic view, current offers fall short by about a third of the reductions needed by 2020 for a pathway to a ceiling of 450 parts per million of CO_2 equivalent.

Copenhagen then would only be a beginning. It is likely not even to be that, since the US administration is unable to make binding commitments and developing countries are unwilling to do so. Yet Copenhagen seems the end of the beginning. Something close to agreement exists that the world should act. There is, equally, agreement that, despite the rhetoric, little useful has been achieved so far. The time for action is now—if not at Copenhagen, then soon after.

Unfortunately, this does not mean that the right sort of agreement will emerge. The policies we employ must be as effective and efficient as possible. What does that mean? I would emphasize three criteria.

First, we need prices for carbon that apply over relevant planning horizons. That price cannot be fixed forever, but must change with events. But it needs to be far more stable than in the European Union's market for permits (see chart). A tax seems more attractive to me than "cap and trade", for this reason.

Second, where the abatement occurs must be separated from who pays for it. Abatement needs to happen where it is most efficient. That is why emissions of developing countries must be included. But the cost should fall on the wealthy. This is as much because they can afford it as because they produced the bulk of past emissions.

Finally, we need to develop and apply innovations in all relevant technologies. A paper from the Bruegel think-tank argues, persuasively, that merely raising prices on carbon emissions would reinforce the position of established technologies. We need large-scale subsidies for innovation as well.

New Words and Expressions

palaver [pəˈlævə] *n.* idle talk 闲聊；长时间闲谈
abject [ˈæbdʒekt] *adj.* (of conditions) wretched; miserable (指境况)悲惨的；可怜的
stark [stɑːk] *adj.* complete; downright 完全的

mitigation [ˌmitiˈgeiʃən] *n.* to make less severe, violent or painful 使缓和；使减轻；使镇静

ameliorate [əˈmiːljəreit] *vt.* (formal)(cause to) become better（正式用语）改善；改良；变好

palatable [ˈpælətəbl] *adj.* agreeable to the taste or (fig) to the mind 可口的；美味的；(喻)怡人的

paltry [ˈpɔːltri] *adj.* worthless; of no importance; contemptible 无价值的；不重要的；微不足道的；可鄙的

limp [limp] *vi.* walk lamely or unevenly as when one leg or foot is hurt or stiff 跛行；一瘸一瘸地走

contentious [kənˈtenʃəs] *adj.* quarrelsome; likely to cause contention 好争论的；可能引起争论的

armageddon [ˌɑːməˈgedn] *n.* (fig) any dramatic conflict 任何大决战

abatement [əˈbeitmənt] *n.* to make or become less; decrease 减少；减小；减退

concerted [kənˈsɜːtid] *adj.* planned, performed, designed together 一致的

Exercises

I. Answer the following questions.

1. What are the disconcerting conclusions provided by Isabel Galiana and Professor Chris Green of McGill University in July 2009?

2. What are the three criteria emphasized by the author?

3. What is the conclusion arrived in the Copenhagen summit by the author?

4. What is the result of the accord from the Bella Centre?

5. What is the stark lesson of Copenhagen?

II. Paraphrase the difficult sentences or language points.

1. The elephantine gathering that was the Copenhagen climate summit has laboured mightily and brought forth…a mouse.

2. The problem, particularly for China, India, and the rest of the developing world, is that there simply are not any affordable alternatives.

3. Tackling the risk of climate change is the most complex collective challenge humanity has ever confronted.

4. Never has the fundamental bankruptcy of the carbon-cutting strategy seemed more obvious.

5. Well, call me a cock-eyed optimist, but copenhagen's failure strikes me as being too abject to ignore.

III. Choose the word or phrase that best explains the meaning of the underlined part from the text.

1. After 12 days of protests, posturing and seemingly endless <u>palaver</u>, …
   A. quarrel   B. talk   C. palatal

2. Well, call me a cock-eyed optimist, but Copenhagen's failure strikes me as <u>being too abject to ignore.</u>

A. I can ignore Copenhagen's failure because it is very abnormal.

B. I can not ignore Copenhagen's failure because it is very miserable.

C. I can not ignore Copenhagen's failure because it is very abnormal.

3. Never has the fundamental bankruptcy of the carbon-cutting strategy seemed more obvious.

A. The fundamental bankruptcy of the carbon-cutting strategy has not seemed more obvious.

B. The fundamental bankruptcy of the carbon-cutting strategy has never seemed more obvious.

C. The fundamental bankruptcy of the carbon-cutting strategy seemed the most obvious.

4. The stark lesson of Copenhagen is that the world is neither willing nor able to go cold turkey when it comes to ending its addiction to fossil fuels.

A. to step on cold turkey   B. to withdraw suddenly   C. to sell turkey

5. My view that decisive action is justified is contentious.

A. contagious   B. quarrelsome   C. contrary

6. But we cannot—and, self-evidently, should not—rely on economic armageddon.

A. battle   B. argument   C. augmentation

7. Tackling the risk of climate change is the most complex collective challenge humanity has ever confronted.

A. Dealing with the risk of…

B. Taking the risk of…

C. Facing the risk of…

8. The forces of negativity and scepticism, whether self-interested or naive, must not prevail if we are to reduce the threat to the planet's future without sacrificing future economic growth.

A. gain victory   B. preventive   C. potential

9. If this money were to be spent on helping developing countries adapt to climate changes, …

A. If this money were to be spent on helping developing countries adopt to climate changes, …

B. If this money were to be spent on helping developing countries suit with climate changes, …

C. If this money were to be spent on helping developing countries adduct to climate changes, …

10. Perhaps now, as they limp home from Copenhagen, our leaders will recognise the deep flaws in their current approach and chart a smarter course.

A. … and describe a smarter course.

B. … and chant a smarter course.

C. … and charter a smart course.

Ⅳ. **Choose the best phrase or expression in the text from the following list to fit in each of the following blanks. Change the word form where necessary.**

be feasible to, what if, stir up, at best, commit to, range from …to…, account for, thanks to, head for, given…,

1. _____ your help we were successful.

2. He has refused to listen to his parents' suggestion and _____ disaster.

3. _____ good health, I hope to finish the work this year.

4. He _____ himself _____ support his brother's children.

5. It is _____ reconstruct the destroyed city if we choose to do it.

6. The prices of the commodities _____ 5 *yuan* _____ 5,000 *yuan*.

7. _____ every one tries to save every drop of water?

8. We can't arrive before Friday _____.

9. Discontented men _____ trouble among the crew.

10. His illness _____ his absence.

Ⅴ. **Translate the following into English.**

1. 但是,第15届联合国气候变化会议的可悲成果,仍应使我们怀抱希望。为什么呢? 因为这次会议的失败或许正是唤醒世界的一记必要的警钟——泼到我们头上的冷水,或许终于促使我们正视现实,明白要抑制气候变化,什么会起作用,什么不会起作用。

2. 因此我心存希望,在全球变暖方面,政治领导人或许终于要面对以下事实:如果我们确实希望解决问题,我们就必须采取新的方法。承诺减少碳排放或许会使我们显得高尚,但其意义不过如此。假如我们确实希望让这个星球变凉,我们就需要技术上更高明、政治上更可行、经济上更有效的策略。

3. 记住,到2050年,全球能源需求预计将会翻倍。这意味着,假如我们希望减少(如果不是全然戒除)对化石燃料的使用,同时避免让全球经济陷入瘫痪,我们就必须把对绿色能源技术的依赖程度提高几个数量级。

4. 但仅仅争辩科学具有不确定性是不够的。鉴于存在的风险,在听信怀疑论者之前,我们必须确信科学是错误的。等到我们发现它没有错,再要采取有效行动,可能就为时已晚了。我们只有一个地球,无法重复进行实验。

5. 因此,哥本哈根将仅仅是个开始。鉴于美国政府不能做出有约束力的承诺,而发展中国家不愿做出此类承诺,它或许连个开始都谈不上。不过,哥本哈根似乎标志着序幕已经拉开。人们已经达成共识:世界应当采取行动。同样达成共识的是,尽管口头表态不绝于耳,但迄今取得的实际进展寥寥。采取行动的时机就是眼下——如果不是在哥本哈根会议上,那就是在会后不久。

6. 最后,我们需要在所有相关技术领域开发和应用创新成果。欧洲智库Bruegel的一份报告极具说服力地提出,仅仅提高碳排放价格,会巩固成熟技术的地位。我们还需对创新进行大规模补贴。

7. 为举办这次大象级的会议,人们大费周章,取得的成果却小如老鼠。

8. 你可以把我视为一位荒唐的乐观主义者，但哥本哈根会议失败得如此之惨，不容我们对此不闻不问。

9. 哥本哈根的一大教训是，世界既不愿，也无法骤然中止对化石燃料的依赖。

10. 为应对这一现实，哥本哈根协议做出一项含糊的承诺：发达国家最终每年将捐出1 000亿美元，用于帮助穷国应对气候变化。

Ⅵ. Translate the following sentences into Chinese：

1. After 12 days of protests, posturing and seemingly endless palaver, the elephantine gathering that was the Copenhagen climate summit has laboured mightily and brought forth…a mouse. As vague as it is toothless, the accord on curbing greenhouse gas emissions that emerged from the Bella Centre this weekend imposes no real obligations, sets no binding emissions targets and requires no specific actions by anyone.

2. In a paper for the Copenhagen Consensus Centre in July 2009, Isabel Galiana and Professor Chris Green of McGill University examined the state of non-carbon based energy today—including nuclear, wind, solar and geothermal energy—and came to some disconcerting conclusions. Based on present rates of progress, they found that, taken together, alternative energy sources could, if hugely scaled up, get us less than halfway towards a path of stable carbon emissions by 2050, and only a fraction of the way towards stabilisation by 2100.

Writing

Personal Statement

Directions：Personal statements are also called "application essays" or "statements of purpose". Personal statements are most important when you are applying to an extremely competitive program, where all the applicants have high test scores and GPA's.

The best way to do this is to use a set of headings and write bullet points about how you relate to these headings. Here are some headings to think about.

a. What you want to study at university and why
- Specific aspects of the courses that interest you
- Examples of coursework you have completed
- Practical work you have enjoyed

b. Experiences that show you are a reliable and responsible person
- Part-time job
- Business enterprise
- Community and charity work

c. Your interests and skills
- What you like to do in your free time
- Sport and leisure activities
- Subjects you study which are not examined

d. Personal goals of your statement

- Not sound arrogant and pretentious
- I would try not to start any sentences with I
- Try and have an interesting phrase to start and finish on

Language of the statement

You need to use language which makes you sound enthusiastic about your courses and an interesting person. If you're still wondering what sort of language to use look at existing personal statements, prospectuses and sentences on the web which you think fit your views.

Structure of the statement

Most statements are written in an essay format. For example:

Paragraph 1: Introduction to my subject, the parts I'm interested in and why

Paragraph 2: What I had done related to my subject which wasn't on the UCAS form

Paragraphs 3 and 4: Work experience and things I had done in school

Paragraph 5: My interests outside of school (also contained my responsibilities)

Paragraph 6: My goal of going to university and closing comment

A good start will interest the reader and cause them to read the statement properly rather than just scanning it. A good ending will mean the reader remembers what you wrote, and hopefully will recommend you. It's a good idea to start with why you want to take your subject, and finish with why you want to go to university or what you want to do next.

Writing the Statement

Remember the aims of a personal statement. You need to show the admissions tutor why you should be accepted on your chosen course at your chosen university. In addition to what you say in your statement, the language you use and the way it is laid out will be judged as well.

Also remember you only have a limited amount of space, but don't let this put you off too much.

Be positive and interesting, if there is something you are unhappy about, try to portray it in an attractive light.

Before you go, have a look at the websites and prospectuses of universities you are applying for, and see if they say anything about writing personal statements. This information would probably be written by the admissions tutors, and would give you a much better idea of what sort of things to put down.

Now you're ready to go. You want to write in a way that is informative, interesting and useful. Along with writing about what you've done, try and explain why you did it, or what you think you learned from it.

For example:

I currently have a part time job and this has taught me much about teamwork, responsibility and time management in the workplace.

After writing the statement

First read through what you've written slowly and try to read it from someone else's point of view. Make sure it's easy to read and not confusing, make sure you've said everything you want to say.

Next get other people to read it, mainly your family, friends, teachers and anyone else who you think will be able to give you a good opinion. As well as checking for spelling and grammar mistakes, they will be able to tell you if they think there is anything you've missed out.

Sample:

My interest in science dates back to my years in high school, where I excelled in physics, chemistry, and math. When I was a senior, I took a first—year calculus course at a local college (such an advanced—level class was not available in high school) and earned an A. It seemed only logical that I pursue a career in electrical engineering.

When I began my undergraduate career, I had the opportunity to be exposed to the full range of engineering courses, all of which tended to reinforce and solidify my intense interest in engineering. I've also had the opportunity to study a number of subjects in the humanities and they have been both enjoyable and enlightening, providing me with a new and different perspective on the world in which we live.

In the realm of engineering, I have developed a special interest in the field of laser technology and have even been taking a graduate course in quantum electronics. Among the 25 or so students in the course, I am the sole undergraduate. Another particular interest of mine is electromagnetics, and last summer, when I was a technical assistant at a world—famous local lab, I learned about its many practical applications, especially in relation to microstrip and antenna design. Management at this lab was sufficiently impressed with my work to ask that I return when I graduate. Of course, my plans following completion of my current studies are to move directly into graduate work toward my master's in science. After I earn my master's degree, I intend to start work on my Ph. D. in electrical engineering. Later I would like to work in the area of research and development for private industry. It is in R & D that I believe I can make the greatest contribution, utilizing my theoretical background and creativity as a scientist.

I am highly aware of the superb reputation of your school, and my conversations with several of your alumni have served to deepen my interest in attending. I know that, in addition to your excellent faculty, your computer facilities are among the best in the state. I hope you will give me the privilege of continuing my studies at your fine institution.

Writing task: Imagine you will go to America to further your study, so write a personal statement of yourself.

Reading Practice

Passage

Insurance

The package of insurance services available is flexible and can be tailored to suit your needs. In most cases, there is also the added benefit of an option to pay premiums in monthly installments which spreads the costs evenly over the year and will help to improve your cash flow.

Insurance for Business

Protecting your business

Barclays is committed to providing a comprehensive range of business services. Barclays Financial Services Ltd. is dedicated to providing insurance services which can protect the interests of those who are self-employed or running their own businesses.

Cover for your property and your business income

In addition to the basic protection you will need for your business property, including buildings, contents, stock and equipment, we can offer protection against accidental damage.

We can provide cover to help protect you against the resulting loss of income.

Legal liabilities to employees and the public

If you employ someone, even part time, you are required by law to provide insurance cover against injury to employees arising from their employment. You may have to pay damages if, during the course of your business activities, you or your products or services cause injury or loss to customers or to the public.

Barclays can provide protection to cover your legal liabilities to employees and the general public.

Loss of key people

Life assurance and disability insurance arranged through Barclays can provide a business with cash to help replace lost income until replacement personnel can be found and trained. Most business owners are themselves key to the success of their business and are likely to require income protection insurance to maintain their own income in the event of long term disability.

Share protection insurance

If your business is formed as a partnership or limited company, you may also need to consider share protection insurance. If a partner or co-director were to die, the insurance would safeguard the remaining business owners by providing them with the cash which they may need to buy the deceased's share of the business.

This type of arrangement can also be used to assist in buying out the interest of a retiring partner or director.

Travel Insurance

It's important to take out insurance well before going abroad to cover you for problems which can arise, such as becoming ill, losing your money or mislaying your luggage. Our travel policy is specially negotiated by Barclays Insurance (our insurance broking subsidiary) and provides wide cover at a cost you can afford, so you are well protected should disaster strike.

Protection for Your Home and Its Contents

Your home and its contents are probably the biggest investments you'll ever make, so it makes sense to protect them against risks such as fire, theft, storm, flood and accidental damage.

Now peace of mind is no more than a phone call away. Call Barclays Personal Insurance Centre on 081-667 1771 and find out how we can take care of all your house-hold insurance needs.

Our policies include: (a) new for old cover; (b) a choice of different levels of protection; (c) 24 hour helplines for domestic emergencies, glass replacement and legal advice; (d) options to cover your possessions away from home, and to include your buildings.

Motor Insurance

As the Barclays Motor Insurance Scheme is specially arranged by the insurance broking arm of Barclays Financial Services you can be confident that you'll have one of the best names behind you and your car.

Discounts are available depending on your age and type of car, and whether you are prepared to restrict the number of drivers, or pay the first part of any claim for damage to your vehicle.

If your car is currently insured through another insurance company, our scheme allows you to transfer your no claim bonus.

Ⅶ. **Answer the following questions:**

    1. How can Barclays insurance services help to protect your business?

    2. If you are an employer in a firm, what does the law require you to do for your employees?

    3. Before going abroad, which kind of insurance can provide you with help?

    4. What do Barclays home and its contents insurance policies include?

China Should Speed Up the Yuan's Rise

Many of the common arguments for and against the revaluation of the yuan are misguided. China would clearly be better off with a stronger currency—for its own sake, and not just as a means of preventing global pressure—and would do well to move faster than the present pace. I'll get to the "real" case for revaluation shortly. But first, we need to address the most common myths about the Chinese exchange rate.

It's Not About "Manipulation"

Let's recall how a fixed (or quasi-fixed, in China's case) exchange-rate system works. China's central bank, the People's Bank of China, publishes a daily exchange-rate quote and stands ready to trade the yuan against foreign currency at or near that published rate. When there is an excess of dollars on the market, either because of a trade surplus or net capital inflows, the PBOC purchases those dollars by issuing new yuan; when dollars are in short supply, the PBOC sells its own dollar reserves to make up the difference, removing yuan liquidity from the market in the process.

Over the past few years, the rising trade surplus means that the People's Bank has been a continual net buyer, accumulating nearly $30 billion a month in official foreign reserves for a cumulative total of $1.2 trillion as of March 2007. This fact has led to criticism that China consciously set the yuan peg at a level that makes exports hypercompetitive and thus automatically generate enormous trade surpluses. But this doesn't necessarily follow. Under a fixed exchange-rate regime, central banks essentially commit to live with what the market delivers to their doorstep, and in a technical sense the recent flood of dollars is simply what the market has brought to China.

In fact, when looking at policy intent it helps to keep two points firmly in mind. First, when the government first initiated the peg in 1997 it wasn't to keep the yuan from rising. Rather, it was to keep the currency from collapsing. The end of the Chinese bubble in 1995—1996 left the economy with a huge burden of bad debts at home and abroad. Profits were disappearing and real growth had probably slowed to low single-digit levels. Against this backdrop, the onset of the Asian financial crisis convinced many investors that the yuan would be the next domino to fall, and short-term capital began to flow out of the economy at an unprecedented pace. The authorities' decision to institute a de facto peg against the dollar was explicitly billed as a commitment not to devalue the yuan. As late as 2003, when then Premier Zhu Rongji officially retired from government service, he considered holding the yuan peg to be one of his crowning achievements, and one of China's biggest contributions to global stability.

Secondly, the Chinese government has been as embarrassed as anyone else by the skyrocketing mainland trade balance. As late as mid-2004 China was running a trade deficit, and there was no sense whatsoever that the yuan might be structurally undervalued. It wasn't until early 2005 that the trade surplus began to career upwards to unprecedented heights—a trend that caught not only the government but also most outside observers by surprise. Consider the authorities' position: At the beginning of this decade the yuan was trading around eight to the dollar and most economists were imploring them to keep the peg in order to avoid devaluation. Six years later, the exchange rate is still roughly eight to the dollar, but now foreign policy makers are screaming that the yuan is the most undervalued currency in the world.

This is hardly a case for manipulation. "Whiplash" is more the operative word, as China struggles to come to grips with the massive changes of the past few years.

Exports Won't Slow

For those who closely follow the mainland economy, the last few years have provided another interesting spectacle. Remember that the yuan has been strengthening gradually against the dollar, by 2% in 2005, another 4% in 2006 and at a 6% year-on-year pace so far this year. At the same time, Chinese rural migrant wages, which were rising leisurely at 3% to 4% per year at the beginning of the decade, are now shooting up by 10% or even 15% annually as factories come to terms with a dwindling supply of young, single farm workers.

This double-edged sword of an appreciating currency and rising labor costs should have imposed palpable damage on China's traditional export sectors: toys, clothing, furniture, appliances and electronics processing. However, according to industrial earnings and profit statistics, overall light manufacturing margins have been as steady as a rock, with no signs of pressure so far.

Why? Because exporters simply passed on the costs to overseas buyers. In a world where individual country figures rarely tally on pricing trends, one of the startling facts is that Chinese, Hong Kong area, U.S., Japanese and European data all agree that mainland export prices have started to rise in the past three years. From 1995 to 2003, dollar prices in traditional manufacturing industries like clothing and toys were falling on the order of 3% to 4% per year. Since 2004, however, those same prices have been rising by 3% to 4% per year, a very visible turnaround from the previous picture. Exactly the same is true for it electronics. According to partner country data, Chinese electronics prices used to fall by 6% to 10% per year in dollar terms. Now they are barely falling at all and mainland data actually show a sharp increase in prices since the beginning of the year.

Why haven't Chinese exporters felt more pain? The answer is that they're very big. Visitors to mainland factories often return with stories of small suppliers fighting for survival on razor-thin margins in an overly competitive environment. This may be true for individual companies, but on an aggregate level China now has an enormous market share: 70% to 80% of total U.S. imports of toys, footwear and other low-end products, nearly 40% of total apparel imports and 35% of it electronics. In this environment, it's very easy to pass on domestic cost pressures.

Of course, rising wages and a rising currency will eventually bring about the end of traditional low-end manufacturing in China, as production migrates to cheaper markets like Vietnam, India and Indonesia. But it's not happening very fast. In fact, one of the most surprising trends in Asia is that neighboring countries have taken advantage of the "breathing space" offered by China to raise their own prices as well.

So for the next few years, at least, don't look for yuan revaluation to slow the mainland export juggernaut. As best I can tell, the main impact would simply be to raise prices for global consumers.

No Jobs Savings

This doesn't mean that an appreciating currency wouldn't help lower China's trade surplus—it would, mostly through stimulating import purchases. However, I do find it more than a little ironic that the country protesting the loudest over the yuan peg has arguably the least to gain from its removal.

A few numbers here should help put the U. S.-China relationship in perspective. In the three-year span from the first half of 2004 to the first half of 2007, the monthly mainland trade surplus jumped by nearly $20 billion. How much of that shift came from net exports to the U.S.? The answer is around $6 billion, broadly in line with the overall U. S. share in Chinese exports. On a nominal dollar basis, the lion's share of China's net trade expansion has been borne by the rest of the world.

The next point to note is that much of that $6 billion monthly figure actually comes indirectly from China's neighbors as well. The bilateral U.S. trade deficit with China has grown from essentially zero in 1990 to 2% of GDP this year, but, tellingly, the U.S. deficit with all of Asia actually expanded by less, or only 1.5% of GDP. The reason is that many of the goods showing up on U.S. shores with a "Made in China" label used to say "Made in Taiwan" or "Made in Korea." Now, as processing and assembly functions have shifted to the mainland, the headline bilateral U.S. deficit has rather artificially shifted in favor of China as well. Once I account for this "intra-Asian" effect, it turns out that most of the real increase in the U.S. trade deficit comes from elsewhere, including the Organization of Petroleum Exporting Countries, Europe, Canada and Mexico.

Nor is there compelling evidence that Chinese producers are suddenly taking U.S. jobs. Much has been made of the fact that the manufacturing share of U.S. non-farm employment dropped from 16% in 1990 to 10% this year—but remember that the share had already dropped from 32% in 1950. As it turns out, the U.S. economy loses manufacturing jobs at a straight-line pace of 4% per decade, both before and after China's arrival on the scene. Moreover, traditional low-end light industries where mainland penetration has increased the fastest were already decimated in the U.S. decades ago, accounting for only 1.7% of total employment as of 1990. All told, it would be unrealistic to expect even the most aggressive yuan strengthening to have any significant macro impact on the U.S. economy.

Another important fact is that China's gradual approach to moving the currency is not exactly threatening stability at home in the mainland. Many analysts describe an economy where massive foreign-exchange inflows are flooding into domestic liquidity, overwhelming the central bank's ability to carry out monetary sterilization operations and pushing both real growth and asset valuations into extreme bubble territory.

So why doesn't China go? To date, the government has resisted calls for a large one-off move as well as much faster appreciation on the grounds that such a move would be destabilizing. And I do have sympathy for this view if we talk about a revaluation strictly defined—i.e., a sudden, overnight move of 15% to 20% in the yuan exchange rate against the dollar. This could have a disastrous impact on exporters whose contract prices were set at the old exchange rate, especially with the relative lack of formal hedging mechanisms.

So not only have Chinese exporters lived very comfortably with mild trend appreciation to date against the dollar, they've actually been gaining competitiveness against their neighbors whose currencies have been strengthening even faster. And to reiterate the point I made earlier, mainland producers are far more likely to pass costs along to consumers than any other Asian country.

On another front, a few prominent economists argue that China is giving up its "monetary anchor" by letting the currency float—but as far as I can tell, the country never really had one in the first place. The exchange rate plays a significant price-setting role in small, open trading systems, but China is a very large, domestically driven economy with a much smaller traded sector than in other regional neighbors. A currency peg certainly didn't prevent the mainland from careening between massive inflation and sharp deflation in the 1990s, and there's no reason to expect that it would today.

A final, more nuanced argument concerns speculative pressure, i. e., the view that China can't move too fast or else investors will start to see a "one-way bet" and flood the country with capital inflows. This is a valid point in theory, but in practice I've never seen evidence that single-digit rates of yuan have led to any sizeable capital movements. In fact, the main driver of "hot" portfolio flows to date has been asset-market returns.

Expectations of a looming revaluation helped pull money into the country during 2003-05, but the real draw was the Shanghai property market, where the price of luxury flats was going up by 70% to 80% a year. By contrast, hot money flowed out of China in late 2005 and 2006, despite the fact that the yuan was strengthening at an 8% year-on-year rate late last year. It wasn't until the domestic stock market really began to boom, with 10% to 20% monthly returns, that we finally saw portfolio flows coming in again over the past six months.

Given the real transaction costs involved in evading capital controls and moving money in and out of the country, the authorities have little to fear from letting the yuan move at a 10% year-on-year pace in the near term. Will it happen? As of this writing, China is not quite there yet—but I believe the benefits of faster currency adjustment will gradually and steadily make themselves apparent.

New Words and Expressions

foresee [fɔːˈsiː] *v.* to see or know beforehand 预知，先见

routine [ruːˈtiːn] *n.* a prescribed, detailed course of action to be followed regularly; a standard procedure 例行公事，惯例

pundit [ˈpʌndit] *n.* a source of opinion; a critic 提出意见者；批评家

confound [kənˈfaund] *v.* to cause to become confused or perplexed 使困惑

rudimentary [ruːdiˈmentəri] *adj.* of or relating to basic facts or principles; elementary 基本的，初步的

manipulation [məˌnipjuˈleiʃən] *n.* shrewd or devious management，especially for one's own advantage 操纵

cumulative [ˈkjuːmjuˌleitiv] *adj.* increasing or enlarging by successive addition 渐增的

peg [peg] *v.* to fix (a price) at a certain level or within a certain range 稳定行情或价位

hyper- [ˈhaipə] *pref.* excessive; excessively 过度的；过度地

regime [reiˈʒiːm] *n.* a prevailing social system or pattern 体制

implore [imˈplɔː] *v.* to appeal to in supplication; beseech 恳求

onset [ˈɔnset] *n.* a beginning; a start 开始

domino [ˈdɔminəu] *n.* a small, rectangular, wood or plastic block, the face of which is divided into halves, each half being blank or marked by one to six dots resembling those on dice 多米诺骨牌

unprecedented [ʌnˈpresidəntid] *adj.* having no previous example 没有前例的

de facto [diːˈfæktəu] *adj.* actually exercising power though not legally or officially established 实际上存在的

explicit [ikˈsplisit] *adj.* fully and clearly expressed; leaving nothing implied 明白的，清楚的

skyrocket [ˈskaiˌrɔkit] *v.* to rise or cause to rise rapidly and suddenly 暴涨，猛涨

careen [kəˈriːn] *v.* to lurch or swerve while in motion 蹒跚而行

whiplash [ˈhwiplæʃ] *n.* the lash of a whip 鞭打

dwindling [ˈdwindliŋ] *adj.* decreasing, declining, diminishing, shrinking 减少的

tally [ˈtæli] *v.* to cause to correspond or agree 符合，吻合

palpable [ˈpælpəbl] *adj.* easily perceived; obvious 明白的

turnaround [ˈtɜːnəˌraund] *n.* a shift or change in opinion, loyalty, or allegiance 转变，变卦

razor [ˈreizə] *n.* a sharp-edged cutting instrument used especially for shaving the face or removing other body hair 剃刀

aggregate [ˈæɡriɡeit] *adj.* constituting or amounting to a whole; total 聚集的；合计的

juggernaut [ˈdʒʌɡənɔːt] *n.* an overwhelming, advancing force that crushes or seems to crush everything in its path 骇人的(毁灭)力量

nominal [ˈnɔminəl] *adj.* existing in name only 名义上的

bilateral [baiˈlætərəl] *adj.* affecting or undertaken by two sides equally; binding on both parties 双边的，双方的

telling [ˈteliŋ] *adj.* having force and producing a striking effect 有效的

decimate [ˈdesimeit] *v.* to inflict great destruction or damage on 毁损

aggressive [əˈɡresiv] *adj.* inclined to behave in a hostile fashion 侵犯的

sterilization [sterəlaiˈzeiʃən] *n.* the act or procedure of sterilizing 消毒，灭菌；[金融]冲销（不令其发生作用）

one-off *adj.* happening, done, or made only once 一次性的

hedge [hedʒ] *v.* to minimize or protect against the loss of by counterbalancing one transaction, such as a bet, against another 两面下注，套期保值

baht [bɑːt] *n.* a basic unit of currency in Thailand 铢(泰国货币单位)

volatile [ˈvɔlətail] *adj.* tending to vary often or widely, as in price 易波动的，不稳定的

reiterate [riːˈitəreit] *v.* to say or do again or repeatedly 重申；重复

nuance [ˈnjuːɑːns] *n.* expression or appreciation of subtle shades of meaning, feeling, or tone 微妙之处

portfolio [pɔːtˈfəuljəu] *n.* a group of investments 一组投资

loom [luːm] *v.* to come into view as a massive, distorted, or indistinct image. See Synonyms at appear 隐约地出现

evade [iˈveid] *v.* to escape or avoid by cleverness or deceit 躲避

Exercises

Ⅰ. **Answer the following questions.**

1. Why does the People's Bank of China establish the fixed exchange-rate system?

2. According to the author, will the yuan revaluation help to slow the mainland export?

3. Will America gain from the appreciation of yuan? Why?

4. Have the low-end light industries in America been threatened by mainland China? Why?

5. Why does the Chinese government refuse to let the currency float?

Ⅱ. **Paraphrase the difficult sentences or language points.**

1. … central banks essentially commit to live with what the market delivers to their doorstep…

2. The authorities' decision to institute a de facto peg against the dollar was explicitly billed as a commitment not to devalue the yuan.

3. All told, it would be unrealistic to expect even the most aggressive yuan strengthening to have any significant macro impact on the U. S. economy.

4. On a nominal dollar basis, the lion's share of China's net trade expansion has been borne by the rest of the world.

5. Expectations of a looming revaluation helped pull money into the country during 2003-05, but the real draw was the Shanghai property market, where the price of luxury flats was going up by 70% to 80% a year.

Ⅲ. **Choose the word or phrase that best explains the meaning of the underlined part from the text.**

1. …when dollars are in short supply, the PBOC sells its own dollar reserves to <u>make up</u> the difference, removing yuan liquidity from the market in the process.

   A. put together   B. make good a deficit   C. compensate for

2. Under a fixed exchange-rate regime, central banks essentially commit to <u>live with</u> what the market delivers to their doorstep, and in a technical sense the recent flood of dollars is simply what the market has brought to China.

   A. resign oneself to   B. put up with   C. purchase

3. The authorities' decision to institute a de facto peg against the dollar was <u>explicitly</u> billed as a commitment not to devalue the yuan.

A. superficially   B. potentially   C. obviously

4. This is hardly a case for manipulation. "Whiplash" is more the operative word, as China struggles to <u>come to grips with</u> the massive changes of the past few years.

A. fight against   B. confront squarely   C. avoid deliberately

5. At the same time, Chinese rural migrant wages, which were rising leisurely at 3% to 4% per year at the beginning of the decade, are now shooting up by 10% or even 15% annually as factories <u>come to terms with</u> a dwindling supply of young, single farm workers.

A. recognize

B. refuse to admit

C. reach mutual agreement with

6. Of course, rising wages and a rising currency will eventually bring about the end of traditional <u>low-end</u> manufacturing in China, as production migrates to cheaper markets like Vietnam, India and Indonesia.

A. cheapest   B. fundamental   C. immature

7. The answer is around $6 billion, broadly <u>in line with</u> the overall U. S. share in Chinese exports.

A. in accordance with   B. on the basis of   C. against

8. The bilateral U. S. trade deficit with China has grown from essentially zero in 1990 to 2% of GDP this year, but, <u>tellingly</u>, the U. S. deficit with all of Asia actually expanded by less, or only 1.5% of GDP.

A. obviously   B. fortunately   C. frankly

9. In fact, there is only one measure that can fundamentally <u>reverse</u> the situation and cull excess heavy industrial capacity growth.

A. abolish   B. change thoroughly   C. reconsider

10. A final, more <u>nuanced</u> argument concerns speculative pressure, i. e. , the view that China can't move too fast or else investors will start to see a "one-way bet" and flood the country with capital inflows.

A. impressive   B. subtle   C. distinctive

Ⅳ. **Choose the best phrase or expression in the text from the following list to fit in each of the following blanks. Change the word form where necessary.**

foresee	implore	unprecedented	bilateral	overwhelm
career	loom	nominal	volatile	account for

1. The early 90's finds an _____ tide of rural workers flooding into big cities in China.

2. A _____ account is a temporary account used to keep track of amounts in various accounts for a period of usually one year. The accounts are closed at the

end of a period.

3. Already today, less than forty years later, as computers are relieving us of more and more of the routine tasks in business and in our personal lives. We are faced with a less dramatic but also less _____ problem.

4. Don't just win the match; _____ your opponents by about 20 goals to nil.

5. Sharp appreciation or depreciation of the currency over a period or, the exchange rates of the currency being highly _____, could lead to a major impact on cost and savings.

6. Hoyer said both parties will need to educate the country about its _____ fiscal obligations and must be willing to discuss all types of fiscal solutions.

7. During hard economic times, American businesses often _____ government to ease up on regulations to help them survive. In China, officials are more than happy to oblige.

8. A _____ trade agreement is usually signed between countries so that they can reduce tariffs and quotas on items traded between themselves.

9. The United States is Vietnam's largest trading partner, _____ nearly a quarter of exports.

10. As Jack speeds to the gate, guards shoot at the van, causing it to _____ to a halt.

Ⅴ. Translate the following sentences into English.

1. 对资本与企业的如此大规模的非个人操纵大大地增加了作为一个阶级的持股人的数量及其地位的重要性。

2. 官员和商人在那里求神保佑探险者们一路平安。

3. 通货膨胀的意思是,按人口的名义收入或货币收入的增长比按人口的实际产量的增长要快。

4. 这件工作大部分都是你做的,当然你要拿最大部分的利润。

5. 今天所做出的选择可能是高代价的,或者在未来是不可逆转的。

6. 这次不寻常的选举结果使得政府不知所措。

7. 骨牌效应是由一件事引发一系列相似事件的累积效应。

8. 尽管利息付款的数额很大,有些国家并未根据国民收入的减少而减少公共支出的其他项目。

9. 这份协议清楚地说明了必须在每个月十号付房租。

10. 国际营销提供了一种方式来对抗外国竞争者在国内咄咄逼人的竞争。

Ⅵ. Translate the following into Chinese.

1. Against this backdrop, the onset of the Asian financial crisis convinced many investors that the yuan would be the next domino to fall, and short-term capital began to flow out of the economy at an unprecedented pace. The authorities' decision to institute a de facto peg against the dollar was explicitly billed as a commitment not to devalue the yuan.

2. On another front, a few prominent economists argue that China is giving up its "monetary anchor" by letting the currency float—but as far as I can tell, the country never really had one in the first place. The exchange rate plays a significant price-setting role in small, open trading systems, but China is a very large, domestically driven economy with a much smaller traded sector than in other regional neighbors.

Writing

Inquiry letter

Directions: The inquiry letter is useful when you need information, advice, names, or directions. Be careful, however, not to ask for too much information or for information that you could easily obtain in some other way, for example, by a quick trip to the library. There are two types of inquiry letters: solicited and unsolicited.

You write a solicited letter of inquiry when a business or agency advertises its products or services. For example, if a software manufacturer advertises some new package it has developed and you can't inspect it locally, write a solicited letter to that manufacturer asking specific questions. If you cannot find any information on a technical subject, an inquiry letter to a company involved in that subject may put you on the right track. In fact, that company may supply much more help than you had expected (provided of course that you write a good inquiry letter). If you need to find the names and addresses of businesses related to your report project, see the section on finding information in libraries.

Your letter of inquiry is unsolicited if the recipient has done nothing to prompt your inquiry. For example, if you read an article by an expert, you may have further questions or want more information. You seek help from these people in a slightly different form of inquiry letter. You must construct the unsolicited type more carefully, because recipients of unsolicited letters of inquiry are not ordinarily prepared to handle such inquiries.

In an unsolicited letter, identify who you are, what you are working on, and why you need the requested information, and how you found out about the individual. If you have quite a number of questions, consider making a questionnaire and including a stamped, self-addressed envelope. In an unsolicited letter, try to find some way to compensate the recipient for the trouble, for example, by offering to pay copying and mailing costs, to accept a collect call, to acknowledge the recipient in your report, or to send him or her a copy of your report. In closing an unsolicited letter, express gratitude for any help that the recipient can provide you, acknowledge the inconvenience of your request, but do not thank the recipient "in advance."

$$\underline{\hspace{2cm}} \quad \text{Better Widget Makers, Inc.} \quad \underline{\hspace{2cm}}$$

5555 Widget Avenue

Silver City, CO 80456

September 26, 2003

Mr. Russ Hamilton

Vice President, Sales and Marketing

Golden Bread Company

123 Loaf Street

Silver City, CO 80451

Dear Mr. Hamilton:

Construction on the new employee cafeteria at Better Widget Makers, Inc. is nearing completion and I am looking for a supplier capable of fulfilling our weekly bakery needs.

Do you have an information packet that would help me project the cost of doing business with your company? We will need daily deliveries of pastries, pies, dinner rolls and sandwich bread. Our facility operates 24/7, Monday through Friday, with a flextime workforce of 1,500 employees. To complete my operational budget I will need the following information:

- Wholesale price sheets
- Quantity cost breaks
- Annual contract discounts
- Delivery and or any other service charges.

To submit my proposal to the finance committee at their October 20th meeting I will need to receive your information by the 10th. I will also need to meet with you after reviewing the requested materials. Please call me for an appointment at your earliest convenience. My personal extension is 216-8080, #29.

In keeping with long-standing policy we would like to place this contract locally. I look forward to working with you and am hopeful that the Golden Bread Company can fulfill our needs.

Sincerely,

Ida Mae Knott

Purchasing Agent

Writing task: write a letter of inquiry for one of the following occasions.

1. Request the Scholarship offered by The Parrett Scholarship Foundation.

2. Apply a job at Pond's International Division in marketing and public relations for China.

3. Request to send information about lubrication materials for A52 compressors used

in refrigeration manufacturing.

Reading Practice

Passage

China: Latent Risks Fanned by China's Booming Growth Prompt Risk Rating Downgrade

The Chinese economy barrelled to growth of 11. 5% in the third quarter of the year, but the risks associated with the increasingly unbalanced nature of growth have prompted Global Insight to downgrade its economic risk rating from 2. 50 to 2. 75.

Significance

GDP in real terms expanded by 11. 5% year-on-year(y/y) in the third quarter of the year, slowing just marginally from the 12-year-high rate of 11. 9% recorded in the previous quarter.

Implications

Growth continues to be fuelled by external demand and bounding investment growth as private consumption continues to lag. The impact of monetary tightening and administrative adjustments has been minimal.

Outlook

Global Insight forecasts full-year growth at 11. 5%—its highest level since 1993. However, the structure of growth is fuelling risks to economic sustainability over the medium term.

Risk Ratings

Global Insight has downgraded China's economic risk rating from 2. 50 to 2. 75 to reflect the growing weight of structural imbalances in the economy's outlook and the lack of a clear and aggressive policy blueprint to resolve them to date.

Economy Records Still Blistering Growth

Chinese growth maintained blistering momentum in the third quarter, despite slowing marginally from the 12-year-high rate recorded in the previous quarter. The economy is on course this year to record its fastest rate of growth since 1993, while China could supplant the United States as the largest contributor to global growth for the first time ever, according to the International Monetary Fund (IMF). Global Insight forecasts 2007 growth at 11. 5%.

Investment and Exports Still Main Drivers

Inexorable growth in exports and investment continue to drive the economy. Despite gathering headwinds over the global economy, exports have maintained traction, rising by 22. 8% in September alone in y/y terms to US＄112. 5 billion, as imports grew at a more moderate rate of 16. 1%. Foreign-exchange earnings have been further boosted by the continued influx of foreign direct investment(FDI), which rose by 10. 9% on the year in the first nine months to US＄47. 22 billion.

Huge external surpluses continue to fuel robust liquidity growth. Money supply is being inflated by interventions by the People's Bank of China (PBoC) to stem upward pressure on the yuan exchange rate, generated by surging foreign capital inflows. Foreign-exchange gains account for 45% of money supply gains in the nine months through September. High liquidity continues to support robust expansion of credit. During the first three quarters of the year, urban fixed-asset investment (FAI) rose by 25.7%, slowing by just 0.2 percentage point from the 25.9% annual growth rate recorded in the first half, despite monetary tightening and the imposition of administrative controls. Concurrently, retail sales—a key gauge of private consumption—rose by 15.9% over the nine-month period. In inflation-adjusted terms, retail sales rose by 12.3%, indicating that household spending continues to lag significantly as a demand driver. The NBS reports that investment accounted for 42% of GDP growth in the first nine months of the year, against a 37% share for private consumption. This marks a reversal from dynamics at the beginning of the current growth cycle in 2002, when household consumption and fixed capital formation accounted for 44% and 36% of GDP, respectively. By comparison, the share of consumption to GDP in the United States stands at 70% and over 60% in India.

Implications and Outlook

A Growth Phenomenon But Risks Build

It is this changing structure of demand that is fuelling latent risks in China's economic outlook. As investment becomes the largest demand component in the economy, it is beginning to face diminishing rates of returns. Despite huge rates of investment, productivity growth has been relatively weak, highlighting inefficiencies in the economy generated by high and rising levels of excess capacity and the continued heavy presence of the state sector in the current business cycle. Downward pressure has been exerted on prices, undermining the already low margins of domestic firms. Much attention has been garnered by the high rate of inflation, which rose to five-year highs in August. However, pressure has been generated by supply-side constraints, fuelled by interruptions to the food supply.

Asset Bubble Builds

Financial risks are also exacerbated by the current boom in financial markets. Excess liquidity is being ploughed into the stock market by retail investors, with speculation fuelled by so-called "hot money inflows", effectively round-tripping. The benchmark Shanghai A-share's profit/earnings ratio has soared from 16 at the end of 2005 to 73 in September 2007. An asset bubble is clearly forming, compounded by the traditionally volatile nature of China's stock markets, and dominated by short-term trades. A major stock market correction would be unlikely to have a severe impact on the economy comparable to that experienced in Japan in the early 1990s. China's stock markets remain comparatively small in terms of capitalisation despite recent robust growth. Moreover, only a quarter of shares in the Chinese market are liquid and available for trade.

Environmental and Socio-Economic Risks

The economy's extensive growth pattern has also caused additional imbalances. Investment-driven growth is more energy intensive than growth geared to consumption. China's severe environmental degradation is set to become an increasingly acute problem. In addition, investment concentrated in heavy industrial activities has resulted in lower employment generation than consumption-oriented industries.

The potential slowdown in external demand, coupled with the need to maintain growth at high rates to absorb shocks generated by state sector restructuring, will inhibit authorities from allowing more aggressive appreciation in the yuan exchange rate, which could ease upward pressure on the money supply. China's perceived policy self-interest could fuel the current wave of global trade protectionism, further exacerbating external risks.

Authorities recognise the need to re-orient growth from its current export-investment paradigm to greater emphasis on consumption. However, that reorientation will take time given the significant structural challenges it entails ranging from creating a more geographically balanced distribution of growth and a viable social security net to continued downsizing of the state sector to allow for more rapid growth in the more productive and efficient private sector.

Ⅶ. **Answer the following questions**

1. Why has China's productivity growth been relatively weak?
2. Will a major stock market correction in China have impact on the economy comparable to that experienced in Japan in the early 1990s? Why?
3. What risks will Chinese economy's extensive growth pattern bring?
4. Why are the Chinese authorities reluctant to allow more appreciation in the yuan exchange rate?

Recycling the Petrodollars

Exporters of oil are saving more of their recent windfall than in previous price booms. It's hard to spot where the money is going.

Many American politicians and pundits explain their country's enormous current-account deficit by pointing at the surpluses of Asian economies, especially China. Undervalued currencies and unfairly cheap labour, they complain, have undermined America's competitiveness. In fact, looking at the world as a whole, the group of countries with the biggest current-account surpluses is no longer Asia but oil exporters, on which high prices have bestowed a gigantic windfall.

This year, oil exporters could haul in $700 billion from selling oil to foreigners. This includes not only the Organisation of Petroleum Exporting Countries (OPEC) but also Russia and Norway, the world's second—and third—biggest earners. The International Monetary Fund estimates that oil exporters' current-account surplus could reach $400 billion, more than four times as much as in 2002. In real terms, this is almost double their dollar surpluses in 1974 and 1980, after the twin oil-price shocks of the 1970s—when Russia's hard-currency exports were tiny. The combined current-account surplus of China and other Asian emerging economies is put at only $188 billion this year.

Relative to their economies, the oil producers' current-account surpluses are far bigger than China's. Whereas the IMF forecasts China's surplus to be about 6% of GDP this year, it predicts Saudi Arabia's—not much different in money terms, at just over $100 billion this year—to be a whopping 32%. On average, Middle East oil exporters are expected to have an average surplus of 25% of GDP. Russia might record 13% and Norway 18%.

The rise in oil prices represents a big redistribution of income from those who buy oil to those who produce it. Past periods of high prices have not lasted long, but this time oil producers' extra revenues might prove to be more durable. The futures market expects oil to stay expensive, even though the price of a barrel of West Texas Intermediate, an industry benchmark, recently slipped back to around $60.

An Enviable Choice

What will happen to all these petrodollars? In essence, they can be either spent or saved. Either way, a lot of the money can be recycled to oil-consuming economies and thus soften the impact on them of higher oil prices. If oil exporters spend their bonanza, they import more from other countries and thus help to maintain global demand. They are unlikely to spend the lot, however, because they tend to have higher saving rates than oil consumers: saving is around 40% of GDP in the United Arab Emirates (UAE) and Kuwait, for instance. A transfer of income from oil consumers to oil producers will therefore lead to a slowdown in global demand.

If they save their windfall, but invest it in global capital markets, they can finance oil importers' bigger current-account deficits—in effect, lending the increase in fuel bills back to consumers. And by increasing the demand for foreign financial assets, they can boost asset prices and push down bond yields in oil-importing countries. This in turn can help to support economic activity in these economies.

Experience shows that oil booms can be a blessing or a curse for producing economies, depending on how wisely the extra revenue is spent or saved. Too often, past windfalls have been celebrated with budgetary blow-outs, while the abundance of money has encouraged the postponement of economic reforms. This time, however, oil exporters seem to be spending less, instead running larger external surpluses, repaying debts and building up assets. In 1973-1976, 60% of the increase in OPEC's export revenues was spent on imports of goods and services. In 1978-1981, the proportion rose to 75%. But the IMF estimates that only 40% of the windfall in the three years to 2005 will have been spent.

In Russia, the government has taken the sensible step of setting up an oil stabilisation fund, which will be used to reduce its large foreign debt. That said, the country has been more eager than members of OPEC to spend its extra money. Around two-thirds of the increase in Russia's export revenues since 2002 has gone on imports. Some analysts also suspect that the government may yet raid the stabilisation fund for a spending spree. The main concern, however, is that while the economy is flush with cash important structural reforms will be postponed.

In most of the Middle East, governments are being more cautious than usual with their extra revenue. Mohsin Khan, the director of the IMF's Middle East and Central Asia department, reckons that most governments in the region are budgeting on an oil price of only $30 to 40 a barrel for next year. He estimates that governments have on average spent only 30% of their extra oil revenue since

2002, compared with 75% in the 1970s and early 1980s, after previous steep climbs in the oil price. Their average budget surplus has increased from 2% of GDP in 2002 to nearly 15% this year.

Lessons Learned, Perhaps Too Well

Oil-exporting governments seem to have taken to heart the lessons of the 1970s and 1980s. First: don't assume that oil prices will stay high for ever: in real terms, OPEC's annual average oil revenue in 1981—2000 was only one-third of that in 1980. Second, don't waste your windfall. In previous booms, oil-producing countries gaily spent their petrodollars on lavish construction projects that required imported equipment and skilled foreign workers, but did little to create local jobs or to diversify economies. In its recently published Regional Economic Outlook for the Middle East and Central Asia, the IMF advises governments to give priority to spending that will have a more lasting impact on growth and living standards.

In fact, believes Mr. Khan, Middle East oil exporters have greater capacity to spend petrodollars at home than in the 1970s and 1980s, because their populations have been rising rapidly and because their infrastructure needs upgrading after many years of dwindling government revenues. High unemployment means that there is social pressure for more spending on education and health, and for schemes to encourage private-sector employment.

Saudi Arabia, with one of the world's fastest growing populations, has an unemployment rate of perhaps 20%. After nearly two decades of large budget deficits, the government's debt was 100% of GDP by 2000. Even this year, Saudi Arabia's oil revenues per head will be about 70% less in real terms than in 1980, owing in part to a near tripling of its population. It is using some of its extra money to repay debt, and the government has recently raised civil servants' pay by 15%—the first across-the-board increase in more than 20 years.

As well as spending more on health, education and infrastructure, the Middle East also needs to invest in oil production and refining capacity, to ease future supply shortages and so stabilise prices. The International Energy Agency gave warning this week that oil prices will keep rising over the next two decades unless the region's producers invest substantially more than they currently intend.

The IMF is also—unusually—encouraging these economies to be less thrifty. Increased spending will not only, through diversification, allow Middle East countries to support their future economic development, but by boosting imports from the rest of the world it will also allow a more orderly narrowing of global imbalances. This should help to cushion the world economy against the negative impact of rising oil prices.

So far most of the extra money is being saved, not spent, so where is it going? In the 1970s and early 1980s surplus petrodollars were largely deposited in banks in America or Europe. These banks then lent too many of them to oil-importing developing countries, sowing the seeds of Latin America's debt crisis. This time it is proving much harder to track the money, but much more seems to be going into foreign shares and bonds rather than into western banks. This may reflect a greater reluctance to hold deposits in foreign banks, because of the increase in official scrutiny after the terrorist attacks of September 11th, 2001. Figures from the Bank for International Settlements (BIS) show that in 2002 and 2003 OPEC deposits with banks in the BIS reporting area actually fell. Since last year, they have increased, but only modestly. In contrast, Russian bank deposits abroad have risen much more sharply, as have the central bank's official reserves, from $73 billion at the end of 2003 to $161 billion this October.

Russian investment, whether in bank deposits, London property or football clubs, is relatively conspicuous. But even the experts at the IMF and the BIS are finding it hard to track Middle Eastern money, because a large chunk of the surplus is held not as official reserves, but as foreign investment by government oil stabilisation and investment funds and by national oil companies. Official reserves of Middle East oil exporters (including the total net foreign assets of the Saudi Arabia Monetary Agency) have risen by around $70 billion this year, accounting for less than 30% of their current-account surplus.

Follow the Money

One puzzle is that, according to data published by America's Treasury Department, OPEC members' holdings of American government securities fell from $67 billion in January this year to $54 billion in August. But Middle East purchases of American securities are probably being channelled through London. Mr Khan reckons that although the bulk of OPEC's surplus revenues has so far gone into dollar-denominated assets, those assets are increasingly held outside the United States. A big chunk is also going into hedge funds and offshore financial institutions, which are unregulated and so impossible to track.

There has also been a flood of petrodollars into private equity abroad. In January, Dubai International Capital took a $1 billion stake in Daimler Chrysler. In March, it bought the Tussauds Group, a theme-park firm. This month, DP World, Dubai's state-owned ports operator, made a £3 billion($5.2 billion) bid for P&O, Britain's biggest ports and ferries group.

Many smaller private investors in the Middle East are keeping their money closer to home. In the 1970s and early 1980s equity markets barely existed in the Gulf. This time money has flooded into them. Share prices in Saudi Arabia have increased fourfold since 2003, and its bourse now has the largest capitalisation of any emerging stock market. The average price/earnings ratio in the region is over 40 and recent share offerings have been oversubscribed several hundred times. A spectacular property boom is under way in many places, notably Dubai, which has become a regional financial centre and leisure playground. The world's biggest shopping mall is being built there and Emirates, the state's airline, has virtually underwritten the launch of the Airbus A380, ordering no fewer than 45 of the super-jumbos, a third of the total.

Despite the lack of hard data, many economists are sure that a big dollop of petrodollars is going into American Treasury securities. If so, the recycling of money via bond markets could have very different effects on the world economy from the bank-mediated recycling of previous oil booms. If petrodollars not spent flow into global bond markets, they reduce bond yields and thus support consumer spending in oil-importing countries.

New Words and Expressions

windfall ['windfɔ:] *n.* a sudden, unexpected piece of good fortune or personal gain 意外之财,横财

previous ['pri:vjəs] *adj.* existing or occurring before something else in time or order; prior 先前的,先的

spot [spɔt] *v.* to detect or discern, especially visually; spy 辨认,认出

pundit ['pʌndit] *n.* a source of opinion; a critic 提出意见者;批评家

deficit ['defisit] *n.* tthe amount by which a sum of money falls short of the required or expected amount; a shortage 赤字

surplus ['sə:plʌs] *n.* excess of receipts over expenditures 盈余

undermine [ˌʌndə'main] *v.* to weaken, injure, or impair, often by degrees or imperceptibly; sap 逐渐损坏;暗中破坏

bestow [bi'stəu] *v.* to present as a gift or an honor; confer 赠与

gigantic [ʤai'gæntik] *adj.* relating to or suggestive of a giant 巨大的

haul [hɔ:l] *v.* to pull or drag forcibly; tug. See Synonyms at pull 用力拽或牵

whereas [hwɛə'æz] *conj.* while on the contrary 然而

whop [hwɔp] *v.* to defeat soundly; thrash 彻底打败;重创

distribution [ˌdistri'bju:ʃən] *n.* the act of distributing or the condition of being distributed; apportionment 分配,配给

raid [reid] *v.* to make a raid on 袭击

spree [spri:] *n.* a carefree, lively outing 欢闹

revenue ['revənju:] *n.* the income of a government from all sources appropriated for the payment of the public expenses 收入：从各种来源的政府收入拨给支付公共支出的费用

barrel ['bærəl] **n.** a large, cylindrical container, usually made of staves bound together with hoops, with a flat top and bottom of equal diameter 桶

benchmark ['bentʃmɑːk] **n.** a standard by which something can be measured or judged 基准点

bonanza [bəu'nænzə] **n.** a source of great wealth or prosperity 富源

asset ['æset] **n.** a valuable item that is owned 资产

blow-out [bləuaut] **n.** a sudden rupture or bursting, as of an automobile tire 爆裂

postpone [pəust'pəun] **v.** to delay until a future time; put off 延迟

reckon ['rekən] **v.** to consider as being; regard as 认为

assume [ə'sjuːm] **v.** to take for granted; suppose 想当然

gaily ['geili] **adj.** in a joyful, cheerful, or happy manner; merrily 欢快地

lavish ['læviʃ] **adj.** characterized by or produced with extravagance and profusion 奢侈的

infrastructure ['infrə,strʌktʃə] **n.** the basic facilities, services, and installations needed for the functioning of a community or society, such as transportation and communications systems, water and power lines, and public institutions including schools, post offices, and prisons. 基础设施

dwindle ['dwindl] **v.** to become gradually less until little remains 逐渐减少

diversification **n.** the act of introducing variety; the condition of being varied 变化，多样化

cushion ['kuʃən] **v.** to protect from impacts or other disturbing effects 保护

to mitigate the effects of; absorb the shock of 减缓……的后果；吸收……的冲击

sow [səu] **v.** to scatter (seed) over the ground for growing 撒种

reluctance [ri'lʌktəns] **n.** the state of being reluctant; unwillingness 勉强

scrutiny ['skruːtini] **n.** close observation; surveillance 仔细的观察

conspicuous [kən'spikjuəs] **adj.** easy to notice; obvious 易见的

bulk [bʌlk] **n.** a distinct mass or portion of matter, especially a large one 大块，大量

denominate [di'nɔmineit] **v.** to issue or express in terms of a given monetary unit 以……面值发行

chunk [tʃʌŋk] **n.** a thick mass or piece 厚块或大片

offshore ['ɔf'ʃɔː] **adj.** located or based in a foreign country and not subject to tax laws 海外的

ferry ['feri] **n.** to transport (people, vehicles, or goods) by boat across a body of water 渡运

bourse [buəs] **n.** a stock exchange, especially one in a continental European city 交易所

dollop ['dɔləp] **n.** a large lump or portion of a solid matter 大块，大团

Exercises

Ⅰ. **Answer the following questions.**

1. What is the trend of world economy according to the author?

2. How could the oil exporters help to improve world economy? Do they intend to use

their petrodollars to finance oil importers' deficits?

3. What lessons have been learned by oil-exporting governments? Why does the author say that they have learned "too well"?

4. Where do the petrodollars flood into in recent years?

5. How do the oil booms change the economy of Saudi Arabia?

Ⅱ. **Paraphrase the difficult sentences or language points.**

1. In fact, looking at the world as a whole, the group of countries with the biggest current-account surpluses is no longer Asia but oil exporters, on which high prices have bestowed a gigantic windfall.

2. Too often, past windfalls have been celebrated with budgetary blow-outs, while the abundance of money has encouraged the postponement of economic reforms.

3. Some analysts also suspect that the government may yet raid the stabilisation fund for a spending spree.

4. The International Energy Agency gave warning this week that oil prices will keep rising over the next two decades unless the region's producers invest substantially more than they currently intend.

5. Mr Khan reckons that although the bulk of OPEC's surplus revenues has so far gone into dollar-denominated assets, those assets are increasingly held outside the United States.

Ⅲ. **Choose the word or phrase that best explains the meaning of the underlined part from the text.**

1. Undervalued currencies and unfairly cheap labour, they complain, have undermined America's competitiveness.

   A. destroyed completely

   B. weakened the foundation of

   C. ruined

2. Either way, a lot of the money can be recycled to oil-consuming economies and thus soften the impact on them of higher oil prices.

   A. In any case   B. At least   C. By the way

3. Some analysts also suspect that the government may yet raid the stabilisation fund for a spending spree.

   A. carnival   B. ceremony   C. celebration

4. Official reserves of Middle East oil exporters have risen by around $70 billion this year, accounting for less than 30% of their current-account surplus.

   A. explaining

   B. bringing

   C. forming the total of the amount of

5. Mr Khan reckons that although the bulk of OPEC's surplus revenues has so far gone into dollar-denominated assets…

A. beckons   B. points out   C. considers

6. A spectacular property boom is <u>under way</u> in many places, notably Dubai, which has become a regional financial centre and leisure playground.

    A. in great progress   B. getting started   C. on the way

7. Russian investment, whether in bank deposits, London property or football clubs, is relatively <u>conspicuous</u>.

    A. ridiculous   B. attractive   C. distinctive

8. A big <u>chunk</u> is also going into hedge funds and offshore financial institutions, which are unregulated and so impossible to track.

    A. amount of money   B. investment   C. portfolio

9. These banks then lent too many of them to oil-importing developing countries, <u>sowing the seeds of</u> Latin America's debt crisis.

    A. laying the basis of

    B. leading to the unpleasant situation of

    C. preparing for

10. This should help to <u>cushion</u> the world economy against the negative impact of rising oil prices.

    A. caution   B. remind   C. protect

Ⅳ. **Choose the best phrase or expression in the text from the following list to fit in each of the following blanks. Change the word form where necessary.**

point at	as a whole as	as much as	push down	in turn
take to heart	in contrast with	adjust to	build up	so far

1. Furthermore, it is obvious that the strength of a country's economy is directly bound up with the efficiency of its agriculture and industry, and that this _____ rests upon the efforts of scientists and technologists of all kinds.

2. Astronauts in flight must _____ weightlessness.

3. In fact, women talk almost three times _____ men, with the average woman chalking up 20000 words in a day.

4. ART is nothing but ART, which rises from ugly reality and displays all its sanctity _____ reality.

5. It is rude to _____ people.

6. What advice should new graduates _____ as they set out in search of employment opportunities?

7. China _____ some insurance during its long boom because its fiscal policies have been pretty conservative.

8. Is this true just in this country, or in the world _____ ?

9. Even on the most charitable analysis, it has not been a great success _____ .

10. Fears that an economic slowdown in the United States could spread to other parts of the world and lead to lower energy consumption _____ oil prices _____ sharply for the second day on Wednesday.

V. Translate the following sentences into English.

1. 我们已经知道,遇到任何有可能损害我们公司声誉的情况,都要立刻告知高层管理人员。

2. 让孩子感到家庭是世界上最幸福的地方,这是以往有涵养的大人明智的做法。这种美妙的家庭情感,在我看来,和大人赠给孩子们的那些最精致的礼物一样珍贵。

3. 伊拉克官员说,他们推迟了原定星期六举行的一次重要的全国性会议。

4. 科学家们正在作一项迄今为止没人做过的实验。

5. 乐观主义假定或企图证明宇宙存在是为了使我们快乐;悲观主义则假定或企图证明那是为了使我们不快乐。

6. 俄罗斯开始进一步限制对伊朗核计划提供技术和设备,但它不愿放弃利益丰厚的合同。

7. 自 2005 年以来,中国政府已让人民币对美元升值超过 20%。

8. 由于数千年来所处生态体系的变化,野生植物和动物日益多样化。

9. 气候变化特使表示,未来 20 年里,中国的排放量将占到二氧化碳排放增量的 50%,到 2020 年,中国温室气体排放量将比美国多 60%。

10. 随着美国以及海外石油价格的飙升,销售量逐步下滑。

VI. Translate the following into Chinese.

1. Experience shows that oil booms can be a blessing or a curse for producing economies, depending on how wisely the extra revenue is spent or saved. Too often, past windfalls have been celebrated with budgetary blow-outs, while the abundance of money has encouraged the postponement of economic reforms.

2. Despite the lack of hard data, many economists are sure that a big dollop of petrodollars is going into American Treasury securities. If so, the recycling of money via bond markets could have very different effects on the world economy from the bank-mediated recycling of previous oil booms.

Writing

Directions: Outline of an ad

Start-up businesses tend to advertise in print—in newspapers, magazines or other publications.

Successful print ads are usually written around a few basic elements.

1.1 The headline—a strong statement featuring the major selling point (eg cheaper, faster).

1.2 The illustration (optional)—reinforcing the claim in the headline (eg showing how your product works).

1.3 The body copy—the main text which persuades the reader to buy your product.

1. 4 The tag-line—summing up the product or the company's philosophy (eg 'Just do it').

1. 5 The call to action—telling the reader what to do next.

1. 6 The company details—name, address, phone number, email and web addresses and logo (if you have one).

Look at the advertising around you. Decide what sort of ad would work best for your business and what would make the ad stand out.

Sample 1: A GOOD AD

SUPERB
AUSTRALIAN
WINES
…at sensible prices
Philglas & Swiggot
Independent Wine Merchant
21 Northcote Road
Clapham Junction
Tel: 020 7924 4494
Award-winning wines
Case discounts
Weddings and parties supplied
Free glass loan
Ice and cool box loans
Friendly and helpful advice

SPECIAL OFFER
Penfolds Koonunga Hill
Shiraz-Cabernet
£4. 50
during
July

At a glance, the reader can understand what this ad is about and decide whether to read it.

Note the use of different type sizes and areas of white space. These emphasize key points and make the ad seem clear, bright and attractive.

Sample 2: A BAD AD

SAVE MONEY BY BUYING YOUR WINE FROM US!

We stock an enormous range of superb wine from Australia (our home country) and New Zealand, and our prices are sensible.

Choose from our specialist wines or save money by buying wine by the case. You can order wine by post. We also supply weddings and parties, including free glass loan and ice and cool box loan.

We offer friendly and helpful advice and unusual characterful good quality wines.

Philglas & Swiggot
Tel: 020 7924 4494

The reader is put off straight away by too many words and the grey, cluttered look of this ad.

Exercise:

Please write an advertisement for one of the following products or services:

digital camera, Chinese restaurant, luxury car, desktop computer, fitness center, beauty salon, real estate, cell phone, toothpaste, razor, face lotion

Reading Practice

Passage

Seismic Shock as Demand Shifts East

As the decision-makers in the world's energy sector meet at the International Energy Forum in Cancún, Mexico, this week, they represent an industry facing great change. How it reacts to this change is likely to define the landscape of the world's energy demand and supply for many years to come. With that change may come geopolitical shifts.

First, some consumers in the west—and the politicians that represent them—are starting to view "green" sources of energy in a more favourable light than the fossil fuels that have hitherto largely powered the industrialised world. Second, and perhaps more importantly, the oil industry—and specifically Opec, the producers' cartel—is facing a significant shift in demand from west to east. Demand from the customers Opec has supplied for the past 50 years is stagnating, as market saturation and environmental policies move the US and Europe away from oil.

However, energy-hungry Asian nations, such as India and particularly China, are taking their place, refocusing the organisation's attention eastward. Noé van Hulst, secretary-general of the International Energy Forum, says the shift is of "overwhelming importance". "The Middle East is looking east more and more, that is where the growth [in demand] is," he says.

In the past three years, China doubled its consumption of Saudi oil imports. These recently surpassed 1m barrels a day (b/d). The increase came as Saudi exports to the US—long its biggest and most important customer—slipped below 1m b/d. In January, demand from China grew so much—by 28 per cent compared with the year before—that the International Energy Agency, the energy watchdog of the western world, called it "astonishing".

Meanwhile, the US imported increasing amounts of oil from Canada and Africa and, in Washington, politicians continued to pursue energy legislation that would put a cap-and-trade system in place for carbon emissions.

In Europe, the economic slump, combined with high petrol taxes, biofuels and emissions targets, pushed demand into reverse last year. The IEA reckons that even without any new policy measures to raise fuel efficiency or encourage biofuels, US oil demand will fall by 0.7 per cent a year over the next 20 years. In Japan, the annual decline is 1. 8 per cent and in western Europe it is 0. 4 per cent.

When AliNaimi, Saudi Arabia's energy minister, takes his morning jogs around Vienna when he is there for Opec meetings, most of the conversation with the journalists trailing him now centres around China's economy. Mr Naimi is also no longer under orders from Riyadh to ensure Saudi Arabia is the US's number one oil supplier—a policy that at one point led to strain within Opec, pitting Riyadh against Caracas. It is little wonder his priorities have shifted. Demand recovery from China, and Opec's decision to withhold some of its own oil production, are the two biggest factors that returned oil prices to about $80 a barrel after they had dropped to $32 at the start of 2009 in the wake of the global financial crisis.

Despite these new relationships, the fungible nature of oil will limit the extent to which this economic shift eastward translates into a geopolitical one. One factor assisting any change will be the lack of bitter history—especially of the 1973 oil embargo—between China and Opec. In those days, China was self-sufficient and felt the effect of Opec's actions far less than drivers in the US.

Iraq, a founding member of Opec, plans radically to boost its oil production, which currently hovers around 2. 4m b/d. Last year, it signed several big deals with international oil companies, persuading them to accept minimal fees so as to help repair the country's huge fields.

Today, the market cannot absorb all the oil Opec has the ability to pump. This month Opec reaffirmed those cuts, deciding to keep its output ceiling unchanged. At the meeting, Opec—which, with Iraq, produces about 29m b/d—avoided the thorny question of reintegrating Iraq. But the group knows that its members will have to give up some of their market share eventually. Iraq is Opec's only member without a production quota, a recognition on the part of the cartel that Baghdad has for a long time not been the master of its own industry, because of United Nations sanctions, conflict and occupation.

Mr Shahristani this month said Opec would eventually have to discuss lowering other members' quotas to make room for Iraq. "Opec obviously has to accommodate Iraq's increased production," he says, adding that he did not believe it should be subject to any output restrictions until its production rose to 4m b/d, likely to be reached in 2012. His position could cause tension with Iran. Since the Iran-Iraq war, the two countries have had a gentlemen's agreement to maintain similar quotas within Opec.

As many of the organisation's ministers this week meet their counterparts from consuming countries at the IEF summit in Cancún, the issue of Iraq will be part of the discussions—at least indirectly. Integrating Iraq means that Opec needs to know what kind of demand it can expect. Oil-producing countries will push consuming countries to make their energy policy more transparent—especially legislation that could reduce demand. The issue has already appeared in a report commissioned for the meeting.

Ⅶ. Answer the following questions

1. Why is Opec facing a significant shift in demand from west to east?
2. Why will the oil demand fall in the U. S. and Europe?
3. Will this economic shift eastward translate into a geopolitical one?
4. How does Opec consider the role of Iraq concerning the production quota?

Asian Economy
The Asian Miracle and Modern Growth Theory

Over the past thirty-five years Korea, Taiwan area, Singapore, and Hong Kong area have transformed themselves from technologically backward and poor, to relatively modern and affluent economies. Each has experienced more than a fourfold increase of per capita income over the period. It took the United Kingdom, the United States, France and Germany eighty years or more, beginning in the 19th century to achieve such growth although the Japanese did it even more quickly, between 1952 and 1973. Each now has a large number of firms producing technologically complex products competing effectively against rival firms based in the United States, Japan, and Europe. The growth performance of these countries has vastly exceeded those of virtually all other economies that had comparable productivity and income levels in 1960. On these grounds alone the question of "how they did it" obviously is of enormous scientific and policy importance.

The crisis of 1997 and 1998 may have tarnished the "Asian Miracle". However, their human, organizational, and physical capital remain intact, and GNP at purchasing power parity in Korea and Taiwan area is far above that of their peer countries in 1960 such as Ghana and Mexico. It is important not to forget that their move from poverty and economic and technological backwardness to relative affluence and economic and technological modernity over a space of less than forty years has been something of a miracle. This article argues that the absorption or assimilation of increasingly modern technology has been the critical component of this process.

1. The Policy Context

After brief interludes of import substituting industrialization, Korea, Taiwan area, and Singapore switched to increasingly liberal trade policies while Hong Kong area was always a free trade entrepôt. Korea and Taiwan area provided substantial export incentives while gradually lowering trade barriers. When protection was granted in the home market, especially in Korea, it was tied closely to export performance. The granting of low interest loans was also contingent, especially in Korea, on firms meeting export targets. Firms were able to obtain inputs needed for producing exports at international prices as a result of a tariff rebate system. Subsidized credit was also tied to export success. Hence, individual firms had strong incentives to improve efficiency to enable them to export rather than to engage in rent seeking in the domestic market. A relatively stable macroeconomic environment characterized by limited inflation relative to many developing countries provided the overall context. Rarely did the real effective exchange rate appreciate and such episodes were quickly corrected. Manufacturers were thus able to concentrate on improving productivity rather than coping with rapidly changing relative prices of inputs and outputs. Within this context, the countries in question experienced 5% or more growth in per capita income over a period of 30 to 35 years. The policy environment was obviously a critical component of the success in these countries.

2. Assimilation Theories of Asian Growth

Over the last dozen years a number of different views have been put forth attempting to explain the 'Asian Miracle'. One set of views that we denote by 'assimilation' theories, stresses the entrepreneurship, innovation, and learning, all encouraged by the policy regime, that these economies had to go through before they could master the new technologies they were adopting from the more advanced industrial nations; it sees investment in human and physical capital as a necessary, but far from sufficient, part of the assimilation process. Another which emphasizes physical and human capital accumulation we denote by 'accumulation' theories.

The assimilationist view notes that the technologies that the newly industrialized countries (nics) came progressively to master during the 1970's and 1980's were ones with which, in 1960, they had no experience at all. In addition, the product mix changed dramatically as shown in Table 1 for Taiwan area. For example, in 1960 virtually no electronics goods were produced in Taiwan area but by 1990 these accounted for roughly 21 % of manufacturing exports. To learn to use new technologies and to function effectively in new sectors required the development of new sets of skills, new ways of organizing economic activity, and becoming familiar with and competent in new markets. To do this was far from a routine matter, but involved risk taking entrepreneurship as well as good management. What makes the Asian miracle miraculous is that these countries did these things so well, while other countries were much less successful. To be sure, adopting the technologies of the advanced countries required, among other things, high rates of investment in physical and human capital, and the nics achieved these high rates. But to say that these investments were all that was required offers too limited a perspective on the magnitude of the achievement.

Table 1

Changes in Physical Production Levels

Selected Industrial Products

Taiwan area 1960—1990

Product	1960	1990
Man Made Fibres—millions of tons	1,762	1,785,731
Polyvinyl Chloride—millions of tons	3,418	920,954
Steel Bars—millions of tons	200,528	11,071,999
Machine Tools	0	755,597
Sewing Machines	61,817	2,514,727
Electric Fans	203,843	15,217,438
Television Sets	0	3,703,000
Motorcycles	0	1,055,297
Telephones	0	13,992,431
Radios	0	5,892,881
Tape Recorders	0	8,124,253
Electronic Calculators	0	44,843,192
Integrated Circuits (1,000)	0	2,676,865
Electronic Watches	0	5,115,695
Shipbuilding (tons)	27,051	1,211,607

Source: Taiwan Area Statistical Data Book, 1992, Council for Economic Planning and Development, Taiwan area, Taipei, Table 5-6c.

An emphasis solely on investment assumes that the state of technological knowledge at any time is largely embodied in machinery and codified in blueprints and associated documents and that for a firm to adopt a technology that is new to it, but not to the world, primarily involves getting access to equipment and blueprints. However, only a small portion of what one needs to know to employ a technology is codified in machine manuals, textbooks, and blueprints; much of it is tacit and learning is as much by doing and using as by reading and studying. Most business organization practices and market judgments are even less codified. A large number of case studies have documented this for hundreds of firms in the Asian countries. All arrive at a view that is illustrated by a quotation from Hobday.

East Asian latecomers did not leapfrog from one vintage of technology to another. On the contrary, the evidence shows that firms engaged in a painstaking and cumulative process of technological learning: a hard slog rather than a leapfrog. The route to advanced electronics and information technology was through a long difficult learning process, driven by the manufacture of goods for export.

Such learning and the eventually high levels of productivity with which imported equipment are operated allows the modern sector to gradually increase its share of output, capital, and labor. The sector expands and the relative size of less productive sectors contracts, yielding a growing level of national productivity. This change is a central feature of the model introduced.

The rapidly rising education levels in the nics is a frequently noted phenomenon. Rising human capital can be viewed simply as an increase in the quality or effectiveness of labor, adding a third factor to the conventional production function. An alternative view perceives the effects of sharply rising educational attainments, in particular the creation by these countries of a growing cadre of reasonably well trained managers, engineers and applied scientists as providing a comparative advantage in identifying new opportunities and effectively learning new things. It permits an earlier identification of new product areas and new technologies and makes the transition to them more efficient. Thus education was critical to realizing the change in the sectoral structure in Taiwan.

3. Why is the Issue Important?

The assimilation account stresses learning about, risking operating, and coming to master, technologies and other practices that are new to the country, if not to the world. The 'marshalling of inputs' is part of the story, but the emphasis is on innovation and learning, rather than on marshalling. Under this view, if when one marshals but does not innovate and learn, development does not follow. Our argument has been that it is a mistake to think that the nics did it largely by moving along production functions, and that understanding must involve 'learning' in an essential way. There are many of the essential elements of the appropriate policy regime: fiscal, monetary, and exchange rate policies that make producing for export attractive, and which stimulate savings and investment; significant investments in human capital; competition to keep firm managers on their toes.

But simply getting the macroeconomic environment right will not assure effective economic development. Policy attention needs to be paid to assuring that potential business leaders who are both competent and willing to take risks have access to whatever is needed to run businesses. Since it is impossible to judge winners and losers in advance, entrepreneurs should be encouraged to try, success rewarded, and failure not coddled. And yet since, at the same time, learning to operate effectively in the world of modern practice takes time and effort, the policy environment needs to nurture learning. The successful Asian nics have succeeded until recently, albeit in different ways.

Above all, we think the significance involves perceptions as to the nature of firms and about their processes of learning. To return to our earlier discussion, when a firm 'chooses' to do something that is radically new to it, and to the community in which it resides, this involves risk taking and, if successful, requires effective learning. In turn, learning proceeds at several different levels: that of individual workers and teams of them, that of establishments and firms, and at the level of an industry.

New Words and Expressions

per capita income: the total national income divided by the number of people in the nation 个人平均所得

tarnish ['tɑːniʃ] *v.* to lose or cause to lose the shine 晦暗

parity ['pæriti] *n.* functional equality 同等,相等

entrepôt ['ɔntrəpəu] *n.* transshipment center, a port where merchandise can be imported and then exported without paying import duties 转口港

incentive [in'sentiv] *n.* a motivating influence; stimulus 刺激,动力

contingent [kən'tindʒənt] *a.* dependent on events, conditions, etc, not yet known; conditional 可能发生的,可能的

rebate ['riːbeit] *n.* a refund of some fraction of the amount paid 折扣,返还

tacit ['tæsit] *a.* implied or inferred without direct expression 按惯例的

cadre ['kɑːdə] *n.* core, nucleus 骨干;核心

Exercises

Ⅰ. **Answer the following questions.**

1. Why do people call the Asian growth performance a miracle?

2. What are the characteristics of a positive policy context?

3. What are the basic assumptions of assimilation theories?

4. Learning should proceed at different levels. What are they?

Ⅱ. **Paraphrase the difficult sentences or language points.**

1. It is important not to forget that their move from poverty and economic and technological backwardness to relative affluence and economic and technological modernity over a space of less than forty years has been something of a miracle.

2. The granting of low interest loans was also contingent, especially in Korea, on firms meeting export targets.

3. East Asian latecomers did not leapfrog from one vintage of technology to another.

4. The modern sector grows, and the sector which could not produce as much as the modern sector declines, and such changes lead national productivity to increase.

5. Because it is difficult to predict who will win and who will lose, we should encourage entrepreneurs to try, reward success and tolerate failure.

Ⅲ. **Choose the word or phrase that best explains the meaning of the underlined part from the text.**

1. This article argues that the absorption or <u>assimilation</u> of increasingly modern technology and the change in industrial structure has been the critical component of this process. (Para. 2)

   A. a linguistic process by which a sound becomes similar to an adjacent sound

   B. the process of assimilating new ideas into an existing cognitive structure

   C. the process of absorbing nutrients into the body after digestion

2. A relatively stable macroeconomic environment characterized by limited inflation <u>relative to</u> many developing countries provided the overall context. (Para. 3)

   A. comparative with   B. similar to   C. in relation to

3. <u>Within this context</u>, the countries in question experienced 5% or more growth in per capita income over a period of 30 to 35 years. (Para. 3)

   A. under such circumstances

   B. in such circumstances

   C. under no circumstances

4. But to say that these investments were all that was required <u>offers too limited a perspective</u> on the magnitude of the achievement. (Para. 5)

   A. provides a panoramic view

   B. gives a vanishing point

   C. provides a rather narrow point of view

5. An emphasis solely on investment assumes that the state of technological knowledge at any time is largely embodied in machinery and codified in blueprints and associated documents and that for a firm to adopt a technology that is new to it, but not to the world, primarily involves <u>getting access to</u> equipment and blueprints. (Para. 6)

   A. keeping up with   B. approaching   C. getting in

6. However, only a small portion of what one needs to know to employ a technology is codified in machine manuals, textbooks, and blueprints; much of it is tacit and <u>learning is as much by doing and using as by reading and studying</u>. (Para. 6)

   A. practice is not as important as reading

   B. practice is more important than reading

   C. learning relies on practice as much as on reading

7. On the contrary, the evidence shows that firms <u>engaged in</u> a painstaking and

cumulative process of technological learning: a hard slog rather than a leapfrog. (Para. 6)

    A. carrying out   B. carried in   C. involving with

8. It permits an earlier identification of new product areas and new technologies and makes the transition to them more efficient. (Para. 8)

    A. makes the redemption of them

    B. makes the exchange of them

    C. makes the conversion to them

9. Thus education was critical to realizing the change in the sectoral structure in Taiwan. (Para. 8)

    A. was important   B. was at its best   C. was holding criticism

10. Under this view, if when one marshals but does not innovate and learn, development does not follow. (Para. 9)

    A. shows   B. places in proper rank   C. uses

Ⅳ. **Choose the best phrase or expression in the text from the following list to fit in each of the following blanks. Change the word form where necessary.**

cope with	put forth	account for	be engaged in	in particular
far from	in turn	a number of	in question	in terms of

1. Please _____ your conduct.
2. They looked after their father _____.
3. How well do you _____ tension?
4. He has _____ scientific research for years.
5. His salary was _____ enough.
6. He thought of everything _____ money.
7. _____ people were present.
8. That is not the point _____.
9. They chat about nothing _____.
10. What hypothesis have we _____?

Ⅴ. **Translate the following into English.**
1. 每个国家的个人平均收入在此期间都增长了四倍多。
2. 仅在这种基础上"他们如何做到这点的"就具有极大的科学和政策重要性。
3. 韩国和台湾地区提供了大量出口激励,同时逐渐降低了贸易壁垒。
4. 每个公司有强大的动机提高效率进行出口,而不是在国内市场寻求纯利。
5. 同化理论注意到 20 世纪 70、80 年代新工业国家逐渐掌握的技术是他们在 60 年代时还完全没有经验的。
6. 要完成这些远不仅是一种常规,而涉及冒险的创业精神和良好的管理。
7. 亚洲奇迹之所以神奇在于这些国家和地区做得非常成功,而其他国家却大为不如。

8. 现代部分扩展,生产性不强的其他部分相对规模收缩,带来全国生产力水平的上升。

9. 因此教育对实现台湾地区的部分结构变化非常关键。

10. 同化理论强调学习、控制风险、掌握对本国而言,即使不是对世界而言比较新颖的技术和其他做法。

Ⅵ. Translate the following into Chinese.

1. The crisis of 1997 and 1998 may have tarnished the 'Asian Miracle'. However, their human, organizational, and physical capital remain intact, and GNP at purchasing power parity in Korea and Taiwan area is far above that of their peer countries in 1960 such as Ghana and Mexico. It is important not to forget that their move from poverty and economic and technological backwardness to relative affluence and economic and technological modernity over a space of less than forty years has been something of a miracle.

2. Since it is impossible to judge winners and losers in advance, entrepreneurs should be encouraged to try, success rewarded, and failure not coddled. And yet since, at the same time, learning to operate effectively in the world of modern practice takes time and effort, the policy environment needs to nurture learning.

Writing

How to write a business invitation letter?

Directions: A business invitation letter is a key marketing letter that is typically used to invite clients or customers to special business occasions. When planning a launch, a professional meeting, or even an Open Day at the shop, naturally we want to make it special; we also know that its success and effectiveness rely on how many of our invitees appear. Writing and delivering invitations to customers, would-be customers, or colleagues to attend our important business-related events requires careful attention: While great opportunities lie therein, if done improperly, it can cause undesired results that it is wise to avoid. Usually an invitation letter includes:

1. The name of the person sponsoring the event (who is the host/hostess?)

2. Exactly who is invited (Can someone bring a guest, spouse, child?)

3. What type of social event is being held

4. The date, address, and time of the event

5. Directions or a simple map if the location may be difficult to find

6. What type of dress is appropriate or preferred

7. The phone number and deadline to reply; precede these facts with "RSVP" (French abbreviation for "please reply")

Most of the invitees who receive our business invitation letter will attend our business occasion. A professional and attractive invitation will bring more guests, while a sloppy one at best misses its mark, and at worst harms our business reputation.

Sample: Invitation for Private Preview Showing

January 20, 2010

Mrs. Mary Green
1541 Aberdeen Ave.
Montreal, QC

Dear Mrs. Green:

As one of our longtime valued customers we would like to invite you to our special Private Preview Showing of our Spring Fashion Collection for 2010.

The showing will take place at our downtown store at 4550 Sherbrooke St. West, Thursday evening, February 18, 2010 from 7: 00 pm to 11: 00 pm. Limited free parking will be available in our parking garage on the Mountain Street side of the store.

In addition to the continuous fashion show that will be running all evening long, there will be a number of spring merchandise draws, as well as a door prize for a $2,000 unlimited shopping spree. So, don't miss out on the fun!

For entry into the show and to be eligible for any of the draws you will be required to produce this original invitation with your ticket number printed on it.

In order that we may plan for snacks and refreshments appropriately, if you plan to attend, we ask you to please call Joseph Dane at (514) 982-7893 and advise her by February 12th.

Please note: If Joseph doesn't hear from you by Friday, February 12th we will assume that you are not attending the show and we will issue your ticket number to someone else.

Everyone here at The Fashion House looks forward to meeting you and sharing our Spring Collection with you at our Preview Private Showing.

Yours sincerely,
Linda Cotton
Show Coordinator

Exercise:

Imagine that you're starting an English Enrichment Course business. Prepare an invitation letter for your grand opening.

Reading Practice

Passage

Finance Jobs Hint at Recovery in Asia

HONG KONG—Marco Wong lost his job with Citigroup in Singapore in mid-January. During all the turmoil that engulfed the financial world last year, the cutbacks at the U.S. banking giant were neither unique nor surprising.

But 20 job applications, four interviews and three and a half months later, Mr. Wong was again gainfully employed—as a financial consultant at IPP Financial Advisors in Hong Kong area.

Asia has already emerged more forcefully from recession than the United States and Europe, economic reports over the past month have shown. Now, that upturn here is starting—at least tentatively and in certain sectors—to feed into the job market. Hiring is starting to pick up again, recruiters and bankers say.

Broad unemployment is still rising, a normal pattern even after economies begin to emerge from recession. But economists say that any early signs of job growth are a prerequisite for a more solid-based recovery—one in which more confident consumers, and not just huge government stimulus packages, can play a role in lifting the economy.

While unemployment continues to rise in much of Europe and is expected to top 10 percent in the United States before any improvement materializes, rates in Asia have remained relatively low: 5. 4 percent in Hong Kong area and 3. 3. percent in Singapore.

One relatively weak spot is Japan. The jobless rate hit a seasonally adjusted 5. 7 percent in July, the highest level since the end of World War II and up from 5. 4 percent in June.

But elsewhere, recruitment firms are busy again.

Outside the financial sector, there is anecdotal evidence of hiring in other areas, though it is patchy.

Demand for sales jobs, for example, has picked up across all sectors as companies focus their still scarce resources on jobs that they hope will help generate immediate revenues.

In another example, one senior marketing executive who lost her Singapore-based job with a large U. S. software company, had been in the region for four years. The woman, who spoke on condition of anonymity because she was not authorized to talk to the media, found a job at another U. S. company in the same sector. It took 7 weeks of research, 45 applications and a dozen job interviews.

It is still very much an employers' market. Generous "expat packages"—in which overseas employees have much of their housing and their kids' schooling paid for—are for many a thing of the past.

The most successful candidates have experience in Asia, a network of contacts and language skills. It is difficult for someone to just pack up and move over from New York or London, where the market remains much gloomier.

"Employers are still being extra, extra selective in their talent search," said Mark Carriban, the Asia managing director based in Hong Kong area for Hudson, a recruiting agency. "And what is very prized out here is local market knowledge. "

In fact, many recruiters are already starting to warn that a "talent crunch" could be only months away, with companies again struggling to find people with the right combination of international qualifications, contacts and languages—of which there is a limited supply.

One piece of advice for job seekers, though easier said than done: "Learn Mandarin," Mr. Carriban said.

VII. Answer the following questions

1. What does Marco Wong's case of job-hunting indicate?
2. What is a prerequisite for a more solid-based recovery?
3. What are the unemployment rates in Europe, America and Asia respectively?
4. Is it now an employers' market or an employees' market?

Marketing
Criteria of Marketing Efficiency

Two points of view must be kept in mind in an attempt to analyze marketing efficiency. Such analysis may be directed from the point of view of the individual entrepreneur, or of particular classes of business men. This is commonly called the private point of view. Such investigations as those which have been carried on by the Bureaus of Business Research of Harvard and Northwestern universities are of this kind, as are most of the efforts of the United States Bureau of Markets, and of the Bureaus of Commercial Research maintained by some large business and trade organizations. Other analyses are carried out by investigators who are not interested in increasing the profits of individual firms or of particular classes of private business organization. They take what, for the lack of a better term, we may call the social or public point of view. Their aim is to study the social significance of marketing. In so far as they have any definite aim in mind other than the scientific search for truth, it is to determine how marketing can be carried on in such a way as to improve the economic status of the community as a whole. To such, marketing appears as a great mechanism for bringing goods from producer to consumer. This mechanism functions imperfectly at times and involves expensive processes. Consequently, it is worth study in order to determine whether it can be made to function more effectively and more economically.

The specific lines of research and even the immediate aims of those who take this latter point of view frequently, perhaps usually, coincide with those who are interested only as individuals, or as the representatives of a large class of enterprisers. But whereas those with the individual perspective are interested because they seek a means to increase individual profits, these latter are interested in individual success only in so far as it tends to the development of a more effective and a more economical distributive organization. This point of view is chiefly in mind in the following discussion. In the last analysis, this brings those of us who are individualistic in tendency to the point of view of the consumer. For the social end of marketing, as of production, is to gratify the wants of consumers as effectively and as economically as possible. And so, it is from the point of view of the investigator who sees marketing through the consumer's eyes that the criteria of marketing efficiency are now approached.

What, then, are the criteria for determining the efficiency of our market organization, and of the particular institutions of which it is composed? First among these must be considered the effectiveness with which the distributive service is rendered; then, the cost at which this service is performed, understanding cost to include actual money expenses plus whatever profits are made by those engaged in marketing, whether they be producer, consumer, middleman, or functional agency. And, finally, there must be considered the effect which this cost and these methods of performing this service have upon production and consumption. In other words, to determine the efficiency of our market organization we must answer such questions as these: Does the scheme meet our needs? Do we pay more for the performance of this service, even though it is well done, than we should? What effect does our system of market distribution have upon production and consumption? If the system is effective but costly, it is inefficient. So is it inefficient when it is cheap but ineffective. And even though the mechanism as devised results in the effective and economical distribution of commodities, it is not efficient if it exercises an unfavorable influence on either production or consumption.

It is evident that the first two criteria, service and cost, must usually be studied as one problem, although the emphasis of a particular investigation may be upon service, or upon the actual money cost, or on the trade or speculative profits involved in the performance of the service. The last criterion, the effect of the market organization upon production and consumption, involves some most interesting and illusive considerations. Considerations which the businessman and the economist learned to appreciate only when the great war magnified their difficulty and increased the need for their immediate solution. The price fixers in particular had these problems before them.

Most of the problems we meet, perhaps all of them, raise broad questions of technical efficiency. One group of problems centers about the purely mechanical elements involved in transportation and storage. Among these are problems concerning the effectiveness of the facilities for shipping and warehousing, and concerning the mechanical equipment and physical layout of our markets. The difficulties caused by poor country roads, limited railway facilities, congested terminals, and ill-planned wholesale market areas raise such problems. One of the greatest problems we have to face in the market for agricultural products is found just here. How can we retain the advantages derived from concentrating at these central markets the forces of demand and supply which operate over a wide area, and at the same time eliminate the disadvantages of the physical congestion of the market plants which arises from the resulting tendency to force an enormous supply of actual goods through these markets.

Another group of problems concerns the methods by which title to goods is transferred from producer to consumer. Here are raised a host of questions of the most vital importance. Among them are those which relate to the efficacy of our market news service, upon which we depend to keep demand and supply in equilibrium; those which relate to the adequacy of our price system to properly correlate the various factors in production and marketing; those which relate to the legal protection of the parties to an exchange; those which relate to the great costs involved in our modern methods of buying and selling, including the costs of standardization, inspection and grading, the increased costs of bargaining, and the enormous costs of demand creation.

These two groups of problems concerning the technical efficiency of our market machinery, one arising out of what may be called the purely mechanical efficiency of the plant, the other arising out of what may be called the trade efficiency of the system of bargaining, are the problems which bear directly on those criteria of efficiency which are based on service and cost.

More difficult of analysis but no less important is that group of problems which relates to the reaction of the existing market institutions, mechanical and trade, upon production and consumption. This group includes the question of the effect of the use of standard grades, when it results in improved products and increased stability of income to producers. And here may be considered the effect upon production which occurs when the market organization secures to the producer what he considers to be a "just share" of the final selling price of his produce. Here is raised the whole gamut of questions concerning the results on production and consumption of market competition and of the effects of particular railway rate structures, basing points, postage stamp rates, commodity rates, rates based upon a compromise between value of the product, weight, distance, and the competition of other carriers and of outside markets. Here, likewise can be considered the effect of our finance and warehouse methods upon the production of perishable and seasonable commodities, as well as the reactions to large market areas which have increased the growth of large-scale and specialized production.

Turning to consumption, we find for investigation the tendency for modern distributive methods to make available to consumers a large variety of commodities and the tendency of modern selling methods to create in the mind of the consumer a demand for variety, quality, service, style, and seasonable goods.

Most of the criticism of modern marketing is really pointed directly or indirectly at our competitive regime as it now functions. Even the important problems of the physical efficiency of transportation, and of the physical congestion of central market areas, are very closely bound up with the conditions of competition in a regime of private property. Most of the proposed remedies and reforms propose to eliminate our present competitive system, or they involve proposals leading to an increase in existing forms of control on the part of the government, or to an introduction or enlargement of the control exercised by producers and consumers through some form of cooperation or combination among the members of these classes.

Economists in general hold that economic progress is greater under a regime of competition than it is conceivable it could be under any other known or proposed. Briefly, they hold that the best men and the best processes and policies evolve, and that goods and services that are wanted are produced most effectively and most economically. As applied to marketing this means that the most efficient firms will survive, that the best channels of distribution and the best methods of selling will prevail, and that commodities in amount, kind, and quality demanded will be placed upon the market. Finally, as regards price and cost, competition will reduce price to costs, including a reasonable (socially necessary) profit, but keep it up to a point which will insure the required production. This ideal comes very far from being realized, particularly when conditions are changing so rapidly that attempted solutions of problems of production and marketing are often out of date when they are evolved. In consequence, the process of selection when working through price is for times like the present slow and expensive. For competition is slow to weed out the inefficient producers and distributors, and their methods. But the advocates of the existing system, while recognizing this, hold that it is the best scheme of production and distribution which has been devised, and argue that many of the proposed remedies, such as socialism, the use of combinations tending toward control of particular kinds of production, whether by manufacturers or by agriculturalists, and even by consumers, will bring evils greater than are these wastes of competition.

We have, however, long since reached a point where a large group of investigators take it for granted that the competitive regime imputed to the classical economist's mind is and must be supplemented or abandoned. We have not yet reached a point where the schemes for abandonment as a practical program need seriously be considered. But there is, perhaps, a dominant feeling today that, while we may depend upon competition to maintain and increase private efficiency, that is the efficiency of the individual entrepreneurship, something more is necessary to bring about a proper correlation between individual activities, particularly between the efforts of producers or consumers of specific products, and so to promote general efficiency. As an eminent investigator put it some time ago, "effort within individual or industrial units is carefully planned, between them it is plan-less."

Two types of activity are suggested and in use: governmental assistance, such as is rendered through the crop estimates, and private cooperation as expressed in the combination movement and in consumer and producer cooperation. Both of these can avail to:

1. Improve market news.
2. Limit or increase production, as the condition of the market demands.
3. Improve the physical efficiency of central markets.
4. Improve transportation rates and efficiency.
5. Increase the standardization and the grading of products.
6. Bring about the elimination of unnecessary middlemen.
7. Control excessive profits.

New Words and Expressions

entrepreneur [ˈɔntrəprəˈnəː] *n.* someone who organizes a business venture and assumes the risk for it 企业家

coincide [ˌkəuinˈsaid] *v.* happen simultaneously 同时发生

distributive [disˈtribjutiv] *a.* serving to distribute or allot or disperse 分发的,分配的,分布的

illusive [iˈljuːsiv] *a.* based on or having the nature of an illusion 幻影的,错觉的,虚假的,不牢靠的

magnified [ˈmæɡnifaid] *a.* enlarged to an abnormal degree 放大的

layout [ˈleiaut] *n.* a plan or design of something that is laid out 形式,布局

congested [kənˈdʒestid] *a.* crowded to excess; overfull 拥挤的

efficacy [ˈefikəsi] *n.* capacity or power to produce a desired effect 效力,效能

correlate [ˈkɔːrəˌleit] *v.* to bear a reciprocal or mutual relation 使……相关联

gamut [ˈɡæmət] *n.* a complete extent or range 全部范围

perishable [ˈperiʃəbl] *a.* liable to perish; subject to destruction or death or decay 易腐烂的,易变质的

regime [reiˈʒiːm] *n.* a system of government or a particular administration 组织方法;管理体制

Exercises

Ⅰ. **Answer the following questions.**

1. People with the individual perspective and those with the public perspective may be both interested in individual success. What are the differences between their concerns?

2. What are the criteria that determine the efficiency of market organization, and of the particular institutions of which it is composed?

3. According to most criticism of modern marketing, is it a good way to have a competitive system?

4. Some economists hold that economic progress is greater under a regime of competition than it is conceivable it could be under any other known or proposed. Why is the author against this idea in terms of marketing?

Ⅱ. **Paraphrase the difficult sentences or language points.**

1. For the social end of marketing, as of production, is to gratify the wants of consumers as effectively and as economically as possible.

2. Another group of problems concerns the methods by which title to goods is transferred from producer to consumer.

3. Most of the criticism of modern marketing is really pointed directly or indirectly at our competitive regime as it now functions.

4. Economists in general hold that economic progress is greater under a regime of competition than it is conceivable it could be under any other known or proposed.

5. We have, however, long since reached a point where a large group of investigators take it for granted that the competitive regime imputed to the classical economist's mind is and must be supplemented or abandoned.

Ⅲ. **Choose the word or phrase that best explains the meaning of the underlined part from the text.**

1. They take what, for the lack of a better term, we may call the social or public point of view. (Para. 1)
   A. as we have a good way of naming
   B. as we do not have a more proper way of naming
   C. as we have a better statement

2. In so far as they have any definite aim in mind other than the scientific search for truth, it is to determine how marketing can be carried on in such a way as to improve the economic status of the community as a whole. (Para. 1)
   A. on the contrary   B. besides   C. except

3. For the social end of marketing, as of production, is to gratify the wants of consumers as effectively and as economically as possible. (Para. 2)
   A. the same as the social end of production
   B. as the marketing
   C. because of the production
   D. the same as the marketing of production

4. First among these must be considered the effectiveness with which the distributive service is rendered. (Para. 3)
   A. caused to become   B. interpreted   C. provided

5. The price fixers in particular had these problems before them. (Para. 4)

 A. the person who set the prices

 B. the mechanism that offered the prices

 C. the person who offered the prices

6. Here raised a host of questions of the most vital importance. (Para. 6)

 A. a few   B. a great deal of   C. a little

7. And here may be considered the effect upon production which occurs when the market organization secures to the producer what he considers to be a "just share" of the final selling price of his produce. (Para. 8)

 A. cause to be firmly attached

 B. fill or close tightly with or as if with a plug

 C. assure payment of

8. Even the important problems of the physical efficiency of transportation, and of the physical congestion of central market areas, are very closely bound up with the conditions of competition in a regime of private property. (Para. 10)

 A. are related to   B. are sure of   C. stick to

9. In consequence, the process of selection when working through price is for times like the present slow and expensive. (Para. 11)

 A. For the time being   B. As a result   C. As regards

10. As an eminent investigator put it some time ago, "effort within individual or industrial units is carefully planned, between them it is plan-less. " (Para. 12)

 A. estimated   B. adapted   C. cast

Ⅳ. **Choose the best phrase or expression in the text from the following list to fit in each of the following blanks. Change the word form where necessary.**

in so far as	coincide with	be composed of	in other words	weed out
avail to	even though	a host of	at times	in use

1. His opinions _____ those of his wife.

2. These are medicinal herbs most _____.

3. His language is a bit vulgar _____.

4. They _____ useless books from library.

5. _____ you are a member of our society, you are free to use the facilities.

6. The committee should _____ experts.

7. I shall go _____ it snows.

8. All his efforts _____ nothing.

9. He achieved his goals. _____, he succeeded.

10. I have _____ rivals.

Ⅴ. **Translate the following into English.**

1. 他们的目标是研究营销的社会意义。

2. 对他们而言，营销是将商品从生产者转向消费者的宏大机制。

3. 什么是决定市场组织、组成市场组织的个体单位有效性的标准呢？

4. 我们的营销分配体系对生产和消费起到了什么作用？

5. 很明显前两个标准，即服务与成本，往往应该作为一个问题来研究。

6. 劣质的乡村路、有限的火车设施、拥挤的终点站、计划不佳的批发市场带来的困难造成了这样的问题。

7. 人们提出并使用两种行为方式：政府支持，如通过预测收成，以及个人间的合作，如联合行动、或消费者和生产者的合作。

8. 对现代营销的大部分批评直接或间接指向我们现有的竞争机制。

9. 提高核心市场的切实效率。

10. 去掉不必要的中间商。

Ⅵ. **Translate the following into Chinese.**

1. The specific lines of research and even the immediate aims of those who take this latter point of view frequently, perhaps usually, coincide with those who are interested only as individuals, or as the representatives of a large class of enterprisers. But whereas those with the individual perspective are interested because they seek a means to increase individual profits, these latter are interested in individual success only in so far as it tends to the development of a more effective and a more economical distributive organization.

2. But there is, perhaps, a dominant feeling today that, while we may depend upon competition to maintain and increase private efficiency, that is the efficiency of the individual entrepreneurship, something more is necessary to bring about a proper correlation between individual activities, particularly between the efforts of producers or consumers of specific products, and so to promote general efficiency.

   As an eminent investigator put is some time ago, "effort within individual or industrial units is carefully planned, between them it is plan-less."

Writing

Directions: A recommendation letter should provide information on who we are, our relationship with the person we are recommending, why they are qualified and the specific skills they have. Besides, contact information for follow-up should be provided.

If we are writing a personal recommendation letter, we should include a salutation (Dear Dr. Smothers, Dear Ms. Woolf, etc.). If we are writing a general letter, we can say "To Whom it May Concern" or simply do not include a salutation.

The first paragraph explains our connection with the person we are recommending, including how we know them, and why we are qualified to write a letter to recommend employment.

The second paragraph usually contains specific information on the person we are writing about, including why they are qualified, what they can contribute, and why we are providing a reference letter. If necessary, we can use more than one paragraph to provide details.

When writing a specific letter referring a candidate for a particular job opening, the recommendation letter will include information on how the person's skills match the position they are applying for. We had better ask for a copy of the job posting and a copy of the person's resume so we can target our recommendation letter accordingly.

In the section of summary we briefly sum up why we are recommending the person. State that we "highly recommend" the person or we "recommend without reservation" or something similar.

The concluding paragraph of the recommendation letter contains an offer to provide more information. Include the phone number and email address in the return address section of the letter, or in the signature.

Sample: Recommendation for Laura Addison

To whom it may concern:

It is my pleasure to recommend Laura Addison for employment with your organization. I have known Laura for over two years during which time she worked as a communications assistant in my office. I have been consistently impressed with Laura's attitude and productivity during the time that she has worked in the office.

Laura is both very bright and quite motivated. I am confident that she will devote herself to a position with your organization with a high degree of diligence. She is a quick learner and has shown the ability to digest large volumes of information. She has demonstrated the ability to articulate information and ideas in both the verbal and written forms.

Laura has also been effective in her efforts to engage the media we outreach to. She has been able to write interesting press releases and articles and convince editors to publish those pieces. Laura is willing to take risks. She will reach out to people and involve them with projects. I particularly appreciate Laura's willingness to take initiative to help the office serve its constituents more fully.

I recommend Addison without reservation. I am confident that she will establish productive relationships with your staff and constituents. Please let me know if you have need for additional information about this outstanding young woman.

Sincerely,

Helen Miller

Manager

ABC Company

818-580-5666

helenmiller@gmail.com

Exercise:

Use this letter of recommendation template as a guide for writing your own recommendation letters, making sure all relevant information is included.

Reading Practice

Passage

Text-Message Marketing

The use of text messaging, also called SMS (for short message service), has exploded in this country. Some 3.5 billion text messages are sent and received every day, according to CTIA, the wireless industry trade group. That is more than the number of cellphone calls and a threefold jump from 2007, with some of the biggest increases occurring in people over the age of 30.

Let's review the rules for getting started:

1. Don't even think about doing it the illegal way.

While SMS is less plagued by spam than e-mail, it's not without its bottom feeders. Spammers using automated dialers can hack into the nation's SMS infrastructure through the Web and blast out millions of texts to random cellphone numbers. If you were considering hiring one of these firms to do your marketing, don't. Not only might it expose you to stiffened penalties pending in Congress for text spam, but the vast majority of the messages will never even get through, or through for long, before the cellphone carriers cut you off.

2. Text marketing can be supported by traditional marketing.

Of course, to capture people's cell numbers, you need some way to get their attention. "I tell businesses to think about the resources they already have at their disposal," said Jed Alpert, the founder of Mobile Commons. "If you're a restaurant, you have tabletops. If you have a highly trafficked Web site, or are running billboards or radio spots, those are all good places to let people know about your texting campaign."

The Shedd Aquarium, in Chicago, uses a combination of on-site signs, end-of-aisle displays at local CVS stores with Coca-Cola as co-sponsor, and TV advertising. "We even built in a control group," said Jay Geneske, assistant director of marketing. "For the promotion running on three local TV stations, we just gave out our phone number and Web site. But on the Fox affiliate we gave out our short code and asked people to text in to win. The response to the Fox ad was more than the other three combined."

3. It is better to give than to receive.

"People's mobile number may be the most guarded number they have after their Social Security number," Mr. Lee of Distributive Network points out. "That's why in that first call to action you need to change their mindset from, 'You're going to hit me up with marketing,' to 'You're going to give me exclusive access to something,' or 'You value my opinion.' Voting for the new M&M color is probably the classic example."

Free stuff also helps. Emitations, an online retailer of costume jewelry, is about to start a texting campaign promoting a new product line inspired by the "Twilight" vampire-themed book and movie series. Users who text in to register will receive regular alerts about new releases and sales on products tied to their favorite characters. Just for taking part, though, they'll receive a sampler modeled on the gift bags handed out at Hollywood award dinners.

Ⅶ. Answer the following questions.

1. What are the advantages of SMS over cell phones?
2. Why spammers are not preferred to do marketing?
3. How to support text marketing with traditional marketing?
4. What does the author mean by saying"It is better to give than to receive"?

The Unrepentant Chocolatier

The world's biggest food company is betting on an emerging class of health and nutrition products to spur its growth. But risks abound.

It is a curious blend of kitchen and laboratory. From one room wafts the bittersweet smell of chocolate being gently heated and stirred by chocolatiers. Around the corner it is all science. A double row of cubicles contains human guinea pigs who sniff and taste from little tubs, scoring each on criteria such as sweetness or bitterness to produce complex flavour charts.

This is the science behind Nestlé's 110-year-old chocolate factory next door. It is in these laboratories, where a pinch of art is mixed with SFr25m of technology, that new chocolate recipes are devised. At another Nestlé research centre in Lausanne, meanwhile, researchers have been analysing chocolate as a pharmaceutical product, rather than a treat.

Investment in this kind of research may seem indulgent, particularly in a recession. But it exemplifies Nestlé's strategy for future growth. Peter Brabeck-Letmathe, the firm's chairman, and Paul Bulcke, its chief executive, hope to transform the food company into the world's leading health, nutrition and "wellness" firm. It is tempting to dismiss this as a mere marketing stunt—an effort to make people feel better about eating things they really shouldn't. Yet there is a sound commercial logic behind Nestlé's shift towards health and nutrition.

Sales of foodstuffs that have been intentionally modified and improved by manufacturers to provide claimed health benefits—known as "functional foods"—are, in many cases, growing far more quickly than foods sales as a whole.

Looking further ahead, Nestlé sees great potential in the idea of "personalized" nutrition. Just as drugs companies have long talked of devising drugs that take account of genetic variations between people, the firm wants to do the same with food. That is why it is investing in the nascent fields of metabolomics and proteomics with the aim of providing foods, diets, devices and even services for particular subgroups of the population.

Switching to a New Diet

This shift in emphasis towards health and nutrition will, Nestlé hopes, transform it from a purveyor of low-margin, commoditised foodstuffs into a provider of high-margin products and services. The firm needs new sources of growth. Sales of bottled water, which are about 10% of its business, are falling in rich countries because of the recession. They may yet bounce back, but analysts fret that bottled water, which is now firmly in the sights of environmental groups, may go the way of the fur trade.

Nestlé also seems to be losing market share in other products, though company officials dispute the assertion. Scepticism about Nestlé's prospects can also been seen in its share price: its shares trade at a lower multiple of earnings than those of its main European competitors. One reason is that investors are concerned that it may invest in businesses that are less profitable than the ones it already has.

Investors are also worried that Nestlé has become too large and unwieldy. The firm has 30 product lines from Nescafé coffee and Nesquik milk to Purina pet food. Consumers have been trading down to cheaper, unbranded foods in recent years, potentially undermining the value of owning big brands. So the company has seized upon evidence that incorporating healthier ingredients into its products could help it get its sales moving in rich countries again, and win over hearts and minds in emerging markets, too.

Sales of Nestlé's functional foods grew by 20% in 2008. And on October 22nd the company announced that in the difficult year to September 2009, in which the underlying growth rate (stripping out price changes and currency movements) across its food and beverage product lines was 0.7%, functional foods still managed to eke out growth of 4%. Other companies are benefiting from the same trend. Results released on September 23rd by Danone, a French diary and yogurt company, showed that its bestselling yogurts are those with live bacteria that are said to strengthen immunity or ease constipation. Even drugs companies are eyeing this new market. In March the chairman of Sanofi-Aventis, a French drug firm, mused about acquiring food and nutrition firms as a way to pursue growth.

Few companies, however, are spending the sort of money that Nestlé is to develop foods that are tailored to improve health. Even so, Mr Brabeck-Letmathe's grand plan to reinvent his company must navigate several dangers. Does it make sense to invest in costly, long-term research for a market that may not materialise? Another risk is that a sceptical public will not be convinced by Nestlé's grand health claims, prompting a backlash from the public or activists. There is also a danger that the new strategy might damage the firm's blockbuster legacy brands, such as Nescafé, which have taken decades to build.

Profit or Peril?

Start with the cost of research. If Nestlé were content to battle it out with Kraft, the world's second-largest food firm, in the business of just selling food, then its outlay on research and development (R&D) would be difficult to justify. But Mr Brabeck-Letmathe saw a decade ago that the food industry was becoming a commoditised grind with diminishing margins and little scope for disruptive innovation. So he began pushing Nestlé to develop functional foods with higher profit margins, and he increased spending accordingly.

Richard Laube, the head of Nestlé's nutrition business and a former pharmaceuticals executive, describes a "pipeline" of some 75 research projects. Borrowing terminology from the drugs industry seems appropriate, given the time required to develop these new products. Unlike the quick development cycles usually seen in fast-moving consumer goods, which typically take one to two years, products in Nestlé's nutrition pipeline may take four to six years to develop.

Mr Laube acknowledges that the pursuit of functional foods means that R&D expenditure must go up, not least because regulators on both sides of the Atlantic are taking a tougher line towards them. In October, America's Food and Drug Administration warned that it was reviewing health claims made by food companies; it plans to announce stricter guidelines soon. The European Commission has forged ahead with strict rules on nutrition claims, and is in the process of tightening up the claims allowed on health grounds too. Companies wishing to make claims related to disease will have to provide solid scientific evidence to back them up.

But it will be worthwhile if consumers prove willing, as they seem to be, to pay more for products with health benefits. Another benefit to such long-term research, observes Mr Laube, is that it tends to produce the sorts of innovations that pay dividends for longer than the minor, fleeting improvements made to consumer goods. He points to the formulas for whey protein, used in Nestlé's PowerBar range, and for hypoallergenic baby food. In both cases consumers continue to pay premium prices for these products a decade after their initial introduction.

Nestlé is used to playing a long game. Take Nespresso, an almost instant espresso that is made by machine from a little capsule of coffee. Nestlé started working on the technology in 1970 and filed its first patent in 1976. It was another decade before it was ready to start selling Nespresso pods and machines. Thereafter the business lost money for a decade. But now it is one of

Nestlé's fastest-growing products. "It took off very, very slowly," says Mr Bulcke. "It was 20 years of conviction that got us there."

The tighter regulatory outlook for functional foods could, in fact, benefit Nestlé because few of its rivals have the deep pockets necessary to invest in such research. The Swiss firm could end up in a strong position—provided, that is, it can develop functional foods with genuine benefits that consumers are willing to pay for.

Another risk to Nestlé's strategy is that of overreach, arising from two particular vulnerabilities. One is the legacy of the firm's past scandals involving the sale of milk powder in poor countries, which led to painful boycotts. The other involves the food industry's experience of a backlash against genetically modified (GM) crops.

"Breastfeeding is best! We will salute and say this every day, but the world won't believe us," laments Mr Laube, describing the lingering suspicions harboured by some about the company's behaviour in the developing world. The firm's founder developed its trademark milk substitute not to replace mother's milk, but to feed only those newborns who cannot be breast-fed safely. This is not company propaganda. But the firm was caught in Africa and elsewhere promoting its milk powders so aggressively that they did, in fact, replace mother's milk inappropriately. The firm insists it has mended its ways.

Nestlé's deep reach in the developing world goes back decades and gives it a head start over most of its rich-world competitors when it comes to exploiting growth. Its early embrace of globalisation had less to do with planning than with the coincidence of being based in a small country and selling a highly tradable commodity. As early as 1919 Nestlé's condensed-milk business had exhausted the supply of milk from local farmers, forcing it to open factories in Australia, England, Germany and Norway.

Today less than 2% of Nestlé's sales are in its home market, compared with 60% of Kraft's. Enforced globalisation taught Nestlé far earlier than its rivals just how markedly tastes differ across the world. The legacy of its powdered-milk scandals, however, is that Nestlé actions in poor countries are scrutinised like those of few others. That means any grand new effort to rebrand the firm's offerings as "healthy" will face scepticism, in emerging markets in particular.

Nestlé's strategy this time round is to work more closely with health authorities across the world. Its aim is to localise "wellness" in much the way it has adapted its coffees to various markets. It is, for instance, greatly expanding its efforts to add essential micronutrients to its basic foodstuffs. The firm had dismissed infant cereal as a niche product, but now its researchers are using that product as a "carrier" for probiotics and vitamins for children. It is also developing cheap, single-serving packets of nutrient-rich food for the very poor, another market it had previously stayed out of.

That may help in the poor world, but could Europe's hysteria over Franken foods also stand in the way of Nestlé's wellness products. The firm is treading carefully. Peter van Bladeren, head of Nestlé's main research centre in Lausanne, insists its functional foods will "only improve nature" by adding healthy ingredients: "no weird stuff". And the need to produce solid evidence of benefit to satisfy regulators should reassure shoppers, says Eric Scher of Sanford Bernstein, a research firm.

Stretching the Brand

Finally, there is a risk that Nestlé's new strategy could damage the firm's blockbuster brands, which have taken decades to establish. This could happen in several ways. If some of the firm's functional foods fail to pass muster with the regulators or, worse, turn out to cause harm rather than do good, then consumers could turn against all its products, even those that make no health claims at all.

That points to another potential snag. If a company known for selling indulgence wants to reinvent itself to symbolise wellness, does that not send mixed messages to the consumer? Mr Bulcke insists that there is no contradiction, and that taste will always trump nutritional benefits in the development of new products. Carmakers, after all, see no problem with marketing new cars on the basis that they produce fewer greenhouse-gas emissions without compromising on performance.

Mr Brabeck-Letmathe is convinced that all of Nestlé's brands can be made to fit into the wellness strategy. "You don't have to stretch," he insists, "if the discipline of every product is to be healthier." Every product must undergo what he calls a "sixty-forty-plus" analysis: at least 60% of those tasting it must prefer it to a rival product or the one it is replacing, and it must also be more nutritious. Critics question, however, whether, in the aggregate, Nestlé can deliver on its ambitious health and wellness promises.

New Words and Expressions

unrepentant [ˌʌnriˈpentənt] *adj.* not feeling sorry for wrongdoing 不感到懊悔的，不悔改的

scrutiny [ˈskruːtini] *n.* (instance of) careful and thorough examination 仔细而彻底的检查

nascent [ˈnæsnt] *adj.* (*fml*) beginning to exist; not yet well developed 新生的，尚未成熟的

purveyor [pəˈveiə] *n.* (*fml*) person or firm that supplies goods or services 供应货物或提供服务的人或公司

muse [mjuːz] **v.** to think in a deep and concentrated way, ignoring what is happening around one 沉思，冥想

forge [fɔːdʒ] **v.** move forward steadily or gradually 稳步前进

dividend ['dividend] **n.** share or profits paid to share-holders in a company 红利，股息

boycott ['bɔikɔt] **n.** refusal to deal to trade with (a person, country, etc)（对与某人、某国等交往或贸易的）抵制

salute [sə'luːt] **v.** (*fml*) to honour or express admiration publicly for a person or an achievement 致敬

lament [lə'ment] **v.** feel or express great sorrow or regret for (sb/sth) 为（某人/某物）感到悲痛；痛惜

hysteria [his'tiəriə] **n.** wild uncontrollable emotion or excitement, with laughter, crying or screaming 不能控制的情绪激动；歇斯底里

snag [snæg] **n.** small difficulty or obstacle, usu. hidden, unknown or unexpected 小的困难或障碍（通常只潜在的、未知的或未料到的）

aggregate ['ægrigeit] **n.** total amount 合计，总计

Exercises

Ⅰ. Answer the following questions.

1. What can we know about Nestlé's strategy for future growth?

2. Why did the author say there is a sound commercial logic behind Nestlé's shift towards health and nutrition?

3. What are the potential dangers that Mr Brabeck-Letmathe's grand plan to reinvent his company must navigate?

4. What actually caused Nestlé's early embrace of globalization?

5. What is the author's purpose of talking about Nespresso?

Ⅱ. Paraphrase the difficult sentences or language points.

1. A double row of cubicles contains human guinea pigs who sniff and taste from little tubs, scoring each on criteria such as sweetness or bitterness to produce complex flavour charts.

2. Even drugs companies are eyeing this new market.

3. Companies wishing to make claims related to disease will have to provide solid scientific evidence to back them up.

4. "It took off very, very slowly," says Mr Bulcke. "It was 20 years of conviction that got us there."

5. The tighter regulatory outlook for functional foods could, in fact, benefit Nestlé because few of its rivals have the deep pockets necessary to invest in such research.

6. The firm insists it has mended its ways.

7. Nestlé's deep reach in the developing world goes back decades and gives it a head

start over most of its rich-world competitors when it comes to exploiting growth.

8. It is also developing cheap, single-serving packets of nutrient-rich food for the very poor, another market it had previously stayed out of.

9. If some of the firm's functional foods fail to pass muster with the regulators or, worse, turn out to cause harm rather than do good, then consumers could turn against all its products, even those that make no health claims at all.

10. Critics question, however, whether, in the aggregate, Nestlé can deliver on its ambitious health and wellness promises.

Ⅲ. **Choose the word or phrase that best explains the meaning of the underlined part from the text.**

1. It is tempting to dismiss this as a mere marketing stunt—an effort to make people feel better about eating things they really shouldn't.
   A. acrobatics   B. trick   C. fake

2. Yet there is a sound commercial logic behind Nestlé's shift towards health and nutrition.
   A. evident   B. invalid   C. valid

3. They may yet bounce back, but analysts fret that bottled water, which is now firmly in the sights of environmental groups, may go the way of the fur trade.
   A. are worried   B. are confident   C. are sure

4. Few companies, however, are spending the sort of money that Nestlé is to develop foods that are tailored to improve health.
   A. cut   B. sewed   C. adapted

5. Borrowing terminology from the drugs industry seems appropriate, given the time required to develop these new products.
   A. guaranteed   B. acknowledged   C. taken

6. Mr Laube acknowledges that the pursuit of functional foods means that R&D expenditure must go up, not least because regulators on both sides of the Atlantic are taking a tougher line towards them.
   A. being more susceptible   B. being more credulous   C. being stricter

7. The firm had dismissed infant cereal as a niche product, but now its researchers are using that product as a "carrier" for probiotics and vitamins for children.
   A. aimed at a small specialized market
   B. relating to a large specialized group
   C. aimed at overseas markets

8. Peter van Bladeren, head of Nestlé's main research centre in Lausanne, insists its functional foods will "only improve nature" by adding healthy ingredients: "no weird stuff".
   A. strange   B. usual   C. artificial

9. Finally, there is a risk that Nestlé's new strategy could damage the firm's blockbuster

brands, which have taken decades to establish.

    A. explosive   B. notably cheap   C. notably successful

10. Critics question, however, whether, in the aggregate, Nestlé can <u>deliver on</u> its ambitious health and wellness promises.

    A. break   B. keep   C. dismiss

Ⅳ. Choose the best phrase or expression in the text from the following list to fit in each of the following blanks. Change the word form where necessary.

eke out	take off	incorporate into	take account of		in many cases
turn against	after all	end up		give somebody a head start	muse about

1. Some are momentous and life-changing passages, whilst others are quotidian trips undertaken every day to _____ a living.

2. I have recently picked Art and Design as one of my GCSE options and I wish to carry it further, perhaps into A Level, and hopefully _____ it _____ my career.

3. As they wander round Covent Garden later in the day, Zak, Arun and Sean _____ their futures and what lies ahead for each of them.

4. When Becca sends nasty messages to her online friends, they all _____ her. But it turns out she's been the victim of a hacker.

5. This is a very impressive start to a musical career that looks certain to _____.

6. _____ your children _____ by sending them to nursery school.

7. How amazing that something made hundreds of years ago should _____ in the sand at our feet!

8. Where a child is involved in our work the risk assessment for the activity must _____ their particular health, safety and welfare requirements.

9. _____, for most of our history we humans have been a resolutely land-locked African, Asian and European species.

10. What makes these problems especially hard to deal with is that _____ there is no right or wrong answer, just shades of grey.

Ⅴ. Translate the following into English.

1. 雀巢希望通过这次的重心向保健和营养方向转型能够把公司从一个售卖利润低的、商品化的食品的公司转型为高利润产品和服务的供应商。

2. 人们很容易将此举理解为一种单纯的营销噱头(努力让人们对于吃本不应该吃的食品感觉更好些)。

3. 分析人士担心由于瓶装水现在被环保组织紧紧盯上了,可能会重蹈裘皮贸易的覆辙。

4. 人们对雀巢前景的担忧在其股价上便可见一斑:股票交易时的盈利率低于其主要欧洲竞争对手数倍。

5. 另一个风险是雀巢对保健功效的极力宣传说服不了满怀疑虑的公众,反而招致公众或激进分子的强烈反对。

6. 但是早在十年前 Brabeck-Letmathe 先生就意识到食品行业的利润日益下降,正成为商品化的苦差,可供颠覆性创新的空间很小。

7. 功能性食品更严格的监管前景,实际上,对于雀巢是有利的。因为鲜有竞争对手有如此雄厚的经济实力投资这种研究。

8. 雀巢早期融入全球化并非计划使然,而是出于巧合:恰巧在一个小国家并售卖流通性很高的商品。

9. 这次雀巢的策略是与世界各地的健康权威紧密合作,目的是沿用咖啡适应各地市场的方式将"健康"本地化。

10. 如果雀巢的功能性食品有几项未能通过监管者审核,或者更糟,被证明对人体有害而不是有益。如果真是如此,消费者会抵制雀巢旗下的所有产品,甚至完全非功能性的产品也不能幸免。

Ⅶ. **Translate the following into Chinese.**

1. But it will be worthwhile if consumers prove willing, as they seem to be, to pay more for products with health benefits. Another benefit to such long-term research, observes Mr Laube, is that it tends to produce the sorts of innovations that pay dividends for longer than the minor, fleeting improvements made to consumer goods. He points to the formulas for whey protein, used in Nestlé's PowerBar range, and for hypoallergenic baby food. In both cases consumers continue to pay premium prices for these products a decade after their initial introduction.

2. That points to another potential snag. If a company known for selling indulgence wants to reinvent itself to symbolise wellness, does that not send mixed messages to the consumer? Mr Bulcke insists that there is no contradiction, and that taste will always trump nutritional benefits in the development of new products. Carmakers, after all, see no problem with marketing new cars on the basis that they produce fewer greenhouse-gas emissions without compromising on performance.

Writing   Résumé Writing

Directions:

A résumé is a brief document that summarizes your education, employment history, and experiences that are relevant to your qualifications for a particular job for which you are applying. The Résumé has become an essential part of the work search process. A Résumé is:

- A systematic assessment of your skills in terms of a specific work objective
- A marketing device used to gain an interview

The purpose of the Résumé is to get an interview. It is like an advertisement: it should attract attention, create interest, describe accomplishments and invite a person to contact you.

A general résumé should be a brief summary of your experience, so it should be as concise as possible —no shorter than one full page and no more than three pages (some specific kinds of résumés can be longer).

There are several sections that almost every résumé must have, including objective, education, work experience, and contact information.

1) Objective

The objective should be short and concise, but it must also be user-centered. User-centered objectives are tailored to the specific organization and position.

2) Education

In the education section, state the highest degree you have earned and provide the following details:

- Institution where the degree was granted
- Date of graduation
- Level of degree (B. A. , M. A. , etc.) and field (Electrical Engineering), any minors (English), and your GPA.

3) Work Experience

The section on work experience is usually broken down by company or position. For each, provide the following:

- Name and address of the organization
- Dates of employment
- Position title
- Responsibilities.

4) Contact Information

The contact information section is where you detail how potential employers can get in touch with you. Make sure all information is accurate and current. You should, at minimum, include your name, address, and phone number. Many people also include cell phone numbers, e-mail addresses, and web pages. It is in your best interest to make sure your potential employers can contact you.

5) Optional Sections

In addition to the basic sections, you may also want to include other optional sections to provide a more accurate idea of your skills, achievements, education, etc. These can include the following:

- Computer skills
- Honors and awards
- Languages
- Certifications
- Volunteer experience

- Hobbies and interests
- Foreign travel
- Professional memberships
- Community service, etc.

3. Additional Résumé Tips

- Do not include the word "Résumé" at the top of the page or the date you prepared the document
  - Be sure that your name appears at the top of all pages
  - Include the page number at the top of page two
  - Avoid verbs such as: "assisted", "helped", "aided", "participated" or "involved" as they do not say precisely what you did and the employer will not know what your contribution was.

4. Resume Formats

The two basic resume styles are chronological and functional. Some use features of both and are called combination resumes. Your resume should reflect your goals and unique background.

Combination Resume

This format merges elements of functional and chronological resumes. It accentuates skills and capabilities but also includes positions, employers, and dates within the skill groups. It retains the directness of the chronological format and groups skills into functional categories.

Sample 1:

A sample chronological resume is listed below.

JULIE PURDUE

jpurdue@pu. email. me

Present Address	**Permanent Address**
123 Riverwood Dr.	222 Hometown Dr.
Collegetown, USA 12345	Parentville, USA 45678
(xxx)555-7756	(xxx)444-1111
	(after May 15, 2007)

JOB OBJECTIVE

To obtain a position working with social issues where I can utilize my problem solving skills to assist individuals with financial and daily living issues.

EDUCATION

Purdue University, West Lafayette, IN

Bachelor of Art, Expected Graduation, May 2008

Major: Sociology　　Minor: History

GPA: 3. 75/4. 00

Significant Coursework: Research Methods, Peer Leadership, Social Problems, Professional

Writing.

Computer Skills: Word Processing, Excel, PowerPoint, Front Page

PROFESSIONAL EXPERIENCE

Intern, Department of Housing

Denver, Colorado, May 2006-August 2006

* Assisted supervisor with financial planning booklets
* Presented financial planning workshops for clients
* Consulted with clients on housing choices
* Met with clients to discuss financial issues

Student Assistant, Purdue University Department of Sociology

West Lafayette, IN, September 2006-May 2007

* Compiled and indexed statistical information from housing surveys
* Interviewed individuals with housing problems
* Created list of recommendations for clients with housing problems
* Wrote reports summarizing results of surveys

President, Lambda Lambda Lambda Sorority

Purdue University, West Lafayette, IN, September 2006-present

* Organized meetings for a group of 25 house members
* Coordinated activities and intramural participation during Greek Week
* Proposed new and successful fund raising activities for the house

ACTIVITIES AND HONORS

Sociology Honorary, 2005-present

Scholarship Award, 2006

Dean's list, last six semesters

History Club, 2005-present

Sample 2:

JULIE PURDUE

jpurdue@pu.email.me

Present Address	**Permanent Address**
123 Riverwood Dr.	222 Hometown Dr.
Collegetown, USA 12345	Parentville, USA 45678
(xxx)555-7756	(xxx)444-1111
	(after May 15, 2003)

JOB OBJECTIVE

To obtain a position working with social issues where I can utilize my problem solving skills to assist individuals with financial and daily living issues.

EDUCATION

Purdue University, West Lafayette, IN

Bachelor of Art, Expected Graduation, May 2003

Major: Sociology   Minor: History

GPA: 3.75/4.00

Significant Coursework: Research Methods, Peer Leadership, Social Problems, Professional Writing.

Computer Skills: Word Processing, Excel, PowerPoint, Front Page

PROFESSIONAL SKILLS

Communication/Presentation

* Presented financial planning workshops for clients
* Consulted with clients on housing choices
* Met with clients to discuss financial issues
* Interviewed individuals with housing problems
* Proposed new and successful fund raising activities for the house

Organization

* Compiled and indexed statistical information from housing surveys
* Created list of recommendations for clients with housing problems
* Organized meetings for a group of 25 house members
* Coordinated activities and intramural participation during Greek Week
* Assisted supervisor with financial planning booklets
* Wrote reports summarizing results of surveys

PROFESSIONAL EXPERIENCE

Intern, Department of Housing

Denver, Colorado, May 2001-August 2001

Student Assistant, Purdue University Department of Sociology

West Lafayette, IN, September 2001-May 2002

President, Lambda Lambda Lambda Sorority

Purdue University, West Lafayette, IN, September 2002-present

ACTIVITIES AND HONORS

Sociology Honorary, 2000-present

Dean's list, last six semesters

History Club, 2000-present

Exercise:

Suppose you are asked to draft a resume by using the information in the above samples. Your resume should be a combination one.

Reading Practice

Passage

Fashion Conquistador

Zara's quick turnover lures shoppers, but global expansion could be a strain.

It's fast, it's fashionable, and it's out to conquer the world from a remote corner of northwestern Spain. Inditex, parent of cheap-chic fashion chain Zara, has transformed itself into Europe's leading apparel retailer over the past five years, and is now aiming to rev up growth in Asia and the U. S. But as Chief Executive Pablo Isla maps out plans for global expansion, some are wondering whether Inditex is moving a little too fast for its own good.

Make no mistake: The company's track record is pretty impressive. Since 2000, Inditex tripled its sales and profits as it has doubled the number of stores of its eight brands. (Zara is the biggest, accounting for two-thirds of total revenues.) Now Isla expects to open more than one outlet each day in coming years, for a total of more than 4,000 by 2009, up from 2,800 today. Too fast? No way, says Isla. "We think we can keep up the pace of expansion without endangering profits," he says.

Others aren't so sure. As Zara ventures deeper into far-flung territories, it risks losing its speed advantage. That's because Zara turns globalization on its head, distributing all of its merchandise, regardless of origin, from Spain. With more outlets in Asia and the U. S., replenishing stores twice a week—as Zara does now—will be increasingly complex and expensive. The strain is already starting to show. Costs are climbing and growth in same-store sales is slowing: At outlets open two years or more, revenues were up by 5% last year, compared with a 9% increase in 2004. "The further away from Spain they move, the less competitive they will be," says Harvard Business School professor Pankaj Ghemawat. "As long as Zara has one production and distribution base, its model is somewhat limited." So far, the company has managed to offset that problem by charging more for its goods as it gets farther from headquarters.

Zara has succeeded by breaking every rule in retailing. For most clothing stores, running out of best-selling items is a disaster, but Zara encourages occasional shortages to give its products an air of exclusivity. "We don't want everyone to wear the same thing," Isla says. With new merchandise arriving at stores twice a week, the company trains its customers to shop and shop often.

And forget about setting trends; Zara prefers to follow them. Its aim is to give customers plenty of variety at a price they can afford. Zara made 20,000 different items last year, about triple what the Gap did. Rifling through the racks at Zara's store on New York's Fifth Avenue, Dana Catok, a 25-year-old administrative assistant, says: "At Gap, everything is the same." It's a sentiment echoed by Zara fans the world over.

Collaborations with big-name designers and multimillion-dollar advertising campaigns? Zara eschews both. Instead, it uses its spacious, minimalist outlets—more Gucci than Target—and catwalk-inspired clothing to build its brand. "Our advertising is our stores," says Isla. "The money we save is spent on top locations." Zara is on some of the world's priciest streets: Fifth Avenue, Tokyo's Ginza, Rome's Via Condotti, and the Champs-Elysées in Paris.

The tight control makes Zara more fleet-footed than its competitors. While rivals push their suppliers to churn out goods in bulk, Zara intentionally leaves extra capacity in the system. That results in fewer fashion faux pas, which means Zara sells more at full price, and when it discounts, it doesn't go as deep. The chain books 85% of the full ticket price for its merchandise, while the industry average is 60%. "We have greater flexibility," says Isla. "We can commit to a low level of purchases at the beginning of each season, so that when new trends emerge we can react quickly."

Zara's nerve center is an 11,000-square-foot hall at its headquarters in Arteixo, a town of 25,000 in Galicia. That's where hundreds of twenty something designers, buyers, and production planners work in tightly synchronized teams. It is there that the company does all of its design and distribution and half of its production. The concentrated activity enables it to move a dress, blouse, or coat from drawing board to shop floor in just two weeks—less than a quarter of the industry average.

Ⅶ. **Answer the following questions.**

　　1. What can we know about Inditex's track record from the beginning of this passage?

　　2. Why global expansion could be a strain for Zara?

　　3. Why are the rules in retailing that have been broken by Zara on its way to success?

　　4. What does "fashion faux pas" mean? Why is it crucial for Zara to commit fewer fashion faux pas?

The News Business Tossed by a Gale

It isn't just newspapers; much of the established news industry is being blown away. Yet news is thriving.

Perhaps the surest sign that newspapers are doomed is that politicians, so often their targets, are beginning to feel sorry for them. House and Senate committees have held hearings in the past month. John Kerry, the junior senator from Massachusetts, called the newspaper "an endangered species".

Indeed it is. According to the American Society of News Editors, employment in the country's newsrooms has fallen by 15% in the past two years. Paul Zwillenberg of OC&C, a firm of consultants, reckons that almost 70 British local newspapers have shut since the beginning of 2008. The strain is not confined to English-speaking countries; French newspapers have avoided the same fate only by securing an increase in their already hefty government subsidies.

Broadcast television news is struggling too. Audiences have split and eroded; the share of Americans who watch the early evening news on the old "big three" broadcast networks (ABC, CBS and NBC) has fallen from about 30% in the early 1990s to about 16%. ITV, Britain's biggest commercial broadcaster, is pleading to be excused from its obligation to produce local news.

Yet the plight of the news business does not presage the end of news. As large branches of the industry wither, new shoots are rising. The result is a business that is smaller and less profitable, but also more efficient and innovative.

Deeper but Not Broader

It is not only a matter of people switching from one medium to another. Nearly everybody who obtains news from the internet also commonly watches it on television or reads a newspaper. Technology has enabled well-informed people to become even better informed but has not broadened the audience for news.

Those who do seek news obtain it in a different way. Rather than plodding through a morning paper and an evening broadcast, they increasingly seek the kind of information they want, when they want. Few pay. Robert Thomson, editor-in-chief of the Wall Street Journal, says many have come to view online news as "an all-you-can-eat buffet for which you pay a cable company the only charge."

The main victim of this trend is not so much the newspaper as the conventional news package. Open almost any leading metropolitan newspaper, or look at its website, and you will find the same things. There will be a mixture of local, national, international, business and sports news. There will be weather forecasts. There will be display and classified advertisements. There will be leaders, letters from readers, and probably a crossword.

This package, which was emulated first by broadcasters and then by internet pioneers such as AOL. com and MSN. com, works rather like an old-fashioned department store. It provides a fair selection of useful information of dependable quality in a single place. And the fate of the news package is similar to that of the department store. Some customers have been lured away by discount chains; others have been drawn to boutiques.

The Wal-Marts of the news world are online portals like Yahoo! and Google News, which collect tens of thousands of stories. Some are licensed from wire services like Reuters and the Associated Press. But most consist simply of a headline, a sentence and a link to a newspaper or television website where the full story can be read. The aggregators make money by funnelling readers past advertisements, which may be tailored to their presumed interests.

Although they are convenient, these news warehouses can feel impersonal. So another kind of aggregator has emerged, which offers a selection of news and commentary. Some are eclectic, like the Daily Beast and the Drudge Report— the grandfather of the boutique aggregators. Others are more specific, like Perlentaucher, a German cultural website. The most successful of the lot, and the template for many newly unemployed journalists who have tried to launch websites of their own, is the Huffington Post.

HuffPo, as it is broadly known, employs just four reporters among a total staff of about 60. Much of its news is second-hand. But it boasts an unpaid army of some 3,000 mostly left-wing bloggers. The website feels like a cross between a university common room and a Beverly Hills restaurant (your attitude to HuffPo will depend largely on whether you find this prospect appealing). Arianna Huffington, who runs it, calls it a "community around news".

Old-fashioned news folk increasingly complain that aggregators are "parasites" that profit from their work. They are, in a sense; but parasites can be useful. As the quality of journalism becomes more erratic, the job of sifting stories is increasingly vital. And aggregators drive readers, hence advertising, to original-news websites. Hitwise, another market-research firm, estimates that in March 22% of referrals to news sites came from search engines like

Google, whereas 21% came from other news sites.

The rise of the aggregators reveals an uncomfortable fact about the news business. The standard system of reporting, in which a journalist files a story that is broadcast or printed once and then put on a single proprietary website, is inefficient. The marginal cost of distributing the story more widely is close to nil, but the marginal benefit can be considerable.

The inherent benefit of spreading stories around helps explain why some established news outfits are coming to resemble aggregators. News Corporation set up a website, Fox Nation, which mixes news stories with right-wing commentary. It is intended to become a conservative Huffington Post. Indeed, one of the great successes in both British and American news publishing is the Week, in effect an aggregator that is printed on paper.

Up Go the Walls

General news is likely to remain free on the internet. The crush of similar stories is too great, the temptation of piracy is too strong and the aggregators are too good at sniffing out decent free reports. Yet it has become clear that online advertising alone cannot support good original journalism.

Until recently many print news executives believed that advertising revenues would follow their readers from print to the web. But in the second quarter of 2008 online advertising revenues began to fall. Online advertising money has moved to search—ie, Google—and excess supply has depressed prices of display advertisements. As a result, executives are looking hungrily at the few online outfits that dare ask readers for money.

One is the *Financial Times* which demands registration of anybody wishing to view more than three articles per month and payment from anybody wanting to see more than ten. About 1m people are registered, of whom 109,000 pay. By going easy on casual readers, the *Financial Times* keeps a foot in what John Ridding, the company's chief executive, calls the "giant wave machines" of the internet, such as Google and Yahoo!, which drive traffic to the site. Registered readers are served targeted advertisements, which are more lucrative. It is an attempt to fuse a subscription model with one supported by advertising.

The *Wall Street Journal* takes a shrewd route to a similar destination. Rather than charging certain types of user, it charges for certain types of news. Earlier this week, it offered for nothing a story about swine flu, a review of the new "Star Trek" film and a report on looming cuts at car dealerships. It charged for pieces on Cigna Corporation's pension plan, Lockheed Martin's quarterly lobbying expenditures and a lawsuit against a bottling company which alleges that a board meeting was held improperly. In short, the fun articles are free. The dry, obscure stuff costs money.

The thinking is that broadly appealing articles draw readers to the website, where they can be tempted by advertisers and by the Journal's more selective wares. Most people do not care about pensions in a Philadelphia health-insurance company. But those who are interested in such information are very interested, so much so that they will probably pay a monthly subscription for it. And those who cross the main pay wall may be persuaded to purchase more premium content. The paper is also exploring a "micro-payments" model for individual articles.

Financial news is not the only kind for which people appear prepared to pay. ESPN, a cable sports channel, has erected several pay walls on its website. They protect information that only the most rabid fan would want to know, adhering to the Wall Street Journal's dictum that people's willingness to pay for a story is inversely correlated with the size of its potential audience. The number of profitable news niches may grow as rivals close bureaus or go out of business altogether.

Newspapers and magazines are more likely to be rescued by a careful combination of free and paid-for content than by new technology. Portable news readers such as the Kindle DX, which some have hailed as potential saviours, will help only to the extent that they lure readers from the web, where news is mostly free. At the moment they seem to be doing something else. Ken Doctor of Outsell, a research firm, reckons that the Kindle appeals to baby-boomers who would otherwise read a paper magazine or newspaper. The young prefer their iPhones and their aggregators.

King Comment

On cable television, a different kind of niche product is cleaning up. The right-wing Fox News Channel has become by far the most popular specialist provider of news. This is not surprising. The channel's newscasts and opinion shows are well-produced, and the crumbling of the Republican Party has left conservatives seeking a voice. Rather more surprising is that the left-wing MSNBC now draws more prime-time viewers aged 25 to 54 than the much more established CNN.

Fox and MSNBC provide a mixture of news, interviews and occasionally furious commentary. The aim is to complement and give meaning to the mass of disconnected information that viewers pick up during the day. Viewers know what they are getting; indeed, they rate cable shows as more reliable than newspapers. Against the common charge of partisanship, Mr Griffin, the chief executive of MSNBC, offers what could be the slogan of the cable news industry:

"We're not trying to be all things to all people."

Hot talk may be popular at the moment because Americans are politically polarised. The calmer CNN won the battle for cable viewers on election night and may well do so again in 2012. Yet, as in so much of the news business, a return to normal is improbable. The market for news is likely to remain unstable, favouring different providers at different points in political, economic and even sporting cycles.

Take Real Clear Politics, an American political website, which aggregates news, commentary and opinion polls. It became essential reading during last year's presidential race. At its peak, shortly before the election, it attracted 1.4m unique visitors a month, according to comScore. Since then its popularity has plunged by 75%. For newspapers, magazines and television programmes, with their high fixed costs, such fluctuations would be ruinous.

Not so long ago, news was a highly profitable business. Yet news does not always have to be profitable in order to survive. Even in their diminished state, large newspapers attract rich men who seek political or business clout, or who believe that there is money to be made after all. Rupert Murdoch's fondness for printer's ink has sometimes baffled Wall Street analysts. Still, last month David Geffen, a media mogul, reportedly tried to buy a stake in the parent company of the New York Times.

Less glamorous outfits can also attract benefactors. San Diego has a small, scrappy news website that was paid for at first largely by a local businessman. The Voice of San Diego concentrates on nitty-gritty issues such as water, crime and health care—the sort of stories that local newspapers used to cover extensively.

The spread of digital cameras has also enabled ordinary people to file pictures and news reports directly. They are encouraged in this by established news outlets like CNN, which have come to view citizen journalists as a source of both content and page views. Leonard Brody, the head of NowPublic, a large Canadian news-gatherer, believes that amateurs will eventually liberate journalists from the tedious business of reporting, leaving them free to concentrate on analysis. He means it kindly.

Just now journalists have less competition from crowds than from governments. In Britain local authorities have created newsletters that carry advertising. America's president has proved an especially prolific citizen journalist. People who let Barack Obama's campaign team have their e-mail address last year still receive the occasional missive. The White House posts videos on YouTube that are often more polished than those produced by the news networks.

The decline of once-great newspapers and news programmes is not without cost. It means the end of a certain kind of civic sensibility that was built on broad agreement about what is important and what is not.

New Words and Expressions

hefty [ˈhefti] **adj.** (*infml*)(*fig*) extensive; substantial 大量的；可观的

plight [plait] **n.** a very bad situation that someone is in 困境，艰难

presage [ˈpresiʤ] **v.** (*fml*) to be a sign that something is going to happen, especially something bad 成为……的前兆，预示

emulate [ˈemjuleit] **v.** to do something or behave in the same way as someone else, especially because you admire them 效法

aggregator [ˈægrigeit] **n.** a total considered with reference to its constituent parts 集合体

template [ˈtemplit] **n.** something that is used as a model for another thing 模板，样板

erratic [iˈrætik] **adj.** (*usu derog*) irregular or uneven in quality （品质）无常的，不可靠的

shrewd [ʃruːd] **adj.** well judged and likely to be right 精明的

dictum [ˈdiktəm] **n.** a formal statement of opinion by someone who is respected or has authority 格言，名言

hail [heil] **v.** enthusiastically acknowledge sb/sth as sth 热情地承认某人/某物为……

crumble [ˈkrʌmbl] **v.** (*fig*) gradually deteriorate or come to an end 渐渐垮掉；走向末路

clout [klaut] **n.** (*infml*) power or influence 权力，影响力

baffle [ˈbæfl] **v.** be too difficult for (sb) to understand; puzzle 使（某人）困惑；难倒

mogul [məuˈgʌl] **n.** very rich, important or influential person 富有的、重要的或有势力的人；巨子

missive [ˈmisiv] **n.** (*fml* or *joc*) letter, esp a long or official one 信件；（尤指）长信，公函

Exercises

Ⅰ. Answer the following questions.

1. What are the old "big three" broadcast networks in America?

2. According to the author, what are the Wal-Marts of the news world? How do they make profits? What is their main drawback?

3. What can we know about the style of the website of Huffington Post from the text?

4. How can aggregators be useful now?

5. How does the Financial Times and the Wall Street Journal charge their readers respectively? Which way do you prefer? Why?

Ⅱ. Paraphrase the difficult sentences or language points.

1. ITV, Britain's biggest commercial broadcaster, is pleading to <u>be excused from</u> its obligation to produce local news.

2. Robert Thomson, editor-in-chief of the Wall Street Journal, says many have come

to view online news as "an <u>all-you-can-eat</u> buffet for which you pay a cable company the only charge."

3. The aggregators make money by <u>funnelling readers past</u> advertisements, which may be tailored to their presumed interests.

4. The website feels like <u>a cross between</u> a university common room and a Beverly Hills restaurant (your attitude to HuffPo will depend largely on whether you find this prospect appealing).

5. Old-fashioned news folk increasingly complain that aggregators are "parasites" that profit from their work. <u>They are, in a sense</u>; but parasites can be useful.

6. The crush of similar stories is too great, the temptation of piracy is too strong and the aggregators are too good at <u>sniffing out</u> decent free reports.

7. <u>By going easy on</u> casual readers, the Financial Times keeps a foot in what John Ridding, the company's chief executive, calls the "giant wave machines" of the internet, such as Google and Yahoo!, which drive traffic to the site.

8. On cable television, a different kind of niche product is <u>cleaning up</u>.

9. Against the common charge of partisanship, Mr Griffin offers what could be the slogan of the cable news industry: "We're not trying to <u>be all things to all people.</u>"

10. Still, last month David Geffen, a media <u>mogul</u>, reportedly tried to buy a stake in the parent company of the *New York Times*.

Ⅲ. Choose the word or phrase that best explains the meaning of the underlined part from the text.

1. Paul Zwillenberg of OC&C, a firm of consultants, <u>reckons</u> that almost 70 British local newspapers have shut since the beginning of 2008.

   A. recalls   B. guesses   C. calculates

2. Perhaps the surest sign that newspapers <u>are doomed</u> is that politicians, so often their targets, are beginning to feel sorry for them.

   A. are marked for prosperity

   B. are marked for certain death

   C. are marked for revolution

3. Rather than <u>plodding through</u> a morning paper and an evening broadcast, they increasingly seek the kind of information they want, when they want.

   A. working one's way through something laboriously

   B. working one's way through something efficiently

   C. working one's way through something carefully

4. This package, which was <u>emulated</u> first by broadcasters and then by internet pioneers such as AOL. com and MSN. com, works rather like an old-fashioned department store.

   A. challenged   B. abandoned   C. imitated

5. Indeed, one of the great successes in both British and American news publishing is the Week, in effect an aggregator that is printed on paper.

    A. in a word   B. in general   C. in essence

6. The channel's newscasts and opinion shows are well-produced, and the crumbling of the Republican Party has left conservatives seeking a voice.

    A. trying to express disagreement

    B. trying to express their opinion

    C. trying to arrive atconsensus

7. Yet, as in so much of the news business, a return to normal is improbable.

    A. inappropriate

    B. unlikely to happen

    C. highly likely to happen

8. Even in their diminished state, large newspapers attract rich men who seek political or business clout, or who believe that there is money to be made after all.

    A. influence   B. profits   C. identity

9. The Voice of San Diego concentrates on nitty-gritty issues such as water, crime and health care—the sort of stories that local newspapers used to cover extensively.

    A. impractical   B. frivolous   C. basic

10. The White House posts videos on YouTube that are often more polished than those produced by the news networks.

    A. doctored   B. accomplished   C. professionally made

Ⅳ. Choose the best phrase or expression in the text from the following list to fit in each of the following blanks. Change the word form where necessary.

plod through	in a sense	in effect	so much so that	clean up
adhere to	a cross between	seek a voice	in case	nitty-gritty

1. We have done so much work on making sure we know our roles and what needs to be done—_____ I think every player could now write a book on it!

2. The film conveys much of the _____ of Welsh life and plight of families living on tick—and was the first in Britain to tackle, however tenuously, the tricky subject of racism.

3. He had his camera ready, just _____ he saw something that would make a good picture.

4. It will be consumer demand again that forces the industry to _____.

5. The public need to realise that Loughborough Post Office is, _____, closing as it is now and it's going to re-open as what we would previously have called a "sub-post office".

6. Looking like _____ a tomato and a physalis, these little fruits are eaten green and have a sweet-yet-tart taste that makes them ideal for salads and sauces.

7. What he says is right _____.

8. They offer uniqueness and most importantly offer self-respect for all ethnic women _____, a future, waiting to be heard, waiting to be acknowledged.

9. It calls for Google to _____ a set of "fundamental privacy principles" when creating new services in future.

10. It is such a shame we just _____ life without really reminding ourselves what we have done and been through to get to where we are today

Ⅴ. **Translate the following into English.**

1. 报纸业还是在劫难逃,其中最明显的标志就是:过去一贯为他们所评论的政客们,如今却开始为其感到惋惜。

2. 科技使博识的人更加通晓天下事,但并没有使关注新闻的人群范围有所扩大。

3. 罗伯特·汤马斯,《华尔街日报》的主编,说到有些人将在线新闻视为"一种只需向网络提供商交费,就能无限享用的自助餐"。

4. 这些网站中最成功的同时也是那些最近想尝试自己创立网站的失业记者们的范例的网站,当属《哈分特邮报》。

5. 由于现在新闻的质量得不到保证,所以对于新闻故事的筛选变得愈加至关重要。

6. 其中之一就是《金融时报》规定:想每月阅读三篇以上,需要注册;想每月阅读十篇以上需要缴费。

7. 相对于新科技而言,免费和付费阅读方式的有机结合或许是报纸杂志更好的出路。

8. 而对于被一些人誉为拯救者的便携新闻浏览器—Kindle DX,也只能帮忙做到从网络(网上的新闻大部分是免费的)吸引读者的程度。

9. 这样的起伏波动,对于像报纸、杂志及电视节目这样高固定成本的媒介而言,是毁灭性的。

10. 加拿大一家大型新闻采集公司 NowPublic 的总裁莱昂纳多·布罗迪笑称,他相信总有一天,业余新闻工作者将把专业记者们从纷杂的报道中解救出来,而专注于新闻分析工作。

Ⅵ. **Translate the following into Chinese.**

1. This package, which was emulated first by broadcasters and then by internet pioneers such as AOL. com and MSN. com, works rather like an old-fashioned department store. It provides a fair selection of useful information of dependable quality in a single place. And the fate of the news package is similar to that of the department store. Some customers have been lured away by discount chains; others have been drawn to boutiques.

2. Financial news is not the only kind for which people appear prepared to pay. ESPN, a cable sports channel, has erected several pay walls on its website. They protect information that only the most rabid fan would want to know, adhering to the Wall Street Journal's dictum that people's willingness to pay for a story is

inversely correlated with the size of its potential audience. The number of profitable news niches may grow as rivals close bureaus or go out of business altogether.

Writing

Scientific Poster Design

Directions:

A scientific poster is a large document that can communicate your research at a scientific meeting, and is composed of a short title, an introduction to your burning question, an overview of your trendy experimental approach, your amazing results, some insightful discussion of aforementioned results, a listing of previously published articles that are important to your research, and some brief acknowledgement of the tremendous assistance and financial support conned from others—if all text is kept to a minimum, a person could fully read your poster in under 10 minutes.

A well-designed poster is eye-catching, attractive, and communicates information effectively and economically. The following guidelines have been prepared to help you design your research poster. Keep in mind that this is a general guide. Always check the guidelines for the conference where you will be presenting your poster.

What sections to include and what to put in them:

Title: Should convey the "issue," the approach, and the system (organism); needs to be catchy in order to "reel in" intoxicated passersby. [Maximum length: 1-2 lines.]

Introduction: Get your viewer *interested* about the issue or question while using the absolute minimum of background information and definitions; quickly place your issue in the context of published, primary literature; provide description and justification of general experimental approach, and hint at why your study organism is ideal for such research; give a clear hypothesis. [Maximum length: approximately 200 words.]

Materials and methods: Briefly describe experimental equipment and methods; use figures and tables to illustrate experimental design if possible; use flow charts to summarize reaction steps or timing of experimental procedures; include photograph or labeled drawing of organism; mention statistical analyses that were used and how they allowed you to address hypothesis. [Maximum length: approximately 200 words.]

Results: First, mention whether experiment worked; in same paragraph, briefly describe qualitative and descriptive results; in second paragraph, begin presentation of data analysis that more specifically addresses the hypothesis; refer to supporting charts or images; provide extremely engaging figure legends that could stand on their own; place tables with legends, too, but opt for figures whenever possible. [Maximum length: approximately 200 words, not counting figure legends.]

Conclusions: Remind (without *sounding* like you are reminding) the reader of hypothesis and result, and quickly state whether your hypothesis was supported; discuss why your results are conclusive and interesting; relevance of your findings to other published work; relevance to real organisms in the real world; future directions. [Maximum length: approximately 200 words.]

Literature cited: Follow standard biology format *exactly*; Also, if you haven't read a journal article completely (e. g. , you could only view the abstract online) you may *not* cite it! [Maximum length: approximately 10 citations.]

Acknowledgments: Thank individuals for *specific* contributions to project (equipment donation, statistical advice, laboratory assistance, comments on earlier versions of the poster); mention who has provided funding; be sincere but do not lapse too much into informality in this section; do not list people's titles. Also include in this section *explicit* disclosures for any conflicts of interest and conflicts of commitment. [Maximum length: approximately 40 words.]

Further information: There will be people, hopefully, who want to know more about your research, and you can use this section to provide your e-mail address, your web site address, and perhaps a URL where they can download a PDF version of the poster (edit so that URL is *not* blued or underlined). [Maximum length: approximately 20 words.]

Sample 1:

Now let's consider another template of scientific poster as follows:

Sample 2:

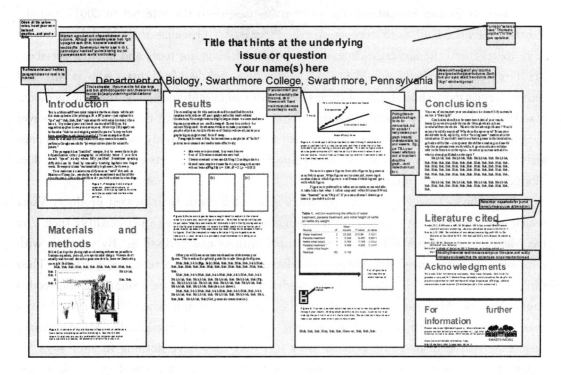

Exercise

Please try to design a scientific poster for your own research.

Reading Practice

Passage

The Universal Diarist

Mena Trott of Six Apart is at the forefront of the shift from mass media to "intimate media".

It all began five years ago with a blog entry about a banjo. Mena Trott had recently graduated as an English major from college and, at 23, was living as an under-employed designer with her husband Ben in San Francisco, passing her time by keeping a personal online diary. One day, on a girly whim, she wrote that she wanted to buy a banjo but that her husband, ever the "tyrant", wouldn't let her. Mena's friends and family, knowing that "Ben is the sweetest guy in the world", recognised the humour, says Ms Trott. But all sorts of strangers suddenly blogged back with angry feminist advice, advising her to get a separate bank account, to tell off her bullying husband, and even to leave him. Ms Trott was livid. "Why can't people take a joke, and who are these people anyway?" she wondered.

It was the seed of a profound insight: that the era of mass media was ending and a new era of "intimate media" had begun. Mr Trott had written some software to make it easier for his wife to update her blog, and they realised that other people might find it useful too. It was an instant success upon its release onto the internet in 2001, and the Trotts have since built their company, called Six Apart (because their birthdays are six days apart), into the largest independent provider of blogging tools and hosting services. Ms Trott is Six Apart's president and public face, while Mr Trott, who is shy and retiring, runs the technical side of things and seasoned executives handle the management. Six Apart's flagship products, Movable Type and TypePad, are popular among "power bloggers" with large audiences, and its third product, LiveJournal, is big among teenage girls who blog for their friends. Collectively, Six Apart's products are used by over 30m bloggers around the world.

These days, however, the Trotts are most excited about their newest product, Vox, which was launched last month. For if a blogging service can have a personality, then Vox has Ms Trott's. Like Ms Trott, Vox is unpretentious and accessible. By contrast with rival services, users need not worry about having to understand technical matters. They can upload pictures, video clips and songs with just a few clicks on a simple, colour-coded page. Also like Ms Trott, Vox celebrates the frivolous and mundane. Much of Ms Trott's personal blog, VoxTrott, is devoted to images of her beloved dog Maddy. Many ordinary people are scared of blogging because they feel that they have nothing to say, says Ms Trott. So her message is that "mundane is interesting". To a handful of people in the world it may mean a lot.

The other thing that keeps many people from blogging is fear for their privacy, she thinks. Hence the third and most important characteristic of Vox. It is intimate. For every item on Vox—a text paragraph, a photo, a link—bloggers can determine if it is to be public or private and, if it is private, exactly who can see it. Ms Trott, for instance, has a daily "Yay Me Update" just for herself, in which she uploads self-portraits from her mobile phone in order to preserve a chronicle of her life for her descendants.

As a firm, Six Apart expects to break even only next year, and it is tiny when compared with giants such as Google, which has a rival blogging service called Blogger, or News Corp, a media conglomerate that offers blogging as one of many features on MySpace, its social-networking site. So the surprise is how well Six Apart holds its own against these industry titans. For some of the large internet companies, blogging seems "like a checkbox", says Ms Trott—ie, something to have because it is fashionable, without caring much about it. She and her husband, however, sincerely regard blogging as a way of life.

Her commitment to the social, not just the commercial, potential of blogging has made Ms Trott an unofficial spokeswoman for the wider phenomenon of new media. Ms Trott is 29 but appears even younger; she is currently practising how to speak clearly with new braces in her mouth. And yet she increasingly has the attention of elder statesmen who are baffled by the rise of blogging and need help in "getting it".

VII. Answer the following questions.

1. What gave Mena Trott the profound insight that the era of mass media had been replaced by a new era of "intimate media"?

2. Is there anything in common between Ms Trott's personality and that of the newest product of Six Apart?

3. What is the most important characteristic of Vox? Do you find this characteristic essential for a blogging software from your own experience?

4. For some of the large internet companies, blogging seems "like a checkbox", says Ms Trott. What does a "checkbox" mean here? What is Ms Trott's purpose of using this metaphor here?

In a Downturn, Provoke Your Customers

NO QUESTION ABOUT IT: This is a tough time to be selling to business customers. The budget allowances simply aren't there. Making matters worse, your customer relationships have lost much of their power. With less money to go around, proposals are subjected to higher levels of review in buying organizations, and the managers you've traditionally dealt with are no longer the decision makers.

In the research and consulting we've done since the 2001 dot-com bust, we've seen how companies have survived and even profited from downturns. Rather than resign themselves to hearing the standard "Sorry, we have no budget for that," some vendors, by using what we call provocation-based selling, persuade customers that the solutions they bring to the table are not just nice but essential.

Provocation-based selling goes beyond the conventional consultative or solution-selling approach, whereby the vendor's sales team seeks out current concerns in a question-and-answer dialogue with customer managers. And it differs dramatically from the most common approach still in use—product-based selling, which pushes features, functionality, and benefits, usually in a generic manner. Provocation-based selling helps customers see their competitive challenges in a new light that makes addressing specific painful problems unmistakably urgent. For many companies that see their old approaches losing power, its time has come.

Learning to Be Provocative

Underlying provocation-based selling is the idea that the vendor should help the customer find investment funds even when discretionary spending appears to have dried up.

This was provocation-based selling at its finest: The vendor identified a process that was critical for customers in the current business environment, developed a compelling point of view on how it was broken and what that meant in terms of cost, and then connected the problem to a solution that the vendor was offering. The approach is challenging to the customer's thinking: Instead of aligning with a company's prevailing outlook, it provides a new angle on the situation. Whereas solution- selling salespeople listen for "pain points" that the customer can clearly articulate, provocation works best when it outlines a problem that the customer is experiencing but has not yet put a name to.

Of course, it isn't easy to arrive at a provocative point of view that will strike the prospective client as original and helpful. But neither is it unrealistic. In the process of selling and supporting their offerings, vendors who have successfully met customer needs in the past have interacted with other companies in the industry, and they naturally bring a different perspective to issues the client has viewed only from within. Moreover, they aren't caught up in the dynamics that often make it hard for a client's own managers to challenge the status quo. This hesitancy to make waves becomes stronger in times of general economic turmoil. When people in your client's organization are too worried about their jobs to present anything original or thought-provoking, it is easier to come across as a much-needed breath of fresh air.

To begin a provocation-based sale, you must do three things well: identify a problem that will resonate with a line executive in the target organization; develop a provocative point of view about that problem; and lodge that provocation with a decision maker who can take the implied action. Let us make a few observations about each step.

Identify a critical issue. For any given prospect or customer, your sales and marketing team can generate a long list of industrywide and company-specific problems that could be better addressed. The key is to find the one that matters so deeply that even in a downturn the money will be found to fix it. Subject any issue you consider to three sets of questions:

- Would it meet the CEO's "keeps me up at night" threshold?
- Is it being ignored, neglected, or ineffectively addressed by existing processes, systems, or services?
- Are you a credible source of advice on the issue?

An excellent way to start the hunt for issues is to note what securities analysts have observed recently, about either the target company or its industry as a whole. When an analyst flags an issue, you can assume that the target company's investors are pressuring management to resolve it—and that proposals that address the issue will get a hearing.

Formulate your provocation. Having identified a high-impact issue, you need to develop an original point of view about it. Otherwise no senior executive will give you time. This may appear to depend on some unpredictable and unmanageable flash of brilliance on your part. In fact it can be approached methodically.

First, go back to your customers, partners, and industry analysts to calibrate your view of the full scope of challenges the industry is facing. From this work, develop a provocation to help your customers recognize the issue, compare their situation to their peer's, and raise the level of urgency across their senior management teams. Finally, develop a multi-phase plan as a road map for how they could adopt your approach to solving the problem.

Lodge your provocation. The delivery of astute points of view must be handled well. Our term "provocation" should not be seen as an invitation to behave disrespectfully. Your statements should clarify the challenge and demonstrate knowledge of the customer's current approach to it. The goal is to disturb the executive's equilibrium—and make the status quo untenable—without putting him or her on the defensive. Presenting specific, well-supported concerns and remedies in a forthright manner keeps the focus on business performance for an executive who is accountable for it.

A provocation-based sale depends on the one crucial meeting in which you present your point of view to a carefully chosen line executive. Do not neglect to rehearse your delivery and anticipate the various directions the conversation might take. A key goal of mock pitches as vendor's training sessions is to find the right balance between being provocative about the issues at hand and being sympathetic to the customer's challenges in dealing with them. Sales teams can often test drive their provocations with advocates lower down in the customer organization or with third parties who are well acquainted with the company. If such an opportunity is available to you, take it; your advocate will then be equipped to set the scene for your session with the executive—or to make the introduction if one is needed. Practice sessions like this are well worth the investment when you consider the stakes. In the limited time you have secured on the executive's schedule, you need to articulate your own perspective on the issue, discover how much urgency the executive assigns to that issue, explain its relation to your company's business, and get the go-ahead to do a diagnostic study.

Proving the Point

Since a diagnostic study provides value to the client, the vendor can choose to charge for it. The study promises a valuable deliverable—a report on the company's vulnerability and resources to deal with the problem in question—with no strings attached.

For you, the diagnostic study has value far beyond the small number of billable hours it represents. It creates a welcome need to conduct a number of interviews with key individuals in the company and to obtain important data with the customer's help. The goal, of course, is to conduct the in-depth analysis needed to underpin your proposal. If you are committed to winning follow-on business, you should use the diagnostic study to establish relationships with every major constituency in the buying process. Discover who your key sponsors are and who your detractors may be, uncover any competitors you must outshine, and learn about any in-house efforts that may be incompatible or competitive with your own.

You'll need a lot of energy to redirect the status quo with incontrovertible fouts that will have come from your conversations with people in the trenches, and total commitment from an executive sponsor if your efforts are to succeed.

Construct the sales proposal that emerges from the diagnostic study in three phases. Phase one is what your company can deliver right away—most often primarily services. Phase two is what it can deliver within the year— usually a customized, solution-oriented adaptation of the offering. Phase three is everything else the customer wants or will need over time to fully address the problem.

Don't race to put a proposal on the table. As long as you are crafting it, you have permission to go back to the organization for more information—and each point of contact is an opportunity to do more selling. Try to defer submitting your proposal until you are confident you have won the deal.

Reaching the Right Ears

Our discussion so far has repeatedly referred to the line executive across the table. Only the resource owners in the client organization—senior executives, typically with P&L responsibilities—can reallocate resources to create the budget for the vendor's offering. Such executives often have elaborate defense mechanisms to shield them from sales pitches.

Start by identifying the right senior-level contact and find a mutual acquaintance who might provide you with a personal referral. Once you've sold the referrer on the provocation you hope to present to the executive, you can ask that person to make the introduction and help you arrange a meeting.

Personal referrals are the stock-in-trade of any good salesperson, especially in a consultative business. But in a period of frozen budgets, no other form of lead generation is worth the time it takes. Your people simply cannot be allowed to pursue poorly qualified leads and chase unclosable deals.

High-level buyers can be reached: through seminars designed for senior executives and by rigorously searching for referrals. Certainly social-networking tools like LinkedIn and Facebook help your company take advantage of its collective professional relationships in like fashion. Some companies will find it worthwhile to create proprietary platforms.

Can Your Sales Organization Adapt?

As you shift into provocation-based selling, the chief source of surprise and perhaps frustration for your veteran salespeople will be the new rhythm of the sales cycle. In the past it usually began with forms of lead generation that seem promising. Unfortunately, the process quickly loses momentum as the team sets up meetings with all those prospects, probes for "pain points," proves the technical feasibility of the proposed solution, and eventually produces a business case and a contract. The cycle bogs down especially in that middle stage, because the vendor is generally put through a number of proof steps before their commercial proposal is entertained.

The provocation-based approach proceeds more deliberately at the outset. Having identified an opportunity, sales and marketing managers delve into the target customer's specific situation and industry, develop a hypothesis about the critical issues to be solved, and plan how to gain access to the appropriate executive. However, once the executive has acknowledged the problem and the need to fix it, the process picks up speed. If a diagnostic study produces the anticipated results and the vendor can demonstrate an ability to solve the problem, both sides can focus on implementation, reviewing the technical feasibility of the proposed solution, the resources needed, and the results to be achieved. In stark contrast to most solution selling, this process gathers momentum at each phase instead of losing it.

Provocation-based selling, in essence, is what companies most value from vendors. In challenging economic times, when budget cutting is the norm, customers expect to buy little if anything. When they are worried about addressing their most acute pain, messages about wonderful opportunities they might exploit fall on deaf ears. By framing a provocation, you can create a readiness to listen and then use your diagnostic study to convert the dialogue into a reprioritization of funds.

Should every sales call your company pays from now on be a provocative one? Probably not. Provocation-based sales cycles are resource intensive; the method makes most sense when a significant business opportunity is at stake. In boom times this would not be your fastest or most direct route to a purchase order. But in a downturn, and with your most important prospects and customers, it will keep you in the game.

New Words and Expressions

downturn ['dauntə:n] **n.** a tendency downward, especially in business or economic activity
衰退；低迷时期

provoke [prəuˈvəuk] **v.** stir to action or feeling 煽动

allowance [əˈlauəns] **n.** amount of sth，esp. money，allowed or given regularly 津贴；补助；分配额

go around **phr v.** (of a number or quantity of sth) satisfy a demand or requirement 满足需求

subject [ˈsʌbdʒikt] **v.** cause sb/sth to experience or undergo sth 经历；遭受

bust [bʌst] **n.** a state of bankruptcy 破产

resign oneself to sth/doing sth **phr v.** be ready to accept and endure sth as inevitable 听任；顺从

vendor [ˈvendɔː] **n.** someone who sells something 卖主；售卖者

whereby [hwɛəˈbai] **adv.** by means of which or according to which 与……一致；通过……，借以

push [puʃ] **v.** persuade people to buy (goods，etc.) or accept (an idea，etc.) 劝人购买或接受

generic [dʒiˈnerik] **adj.** shared by or including a whole group or class; not specific 属的；类的；一般的

in a new/different/bad light **idm.** if someone or something is seen or shown in a particular light，people can see that particular part of their character 以新的,不同的,坏的见解

address [əˈdres] **v.** deal with 处理

discretionary [disˈkreʃənəri] **adj.** available for use as needed or desired 可随意使用的；可自由支配的

dry up **phr v.** (of any source or supply) no longer be available 耗尽，枯竭

compelling [kəmˈpeliŋ] **adj.** drivingly forceful 非常有说服力的

in terms of **idm.** as regards sth；expressed as sth 在某事物方面；以某说法来表达

align [əˈlain] **v.** to organize or change something so that it has the right relationship to something else 调整；使……一致

prevailing [priˈveiliŋ] **adj.** existing or accepted in a particular place or at a particular time 流行的；普遍的

articulate [ɑːˈtikjuleit] **v.** speak (sth) clearly and distinctly 清楚明白地说

put a name to sb/sth **idm.** know or remember what sb/sth is called 知道或记住某人/某事物的名称

strike [straik] **v.** have an effect on sb；impress sb (in the way specified) 对某人产生某种效果；给某人留下印象

interact [ˈintərækt] **v.** (of people) act together or co-operatively，esp. so as to communicate with each other 一起活动或互相合作

be caught up in sth **idm.** be absorbed or involved in sth 被卷入或陷入

the status quo **n.** situation or state of affairs as it is now，or as it was before a recent change 现状；原来的状况

make waves　*idm.* to cause problems，especially when you should not 制造麻烦

turmoil [ˈtəːmɔil] *n.* (instance of) great disturbance, agitation or confusion 骚动；混乱；动乱

resonate [ˈrezəneit] *v.* evoke a feeling of shared emotion or belief 引起共鸣

line executine　*n.* a manager in a company who is responsible for the main activities of production，sales，etc. 主管，业务高管

lodge [lɔdʒ] *v.* present (a statement, etc) to the proper authorities for attention 提出

threshold [ˈθreʃhəuld] *n.* a point separating conditions that will produce a given effect from conditions of a higher or lower degree that will not produce the effect 上限，下限；门槛

flag [flæg] *v.* mark (sth) for particular attention with a special mark or label 标出

hearing [ˈhiəriŋ] *n.* opportunity to be heard 说话或申辩的机会

formulate [ˈfɔːmjuleit] *v.* express (sth) clearly and exactly using particular words 确切地表达

senior [ˈsiːnjə] *adj.* higher in rank, authority, etc. （级别、权位等）较高的

flash [flæʃ] *n.* sudden show of wit, understanding, etc （机智等的）显露；恍然大悟

on the part of sb/on sb's part　*idm.* made or done by sb 由某人做出

approach [əˈprəutʃ] *v.* begin to tackle (a task, problem, etc) 处理

methodically [miˈθɔdikəli] *adv.* in a careful and systematic manner 有条理地，有条不紊地；井然地

calibrate [ˈkælibreit] *v.* make corrections in; adjust 校正；调整

astute [əˈstjuːt] *adj.* clever and quick at seeing how to gain an advantage; shrewd 精明的；机敏的；狡诈的

clarify [ˈklærifai] *v.* (cause sth to) become clear or easier to understand 使清楚易懂；澄清

equilibrium [iːkwiˈlibriəm] *n.* balanced state of mind, feelings, etc. 平静

untenable [ʌnˈtenəbl] *adj.* (of a theory, etc.) that cannot be defended 站不住脚的，不堪一击的

on the defensive　*idm.* expecting to be attacked or criticized 进行防御；采取守势

remedy [ˈremidi] *n.* means of countering or removing sth undesirable 补救方法

forthright [fɔːθˈrait] *adj.* clear and honest in manner and speech; straightforward 言行坦诚的；直率的

accountable [əˈkauntəbl] *adj.* required or expected to give an explanation for one's actions, etc.; responsible 应负责的；可解释的；有责任的

rehearse [riˈhəːs] *v.* give an account of (sth), esp. to oneself; recite 讲述；自述，背诵

mock [mɔk] *adj.* simulated; false; sham 假装的；模拟的；

pitch [pitʃ] *n.* a line of talk designed to persuade （劝诫的）言词

test drive　*v.* drive (a motor vehicle) to evaluate performance and condition 试驾

(training) session [ˈseʃən] *n.* single continuous period spent in one activity （进行某活动连续的）一段时间

be equipped to　*phr v.* provide a person or place with the things that are needed for a particular kind of activity or work 为做某事情整装待发；有能力做

set the scene (for sth) *idm.* prepare for sth; help to cause sth 为某事物作准备；促使

session [ˈseʃn] *n.* meeting or series of meetings 会议

secure [siˈkjuə] *v.* get possession of; acquire 获得；取得

assign [əˈsain] *v.* ascribe; attribute 归于；归属

get the go-ahead *idm.* be given permission to start doing something 得到允许做某事

diagnostic [daiəgˈnɔstik] *adj.* relating to or used for discovering what is wrong with someone or something 诊断的；判断的

deliverable [diˈlivərəbl] *n.* something that a company has promised to have ready for a customer 可以做得到的事；可交付的事物

vulnerability [vʌlnərəˈbiliti] *n.* the state of being exposed to hurt, harm, danger or attack 易受伤；弱点

with no strings attached *idm.* with no special conditions or restrictions 不附带条件；无任何限制

billable [ˈbiləbl] *adj.* capable of being billed 计费的；收费的

underpin [ʌndəˈpin] *v.* form the basis for (an argument, a claim, etc.); strengthen 为(论据、主张等)打下基础；加强；巩固

commit sb/oneself to sth/doing sth *phr v.* make it impossible for sb/oneself not to do sth, or to do sth else, esp because of a promise; pledge sb/oneself 不能不做；保证

constituency [kənˈstitjuənsi] *n.* a group served by an organization or institution; a clientele 主顾；顾客

detractor [diˈtræktə] *n.* someone who says bad things about someone or something, in order to make them seem less good than they really are 诽谤者；恶意批评者

uncover [ʌnˈkʌvə] *v.* make known or disclose (sth); discover 揭露；暴露；发现

outshine [autˈʃain] *v.* shine more brightly than (sb/sth); surpass in obvious excellence; outdo 比……光亮/出色/优异；超越

in-house *adj.* conducted within, coming from, or being within an organization or group 机构内的，组织内的

incontrovertible [inkɔntrəˈvəːtibl] *adj.* so obvious and certain that it cannot be disputed or denied 无可辩驳的；不容否认的

the trenches *n.* the place or situation where most of the work or action in an activity takes place 一线

sponsor [ˈspɔnsə] *n.* one who assumes responsibility for another person or a group during a period of instruction, apprenticeship, or probation 主办者；负责人

customize [ˈkʌstəmaiz] *v.* make or alter to individual or personal specifications 定做

put sth on the table *idm.* sth is offered for consideration or discussion 提交考虑或讨论

craft [krɑːft] *v.* make (sth) skilfully, esp by hand 精工制作

defer [diˈfəː] *v.* delay sth until a later time; postpone sth 延期；推迟

reach sb's ears *idm.* sb finds out about sth, eg news or gossip 传到某人耳朵里

P&L *abbr.* Profit and Loss 益损；盈亏

reallocate [riːˈæləukeit] *v.* change the way of allotting or assigning sth(to sb/sth) for a special purpose 重新配给，重新分配

sales pitch *n.* what a salesperson says in order to persuade someone to buy something from him/her 推销

shield [ʃiːld] *v.* protect sb/sth from harm；defend sb/sth from criticism, attack, etc 保护；庇护

referral [riˈfəːrəl] *n.* (an instance of) the act of officially sending someone to a person or authority that is qualified to deal with them 提及；推荐；参考

be sold on sth/sb；sell sb on *idm.* be enthusiastic about sth/sb 看中

referrer [riˈfəːrə] *n.* a person who refers another 推荐人

stock-in-trade *n.* the resources available to and habitually called on by a person in a given situation 惯用手段

lead generation *n.* a marketing term that refers to the creation or generation of prospective consumer interest or inquiry into a business' products or services 潜在顾客开发流程

lead [liːd] *n.* information pointing toward a possible solution；a clue 线索

seminar [ˈseminɑː] *n.* a meeting where a group of people discuss a particular problem or topic 研讨会

rigorously [ˈrigərəsli] *adv.* carefully, thoroughly, and exactly 严格的，细致的

fashion [ˈfæʃən] *n.* manner or way of doing sth 样子；方式

proprietary [prəuˈpraiətəri] *adj.* manufactured, sold, owned or used exclusively by a particular firm 专利的

frustration [frʌsˈtreiʃn] *n.* the feeling of being annoyed, upset, or impatient, because one cannot control or change a situation, or achieve something 挫败；受挫；挫折

veteran [ˈvetərən] *adj.* having had long experience or practice 丰富经验的，老练的

momentum [məuˈmentəm] *n.* force that increases the rate of development of a process；impetus 动力；冲力；势头

probe [prəub] *v.* investigate or examine (sth) closely 细查，探究

feasibility [fiːzəˈbiliti] *n.* the quality of being doable 可行性，合理性

bog (sth) down *phr v.* (cause sth to) become stuck and unable to make progress (使)陷入困境不能前进

entertain [entəˈtein] *v.* be ready and willing to consider (sth) 愿意考虑

at the outset *idm.* at/from the beginning(of sth) 开端；开始

delve into *phr v.* try to find more information about sth；study sth 探索；钻研

stark [stɑːk] *adj.* clearly obvious to the eye or the mind 显而易见的；明摆着的；鲜明的

value [ˈvæljuː] *v.* have a high opinion of sth/sb 重视

norm [nɔːm] *n.* standard or pattern that is typical (of a group, etc) 标准；规范

if anything *idm.* if there is any difference（used when one is adding something to emphasize what one has just said) 如果有区别的话；如果有什么的话

exploit [ik'sploit] *v.* use，work or develop fully 利用；开发

fall on deaf ears *idm.* be ignored or unnoticed by others 被别人忽视；不受注意

reprioritization [ri'prai̱ɔriti'zeiʃn] *n.* the act of arranging things in a new order of importance；a second，or an altered，prioritization 按重要性重新排序

pay/make a call（on sb） *idm.* visit someone 拜访（某人）

at stake *idm.* to be won or lost；being risked，depending on the outcome of an event 在胜败关头；冒风险

boom [buːm] *n.* sudden increase（in population，trade，etc）；period of prosperity 突然增加；繁荣昌盛时期

Exercises

Ⅰ. **Answer the following questions.**

1. What is provocation-based selling according to the text?

2. How does provocation-based selling differ from solution selling?

3. How can a vendor develop a provocative point of view?

4. Why is the diagnostic study important for a provocation-based sale?

5. What is the new rhythm of the sales cycle of provocation-based selling?

Ⅱ. **Paraphrase the difficult sentences or language points.**

1. With less money to go around，proposals are subjected to higher levels of review in buying organizations，and the managers you've traditionally dealt with are no longer the decision makers.

2. This was provocation-based selling at its finest.

3. Of course，it isn't easy to arrive at a provocative point of view that will strike the prospective client as original and helpful.

4. When people in your client's organization are too worried about their jobs to present anything original or thought-provoking，it is easier to come across as a much-needed breath of fresh air.

5. … and lodge that provocation with a decision maker who can take the implied action.

6. Subject any issue you consider to three sets of questions：

7. Would it meet the CEO's "keep me up at might" threshold?

8. The goal is to disturb the executive's equilibrium—and make the status quo untenable—without putting him or her on the defensive.

9. Practice sessions like this are well worth the investment when you consider the stakes.

10. By framing a provocation，you can create a readiness to listen and then use your diagnostic study to convert the dialogue into a reprioritization of funds.

Ⅲ. Choose the word or phrase that best explains the meaning of the underlined part from the text.

1. In the research and consulting we've done since <u>the 2001 dot-com bust</u>, we've seen how companies have survived and even profited from downturns.
   A. the bankruptcy of 2001 internet companies
   B. the bankruptcy of internet companies in 2001
   C. the evaporation of network bubbles in 2001

2. Moreover, they aren't caught up in <u>the dynamics</u> that often make it hard for a client's own managers to challenge the status quo.
   A. the mechanics   B. the forces   C. the changes

3. Presenting specific, well-supported concerns and remedies in a forthright manner keeps the focus on business performance for an executive who is <u>accountable</u> for it.
   A. responsible   B. explainable   C. considerable

4. A key goal of <u>mock pitches</u> at vendor's training sessions is to find the right balance between being provocative about the issues at hand and being sympathetic to the customer's challenges in dealing with them.
   A. the mimicry of tones
   B. the big talks
   C. the simulation of persuasive talks

5. Sales teams can often <u>test drive their provocations</u> with advocates lower down in the customer organization or with third parties who are well acquainted with the company.
   A. make a preliminary assessment of their provocations
   B. improve their provocations through tests
   C. advance their provocation through tests

6. It creates <u>a welcome need</u> to conduct a number of interviews with key individuals in the company and to obtain important data with the customer's help.
   A. a need welcomed by the company
   B. a need welcomed by the vendor
   C. a need pleasing the vendor

7. Your people simply cannot be allowed to pursue poorly qualified leads and chase <u>unclosable deals</u>.
   A. deals that cannot be ended
   B. deals that can be started
   C. deals that cannot be completed

8. Certainly social-networking tools like LinkedIn and Facebook help your company take advantage of its collective professional relationships <u>in like fashion</u>.
   A. in a possible style
   B. in a similar way

C. in a possible manner

9. In challenging economic times, when budget cutting is the norm, customers expect to buy little if anything.
   A. to buy few things if not anything
   B. to buy few things if not nothing
   C. to buy few things if there is any differences

10. In boom times this would not be your fastest or most direct route to a purchase order.
    A. an arrangement of buying things
    B. an arrangement of things bought
    C. a request to supply goods

IV. Choose the best phrase or expression in the text from the following list to fit in each of the following blanks. Change the word form where necessary.

go around   resign oneself to   be equipped to   in a new light   make waves   on the part of sb   on the defensive   commit oneself to   put sth on the table   set the scene

1. After we had all agreed on the contract, one of the vice-presidents began to _____ _____.

2. Associating beauty with women has put beauty even further _____, morally.

3. China insists that criminals be allowed to study and improve their production skills to make the prisoner look at the world _____ and enable the reformed criminal to contribute to the modernization programme.

4. Menus require more navigational effort _____ users because their contents are not visible prior to clicking.

5. She had to _____ bringing up her baby alone.

6. The study suggests women could _____ use seemingly superficial characteristics "as a cue to pick up on trends in these behavioral strategies," Kruger said.

7. There were never enough chairs to _____ and frequently ladies sat on the steps of the front porch with men grouped about them on the banisters, on packing boxes or on the lawn below.

8. Farmers mounted a "commando operation" to open up the lake's sluice gate and drain off 40 centimetres of water, so _____ for disaster.

9. We are _____ joining with you to advance our many parallel strategic and bilateral interests.

10. When the Hong Kong question was _____ years ago, our government presented the idea of "one country, two systems".

Ⅴ. Translate the following sentences into English.

1. 企业应建立专案团队来解决这一问题,其团队成员由企业各部门的经理组成。

2. 他好不容易从公司的竞争对手那探得的消息却没人理会。

3. 企业鼓励员工提出能让董事会觉得耳目一新的建议,而不是迎合董事会的想法。

4. 电脑网络能帮助营销商开发与他们的目标顾客产生共鸣的信息战略和广告方案。

5. 我们保留因为货物在运输途中遭到损坏而向你方提出索赔的权力。

6. 煽动性观点的形成并不是仅仅依靠灵光一现。实际上,你可以通过对整个行业目前面临的挑战进行梳理和分析,有条不紊地来使观点成形。

7. 经济低迷时期针对企业客户的销售非常艰难,制定一份出色的销售提案尤为重要,提案基于的事实应源自一线人员,并有深入的分析为提案提供支持。

8. 的确,行销人员早已根据直觉知道,在提倡产品及流行时尚方面,某些客户有时就是比其他人来得出色。

9. 友好的劝说是每个推销员的惯用手法。但是许多公司设有防护机制来避开销售人员的推销。

10. 尽管预算有限,公司高管还是被这份没有任何附加条件的解决方案打动,同意予以考虑。

Ⅵ. Translate the following paragraphs into Chinese.

1. Moreover, they aren't caught up in the dynamics that often make it hard for a client's own managers to challenge the status quo. This hesitancy to make waves becomes stronger in times of general economic turmoil. When people in your client's organization are too worried about their jobs to present anything original or thought-provoking, it is easier to come across as a much-needed breath of fresh air.

2. If such an opportunity is available to you, take it; your advocate will then be equipped to set the scene for your session with the executive—or to make the introduction if one is needed. Practice sessions like this are well worth the investment when you consider the stakes. In the limited time you have secured on the executive's schedule, you need to articulate your own perspective on the issue, discover how much urgency the executive assigns to that issue, explain its relation to your company's business, and get the go-ahead to do a diagnostic study.

Writing

Letter of complaint

Directions:

In writing a letter of complaint, the writer should explicitly state the whole story, that is, *what*, *when*, *where*, *why*, and *how*. What is the matter one complains about? When and where did it happen? Why is it dissatisfying or irritating? And how can it be settled? In general, letters of complaint include the following stages.

Provide Background Information Tell the person concerned what happened to you, i. e.

what, *when* and *where*.

Present the Problem Explain the reasons for your discontent, i. e. *why*. Clarify the causes and their effects on you.

Offer a Solution State your solution to the problem, i. e. *how*.

Give a Warning Pressure the person concerned with a warning to handle the problem as you expect. This is optional, depending on how serious the problem is.

End with a Closing End your letter with a formal complimentary closing.

Rules of writing letters of complaint

Content The content should contain enough details so that the receiver does not have to write back requesting more. Legal action is not normally threatened in the first letter of complaint, unless the situation is very serious.

Appropriacy The tone of complaint letters should not be aggressive or insulting, as this would annoy the reader and not encourage them to solve the problem. In addition, questions such as "Why can't you get this right?" should not be included.

Formality Letters of complaint should take a formal format.

Promptness Letters of complaint should be written and sent to the receiver in short time after the problem.

Here is an example of complaint letters for you to study and appreciate.

Example   **Sample letter**

Flat 406 Lucky Mansions
24 Zhongshan Lu
Nanjing

16 April 2010

The Administrative Officer

Exhibition Services

Exhibitions International

238 Zhongyang Lu

Nanjing

Dear Sir/Madam,

I attended your Modern Arts Exhibition 2010 at the National Exhibition center on April 12 and found it impressive and informative. Unfortunately, my enjoyment of the event was spoiled by a number of organisational problems. I explain each of the problems below.

Firstly, I had difficulty in getting a ticket to the exhibition. You set up an on-line application facility, but I found it totally unworkable. Though I spent several hours trying to get a ticket in this way, the computer would not accept my application. Then I turned to your hotline for a ticket, but the line was not answered until I made quite a few attempts.

Secondly, the four-day exhibition was rather short, especially for the public, to which the exhibition was open only on the last two days. Some of my friends complained about the time limitation and they couldn't manage to visit it.

The final point I want to make concerns the information on art works. It is very enjoyable to see a range of excellent art works, but it is also important to be able to take away leaflets on them, so that more information about the art works can be conveyed to attendees who are interested. However, by the time I attended the exhibition all the leaflets had been taken.

Could I please ask you to look into these matters—not only on my behalf but also on behalf of other attendees, and in fact on behalf of your company, too.

I look forward to hearing from you.

Yours faithfully

Maggie Lee

Exercise

You have just returned from a three-day vacation in Hainan, a tour package, which you think is a disaster. Now write a letter to the travel agency to complain about it.

Reading Practice

Passage

Magic Restored

Four years ago Disney was in turmoil, with its then chief executive, Michael Eisner, under siege from shareholders who accused him of stifling the firm's creative culture. Today under Bob Iger, who took over as chief executive in 2005, Disney is enjoying a remarkable and profitable run of hit TV programmes and films. "Disney's creative momentum is so strong now that there's no comparison between it and other big media companies," says Lawrence Haverty, a fund manager at Gabelli Asset Management.

What accounts for this renaissance? Mr Iger's management style is said by many to have unlocked Disney's creativity. "There was already creativity inside Disney, but Bob removed the barriers to it," says Peter Chernin, chief operating officer of News Corporation, a rival media group. "Michael Eisner was all about his own creativity," says Stanley Gold, a former Disney board director who led a campaign to oust Mr Eisner in 2004, referring to the way in which the former boss meddled in the detail of Disney's parks and movies. In contrast, he says, "Bob pushes creative decisions to the people below him."

In addition, Mr Iger's acquisition of Pixar, a studio that insists on creative originality, has sent a signal to people inside and outside Disney. Before Mr Iger took over, says Mr Staggs, Disney had a factory-like process for animation in which a business-development team came up with ideas and allocated directors to them. "With the arrival of the Pixar leadership, Disney has adopted the director-driven development and production approach that Pixar has used so successfully," he says. The full proof of Pixar's impact on Disney's animation will be seen in November when the firm releases "Bolt", the first film developed entirely under the new bosses.

One former Mouseketeer argues that Mr Iger cannot take much credit for Disney's recent string of hits. "All the great new shows from Disney were developed, and many of them launched, when Michael Eisner was leading the company," says David Hulbert, a former president of Walt Disney Television International. "The TV and studio creative cycle lasts several years, so we will have to wait some time yet to see what Bob Iger's cautious, centralised and consensual management style produces," he adds. Disney executives counter that Mr Eisner had made Mr Iger responsible for ABC, the Disney Channel and ESPN, its sports network.

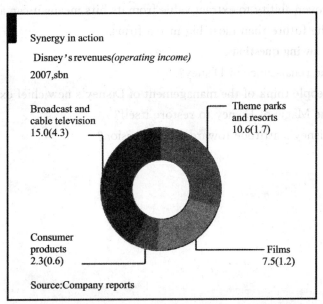

Synergy in action

Disney's revenues *(operating income)*
2007,sbn

Broadcast and cable television
15.0(4.3)

Theme parks and resorts
10.6(1.7)

Consumer products
2.3(0.6)

Films
7.5(1.2)

Source:Company reports

What is certain is that under Mr Iger, Disney has perfected the art of media synergy. The firm has turned "High School Musical", for instance, into a live concert tour, a stage musical, a show on ice, and a series of books and video games. Pixar's "Cars" may have slightly disappointed at the box office, but Disney sold 100m model vehicles on the back of it, plans to build a "Cars Land" attraction in its California Adventure theme park and is developing an online virtual world tie-in.

Disney now has ten"franchises" that it treats in this way, from Mickey Mouse to

Disney Fairies. Every media conglomerate pursued synergy some years ago, but Disney is the only one to have made it work consistently across the whole company. It helps, of course, that so many of its customers are children, who tend to be more receptive to spin-off products than adults.

Mr Eisner certainly pushed synergy hard, but Mr Iger's collaborative management style is better suited to it, insiders say. In Britain, says a Disney executive based in London, the firm's programme-sales group worked hard to sell "High School Musical" to the BBC, even though it contributed relatively little to their own division's bottom line, because exposure on free-to-air TV then bolstered sales of "High School Musical" DVDs, pencil cases and other products. "A few years ago they wouldn't have bothered," says the executive, "but now the key properties are so drummed into us that everyone is behind them."

Not everything is perfect in the Magic Kingdom. Investors worry about the impact of a recession on Disney's theme parks, which accounted for just over a quarter of the firm's revenues in the first fiscal quarter of this year. Mainly for that reason, the firm's share price has fallen by 14% in the past year. Disney says that its American parks are more resilient during slowdowns than those of its rivals. Like its peers, Disney still earns most money from traditional media, and needs to expand its businesses online. But its creative momentum and proven ability to extract value from its hits means it can afford to feel more optimistic about the future than most big media firms.

Ⅶ. Answer the following questions.

1. What is the renaissance of Disney?
2. What do people think of the management of Disney's new chief executive Bob Iger?
3. What is the Magic of Disney to restore itself?
4. What is Disney's attitude towards the recession?

The Founder's DILEMMA

EVERY WOULD-BE ENTREPRENEUR wants to be a Bill Gates, a Phil Knight, or an Anita Roddick, each of whom founded a large company and led it for many years. However, successful CEO-cum-founders are a very rare breed. When I analyzed 212 American start-ups that sprang up in the late 1990s and early 2000s, I discovered that only 40% of founders were still in the corner office by the time the ventures were four years old. We remember the handful of founder-CEOs in corporate America, but they're the exceptions to the rule.

Founders don't let go easily, though. Most are shocked when investors insist that they relinquish control, and they're pushed out of office in ways they don't like and well before they want to abdicate. In fact, the manner in which founders tackle their first leadership transition often makes or breaks young enterprises.

The transitions take place relatively smoothly if, at the outset, founders are honest about their motives for getting into business. Isn't that obvious, you may ask. Don't people start a business to make lots of money? They do. However, entrepreneurs as a class make only as much money as they could have if they had been employees. What's more, in my experience, founders often make decisions that conflict with the wealth-maximization principle.

The reason isn't hard to fathom. There is, of course, another factor motivating entrepreneurs along with the desire to become wealthy: the drive to create and lead an organization. The surprising thing is that trying to maximize one imperils achievement of the other. Entrepreneurs face a choice, at every step, between making money and managing their ventures. Those who don't figure out which is more important to them often end up neither wealthy nor powerful.

Inside the Founder's Mind

Founders are usually convinced that only they can lead their start-ups to success. There's a great deal of truth to that view. At the start, the enterprise is only an idea in the mind of its founder, who possesses all the insights about the opportunity; about the innovative product, service, or business model that will capitalize on that opportunity; and about who the potential customers are.

From the get-go, employees, customers, and business partners identify start-ups with their founders, who take great pride in their founder-cum-CEO status.

New ventures are usually labors of love for entrepreneurs, and they become emotionally attached to them, referring to the business as "my baby" and using similar parenting language without even noticing. Their attachment is evident in the relatively low salaries they pay themselves. Even though they had comparable backgrounds, founders received 20% less in cash compensation than nonfounders who performed similar roles. That was so even after taking into account the value of the equity each person held.

Many entrepreneurs are overconfident about their prospects and naive about the problems they will face. For instance, as to the question: "What are the odds of your business succeeding?" a study of 3,000 entrepreneurs in 1988 showed that 80% of the respondents pegged their chances of success at at least 70%—and one in three claimed their likelihood of success was 100%. Founders' attachment, overconfidence, and naïveté may be necessary to get new ventures up and running, but these emotions later create problems.

Growing Pains

Founders eventually realize that their financial resources, ability to inspire people, and passion aren't enough to enable their ventures to capitalize fully on the opportunities before them. They invite family members and friends, angel investors, or venture capital firms to invest in their companies. In doing so, they pay a heavy price: They often have to give up total control over the enterprise.

Once the founder is no longer in control of the board, his or her job as CEO is at risk. The board's task is straightforward if the founder underperforms as CEO, although even when founders are floundering, boards can have a hard time persuading them to put their "babies" up for adoption. But, paradoxically, the need for a change at the top becomes even greater when a founder has delivered results. Let me explain why.

The first major task in any new venture is the development of its product or service. Many founders believe that if they've successfully led the development of the organization's first new offering, that's ample proof of their management prowess. They think investors should have no cause for complaint and should continue to back their leadership.

Their success makes it harder for founders to realize that when they celebrate the shipping of the first products, they're marking the end of an era. At that point, leaders face a different set of business challenges. The founder has to build a company capable of marketing and selling large volumes of the product and of providing customers with after-sales service. The venture's finances become more complex, and the CEO needs to depend on finance executives and accountants. The organization has to become more structured, and the CEO has to create formal processes, develop specialized roles, and, yes, institute a managerial hierarchy. The dramatic broadening of the skills that the CEO needs at this stage stretches most founders' abilities beyond their limits.

Thus, the faster that founder-CEOs lead their companies to the point where they need outside funds and new management skills, the quicker they will lose management control. Success makes founders less qualified to lead the company and changes the power structure so they are more vulnerable.

Investors wield the most influence over entrepreneurs just before they invest in their companies, often using that moment to force founders to step down. A recent report in *Private Equity Week* pithily captures this dynamic: "Seven Networks Inc., a Redwood City, Calif.-based mobile email company, has raised $42 million in new venture capital funding…. In other Seven news, the company named former Onebox.com CEO Russ Bott as its new CEO."

The founder's moment of truth sometimes comes quickly. One Silicon Valley-based venture capital firm, for instance, insists on owning at least 50% of any start-up after the first round of financing. Other investors, to reduce their risk, dole money out in stages, and each round alters the board's composition, gradually threatening the entrepreneur's control over the company. In such cases, investors allow founder-CEOs to lead their enterprises longer, since the founder will have to come back for more capital, but at some point outsiders will gain control of the board.

Whether gradual or sudden, the transition is often stormy. In 2001, for instance, when a California-based internet telephony company finished developing the first generation of its system, an outside investor pushed for the appointment of a new CEO. He felt the company needed an executive experienced at managing the other executives who oversaw the firm's existing functions, had deeper knowledge of the functions the venture would have to create, and had experience in instituting new processes to knit together the company's activities. The founder refused to accept the need for a change, and it took five pressure-filled months of persuasion before he would step down.

He's not the only one to have fought the inevitable; four out of five founder-CEOs I studied resisted the idea, too. If the need for change is clear to the board, why isn't it clear to the founder? Because the founder's emotional strengths become liabilities at this stage. Used to being the heart and soul of their ventures, founders find it hard to accept lesser roles, and their resistance triggers traumatic leadership transitions within young companies.

Time to Choose

As start-ups grow, entrepreneurs face a dilemma—one that many aren't aware of, initially. On the one hand, they have to raise resources in order to capitalize on the opportunities before them. If they choose the right investors, their financial gains will soar. On the other hand, in order to attract investors and executives, entrepreneurs have to give up control over most decision making.

This fundamental tension yields "rich" versus "king" tradeoffs. The "rich" options enable the company to become more valuable but sideline the founder by taking away the CEO position and control over major decisions. The "king" choices allow the founder to retain control of decision making by staying CEO and maintaining control over the board—but often only by building a less valuable company. For founders, a "rich" choice isn't necessarily better than a "king" choice, or vice versa; what matters is how well each decision fits with their reason for starting the company.

Consider, for example, Ockham Technologies' cofounder and CEO Jim Triandiflou, who realized in 2000 that he would have to attract investors to stay in business. He felt that Ockham would grow bigger if he roped in a well-known venture capital firm rather than an inexperienced angel investor. After much soul-searching, he decided to take a risk, and he sold an equity stake to the venture firm. He gave up board control, but in return he gained resources and expertise that helped increase Ockham's value manifold.

On the other side of the coin are founders who bootstrap their ventures in order to remain in control. For instance, John Gabbert, the founder of Room & Board, is a successful Minneapolis-based furniture retailer. Having set up nine stores, he has repeatedly rejected offers of funding that would enable the company to grow faster, fearing that would lead him to lose control. Gabbert is clearly willing to live with the choices he has made as long as he can run the company himself.

Most founder-CEOs start out by wanting both wealth and power. However, once they grasp that they'll probably have to maximize one or the other, they will be in a position to figure out which is more important to them. Their past decisions regarding cofounders, hires, and investors will usually tell them which they truly favor. Once they know, they will find it easier to tackle transitions.

Founders who understand that they are motivated more by wealth than by control will themselves bring in new CEOs. Such founders are also likely to work with their boards to develop post-succession roles for themselves. By contrast, founders who understand that they are motivated by control are more prone to making decisions that enable them to lead the business at the expense of increasing its value. They are more likely to remain sole founders, to use their own capital instead of taking money from investors, to resist deals that affect their management control, and to attract executives who will not threaten their desire to run the company.

One factor affecting the founder's choices is the perception of a venture's potential. Founders often make different decisions when they believe their start-ups have the potential to grow into extremely valuable companies than when they believe their ventures won't be that valuable. For instance, serial entrepreneur Evan Williams sold his Pyra Labs to Google in 2003 but he brought in outside investors for his next venture Odeo two years later because he thought he had the opportunity to do something more substantial with Odeo. Having ceded control quickly in an effort to realize the substantial potential of the company, Williams has had a change of heart, buying back the company in 2006 and regaining his kingship.

Would-be entrepreneurs can also apply the framework to judge the kind of ideas they should pursue. Those desiring control should restrict themselves to businesses where they already have the skills and contacts they need or where large amounts of capital aren't required. Founders who want to become wealthy should be open to pursuing ideas that require resources. They can make the leap sooner because they won't mind taking money from investors or depending on executives to manage their ventures.

Choosing between money and power allows entrepreneurs to come to grips with what success means to them. Founders who want to manage empires will not believe they are successes if they lose control, even if they end up rich. Conversely, founders who understand that their goal is to amass wealth will not view themselves as failures when they step down from the top job. Once they realize why they are turning entrepreneur, founders must, as the old Chinese proverb says, "decide on three things at the start: the rules of the game, the stakes, and the quitting time."

New Words and Expressions

cum [kʌm] *prep.* also used as; as well as 兼作；和

breed [briːd] *n.* type; kind 类型；种类

start-up *n.* a new small company or business（新建的）小企业

spring up *phr v.* appear, develop, grow, etc. quickly or suddenly 迅速地或突然地出现、发展、生长等

venture [ˈventʃə] *n.* project or undertaking, esp. a commercial one where there is a risk of failure 工作项目或事业；（尤指有风险的）商业，企业

relinquish [riˈliŋkwiʃ] *v.* give up or renounce; surrender 放弃；让出

abdicate [ˈæbdikeit] *v.* formally relinquish (power, a high official position, etc) 正式放弃

at the outset *idm.* at/from the beginning (of sth) 开端；开始

fathom [ˈfæðəm] *v.* understand or comprehend (sb/sth) fully 充分理解；领悟

imperil [imˈperil] *v.* put (sb/sth) in danger; endanger 使……陷于危险；危及

innovative [ˈinəuveitiv] *adj.* new and original 创新的；革新的

capitalize on phr *v.* use sth to one's own advantage; profit from sth 利用；从某事物中获利

get-go *n.* beginning 开始

a labor of love *idm.* task done out of enthusiasm or devotion, not from necessity or for profit 为爱好而做的工作

equity [ˈekwəti] *n.* ordinary stock and share that carries no fixed interest （利息不定的）普通股

odds [ɔdz] *n.* [pl] probability or chance 可能性；机会；

peg [peg] *v.* fix or keep (wages or prices) at a certain level 固定；维持

naïveté [nɑːˈiːvtei] *n.* artlessness or credulity; naivety 天真；幼稚

angel investor phr *n.* an affluent individual who provides capital for a business start-up, usually in exchange for convertible debt or ownership equity 天使投资人

venture capital phr *n.* money made available for investment in innovative enterprises or research, especially in high technology, in which both the risk of loss and the potential for profit may be considerable 风险投资；风险资本

underperform [ˌʌndəpəˈfɔːm] *v.* exhibit a level of performance that is below the standard 表现不佳

flounder [ˈflaundə] *v.* proceed or act clumsily or ineffectually 错乱地做事

paradoxically [ˌpærəˈdɔksikəli] *adv.* in a way that is surprising because it is the opposite of what would be expected 似非而是地；反常地；悖理地

offering [ˈɔfəriŋ] *n.* something offered for sale or patronage 出售物

ample [ˈæmpl] *adj.* (more than) enough; abundant; plentiful 足够的；充足的；富裕的

prowess [ˈprauis] *n.* outstanding skill or ability; expertise 高超的技艺；非凡的才能；专长

managerial [ˌmæniˈdʒiəriəl] *adj.* of, relating to, or characteristic of a manager or management 经理的；管理的

hierarchy [ˈhaiəˌrɑːki] *n.* system with grades of authority or status from the lowest to the highest 等级制度

vulnerable [ˈvʌlnərəbl] *adj.* exposed to danger or attack; unprotected 暴露于危险面前的；易受攻击的；无防御的

wield [wiːld] *v.* exercise (authority or influence, for example) effectively 行使，运用，支配

step down phr *v.* resign (usu from an important position, job, etc) to allow another person to take one's place 辞职

pithily [ˈpiθili] *adv.* in a way sth is intelligent and strongly stated，without wasting any words 有力地；简洁地

dole [dəul] *v.* distribute (esp food，money，etc) in small amounts 少量发放

oversee [ˌəuvəˈsiː] *v.* watch over and control (sb/sth)；supervise 监督，监视

inevitable [inˈevitəbl] *adj.* that cannot be avoided；that is sure to happen 不可避免的；必然发生的；难免的

liability [ˌlaiəˈbiləti] *n.* a handicap 妨碍；不利

trigger [ˈtrigə] *v.* be the cause of a sudden (often) violent reaction；set an action or a process in motion 发动；引发

traumatic [trɔːˈmætik] *adj.* shocking and upsetting，and possibly causing psychological damage 外伤性的；损伤性的

soar [sɔː] *v.* increase quickly to a high level 高涨；飞涨

tradeoff [ˈtreidˌɔːf] *n.* an exchange of one thing in return for another，especially relinquishment of one benefit or advantage for another regarded as more desirable 交易，交换；权衡

sideline [ˈsaidlain] *v.* remove (sb) from a game，team，etc；put out of action 使(某人)退出比赛；使中止活动

retain [riˈtein] *v.* keep；continue to have 保持；保有

vice versa *adv.* the other way round；with the terms or conditions reversed 反之亦然

rope sb in (to do sth) **phr v.** (esp passive) persuade sb (to take part in an activity) 说服某人(参与一项活动)

soul-searching *n.* careful examination of one's thoughts and feelings because one is very worried about whether or not it is right to do something 自省；反省

stake [steik] *n.* a share or an interest in an enterprise，especially a financial share 股份

expertise [ˌekspəˈtiːz] *n.* expert knowledge or skill，esp in a particular field 专门知识或技能

bootstrap [ˈbuːtstræp] *v.* promote and develop by use of one's own initiative and work without reliance on outside help 自力更生

Minneapolis [ˌminiˈæpəlis] *n.* a city in east Minnesota，US and an important industrial centre 明尼阿波利斯市

live with **phr v.** accept or tolerate something 接受或容忍

succession [səkˈseʃən] *n.* (right of) succeeding to a title，the throne，property，etc. 继承(权)

prone (to) [prəun] *adj.* liable to sth or likely to do sth；inclined to do sth 易于某事物；很可能做某事；有……的倾向

at the expense of *idm.* with loss or damage to sth 在损失或损坏某事物的情况下

serial [ˈsiəriəl] *adj.* of，in or forming a series 连续的；一系列的

cede [siːd] *v.* give up one's rights to or possession of sth 割让，让予，放弃

a change of heart *idm* great change in one's attitude or feelings，esp. towards greater friendliness or co-operation 态度或感情的巨大变化

leap [liːp] ***n.*** a rapid increase or change 激增；骤变

come/get to grips with sb/sth ***idm.*** understand or deal with something difficult 应付

amass [əˈmæs] ***v.*** gather together or collect (sth), esp. in large quantities 积累，积聚，收集

Exercises

Ⅰ. **Answer the following questions.**

1. What is the founder's dilemma? And why is it difficult for most founders to make a choice?

2. What are growing pains for entrepreneurs?

3. What does choosing money and choosing power mean to a founder-CEO respectively?

4. How can founders make their choices between power and money?

5. What does success mean to entrepreneurs?

Ⅱ. **Paraphrase the difficult sentences or language points.**

1. We remember the handful of founder-CEOs in corporate America, but they're the exceptions to the rule.

2. New ventures are usually labors of love for entrepreneurs, …

3. boards can have a hard time persuading them to put their "babies" up for adoption.

4. But, paradoxically, the need for a change at the top becomes even greater when a founder has delivered results.

5. The dramatic broadening of the skills that the CEO needs at this stage stretches most founders' abilities beyond their limits.

6. A recent report in *Private Equity Week* pithily captures this dynamic:

7. The founder's moment of truth sometimes comes quickly.

8. He's not the only one to have fought the inevitable;

9. This fundamental tension yields "rich" versus "king" tradeoffs.

10. Founders who want to become wealthy should be open to pursuing ideas that require resources.

Ⅲ. **Use the information in the text to choose the word or phrase that best explains the meaning of the underlined part from the text.**

1. When I analyzed 212 American start-ups that sprang up in the late 1990s and early 2000s, I discovered that only 40% of founders were still <u>in the corner office</u> by the time the ventures were four years old.

    A. in a small office

    B. in the top position

    C. in the difficult situation

2. Founders don't <u>let go</u> easily, though.

    A. give up   B. give out   C. give off

3. Most are shocked when investors insist that they relinquish control, and they're

pushed out of office in ways they don't like and <u>well before</u> they want to abdicate.

    A. completely before   B. long before   C. in all likelihood before

4. In fact, the manner in which founders tackle their first leadership transition often <u>makes</u> or breaks young enterprises.

    A. prepares for   B. turns out to be   C. ensures the success of

5. <u>Even though they had comparable backgrounds</u>, founders received 20% less in cash compensation than nonfounders who performed similar roles.

    A. Even though they had similar backgrounds

    B. Even though they had relatively better backgrounds

    C. Even though they had relatively worse backgrounds

6. The organization has to become more <u>structured</u>, and the CEO has to create formal processes, develop specialized roles, and, yes, institute a managerial hierarchy.

    A. well planned   B. highly organized   C. closely connected

7. "<u>In other Seven news</u>, the company named former Onebox. com CEO Russ Bott as its new CEO. "

    A. In other seven pieces of news

    B. In other news about Seven

    C. In news about other Sevens

8. Because the founder's emotional strengths become <u>liabilities</u> at this stage.

    A. responsibilities   B. financial obligations   C. disadvantages

9. For instance, <u>serial entrepreneur</u> Evan Williams sold his Pyra Labs to Google in 2003 but he brought in outside investors for his next venture Odeo two years later because he thought he had the opportunity to do something more substantial with Odeo.

    A. The entrepreneur who arranges activities in the correct order

    B. The entrepreneur who starts business several times

    C. The entrepreneur who leads the company in a series of periods

10. Once they realize <u>why they are turning entrepreneur</u>, founders must, as the old Chinese proverb says, "decide on three things at the start: the rules of the game, the stakes, and the quitting time. "

    A. why they are becoming entrepreneur

    B. why they are entrepreneur to make decisive changes

    C. why they are entrepreneur with decision-making rights

IV. Choose the best phrase or expression in the text from the following list to fit in each of the following blanks. Change the word form where necessary.

spring up   capitalize on   a labor of love   step down   dole out   rope in   prone to
at the expense of   come to grips with   be open to

1. All these services were provided as _____ no cost except for time and effort through sheer will to make it happen.

2. Although Bill was past retirement age, he refused to _____ and let his son take over business.

3. But these days, fathers aren't laughing over the pressure they face to _____ the dollars on their kids.

4. The owners of the building want to sell and _____ offers.

5. I had to _____ your aunt and put her to no end of trouble to beg Madam Xifeng in the West Mansion to get you this place in the family school.

6. Oil-exporting countries, as they _____ the decline in oil prices, face this issue.

7. The best thing to do with these little passions, if they _____, is to get rid of them.

8. The world of science, prepared for the unexpected, could swiftly _____ Becquerel's chance discovery.

9. To prefer one _____ the other would bring on Civil War and worse disunity than that would result from peaceful partition.

10. Too many in government who decry the "irresponsibility" of the press are _____ ___ judge news less for accuracy than for personal embarrassment.

V. Translate the following sentences into English.

1. 企业募集资源时不得不让出部分利润或一些决策控制权,甚至两者都要让出。

2. 如果你对工作心存感激而非一味抱怨,你会做得更好,更有成果,或许最终也会加薪。

3. 因为经济下滑,年工资增长率已限制在百分之五。

4. 通过相互尊重,共同信任和平等机会,这家公司努力授权其每个雇员最大程度拓展自己的能力,以建立一个充满活力和创造性的团队。

5. 干这种职务的人多半是带工的亲戚,所以他们差不多有生杀予夺的权力。

6. 简而言之,用户必须在产品的易用性和安全性之间做出妥协。

7. 在经过几天的深刻反省后,他改变了心意,决定冒险,把部分股权出售给风险投资公司。

8. 为什么白手起家? 有几个好的原因会促使一个公司考虑用"白手起家"的模式进入市场。

9. 据波士顿 CIBC 的一名分析师说:"在线游戏并不是 AOL 和 RealNetworks 公司的核心业务,但他们不想对微软拱手相让。"

10. 这家公司的创始人很有业绩,在五年内就带领公司取得跳跃式发展。

VI. Translate the following paragraphs into Chinese.

1. Whether gradual or sudden, the transition is often stormy. In 2001, for instance, when a California-based internet telephony company finished developing the first generation of its system, an outside investor pushed for the appointment of a new

CEO. He felt the company needed an executive experienced at managing the other executives who oversaw the firm's existing functions, had deeper knowledge of the functions the venture would have to create, and had experience in instituting new processes to knit together the company's activities. The founder refused to accept the need for a change, and it took five pressure-filled months of persuasion before he would step down.

2. This fundamental tension yields "rich" versus "king" tradeoffs. The "rich" options enable the company to become more valuable but sideline the founder by taking away the CEO position and control over major decisions. The "king" choices allow the founder to retain control of decision making by staying CEO and maintaining control over the board—but often only by building a less valuable company. For founders, a "rich" choice isn't necessarily better than a "king" choice, or vice versa; what matters is how well each decision fits with their reason for starting the company.

Writing

Personal Correspondence by E-mail

Directions:

Personal correspondence refers to letters of separate family members, friends or lovers from one to another in order to exchange information or strengthen emotional bonds with each other. There are two ways of personal correspondence—by traditional letter and by E-mail. Generally speaking, there is minimal difference between writing an email and writing a traditional letter by post. Both ways of letter-writing follow The Five Cs Principles (Consideration, Conciseness, Clarity, Courtesy, Correctness).

Format An electronic mail includes information about the addresser (the "From" line), the addressee (the "To" line), the subject (the "Subject" line), and delivery time. In most cases, the "From" line and time will be filled automatically. The "To" line needs to be filled manually unless it is a response to an incoming email. The "Subject" line gives the receiver a clear idea of the content of the email. The body of an email is written in block style and a blank line should be put between each paragraph.

Content Just as with writing a personal correspondence by traditional letter, writing an email requires an opening stating the purpose of the email, a main body outlining key points or queries and a complimentary closing.

Criteria A good personal email should meet the following requirements:

The subject is clearly and comprehensively stated in the subject line;

The message presented is accurate in content, relevant in meaning, concise and clear in expression, and appropriate in tone that fits the context and the relationship between the addresser and the addressee;

Errors in punctuation, spelling, and grammar do not do harm to the understanding of the message.

Here is an example of personal correspondence by email for you to study and appreciate.

Sample Letter

From: Jimmy (JimmyZhang@hotmail.com)

To: Amy@yahoo.com

Sent: Monday, July 27, 2009 4: 57 PM

Subject: Thank you for your help with our trip

Hi Amy,

I wanted to thank you for all your help with planning our trip to Niagara Falls.

The tour guide you recommended was nice and helpful, and he taught us a lot about the local culture.

The hotel at Niagara Falls was wonderful. The room you booked had plenty of room for all of us and provided a great view of this fascinating scenery. Your advice about to see the Falls at dusk was brilliant.

Another great part of the trip was the ride to Niagara Town. You were certainly right. It is a most beautiful and tranquil town and it is worth visiting.

We will be sure to recommend this tour to our friends and hope to see you again in the future.

Regards

Jimmy Zhang

Exercise

You are going to Suzhou on a business trip next week, where two of your friends are living. Write an email to tell them your trip and ask for a meeting with them during your stay there.

Reading Practice

Passage

A Special Report on Entrepreneurship

VICTOR HUGO once remarked: "You can resist an invading army; you cannot resist an idea whose time has come." Today entrepreneurship is such an idea.

The triumph of entrepreneurship is driven by profound technological change. A trio of inventions—the personal computer, the mobile phone and the internet—is democratising entrepreneurship at a cracking pace. Today even cash-strapped innovators can reach markets that were once the prerogative of giant organisations.

The internet provides a cheap platform for entrepreneurs to build interactive businesses. Meg Whitman grew rich by developing an online marketplace, eBay, where people could buy and sell without ever meeting. An army of pyjama-clad bloggers has repeatedly outsmarted long-established newspapers on breaking stories. Automated news-collecting services such as RealClearPolitics and Memeorandum, using tiny amounts of capital, have established themselves as indispensable tools for news junkies.

The development of "cloud computing" is giving small outfits yet more opportunity to enjoy the advantages of big organisations with none of the sunk costs. People running small businesses, whether they are in their own offices or in a hotel half-way round the world, can use personal computers or laptops to gain access to sophisticated business services.

The mobile phone has been almost as revolutionary. About 3.3 billion people, or half the world's population, already have access to one. The technology has allowed entrepreneurs to break into what used to be one of the world's most regulated markets, telecoms. And many developing countries have been able to leapfrog rich ones by going straight to mobile phones, cutting out landlines.

Thanks to the combination of touch-screen technology and ever faster wireless networks, the mobile phone is becoming the platform of choice for techno-entrepreneurs. Since July last year Apple has allowed third parties to post some 20,000 programs or applications on its "app store", allowing phones to do anything from identifying the singer of a song on the radio to imitating the sound of flatulence. So far around 500m "apps" have been downloaded for about a dollar a time.

These developments have been reinforced by broad cultural changes that have brought entrepreneurialism into the mainstream. An activity that was once regarded as peripheral, perhaps even reprehensible, has become cool, celebrated by politicians and embraced by the rising generation.

Today entrepreneurship is very much part of economics. Economists have realised that, in a knowledge-based economy, entrepreneurs play a central role in creating new companies,

The best and the worst
Ease of doing business rankings

Top ten

2009	2008	Business region
1	1	Singapore
2	2	New Zealand
3	3	United States
4	4	Hong Kong
5	5	Denmark
6	6	Britain
7	7	Ireland
8	8	Canada
9	10	Australia
10	9	Norway

Bottom ten

2009	2008	Business region
172	171	Niger
173	173	Eritrea
174	175	Venezuela
175	176	Chad
176	177	Sao Tome and Principe
177	174	Burundi
178	178	Congo-Brazzaville
179	179	Guinea-Bissau
180	180	Central African Republic
181	181	Congo

Source: World Bank *Doing Business* database

commercialising new ideas and, just as importantly, engaging in sustained experiments in what works and what does not. William Baumol has put entrepreneurs at the centre of his theory of growth. Edmund Phelps, a Nobel prizewinner, argues that attitudes to entrepreneurship have a big impact on economic growth.

Another reason for entrepreneurship becoming mainstream is that the social contract between big companies and their employees has been broken. Under managed capitalism, big companies offered long-term security in return for unflinching loyalty. But from the 1980s onwards, first in America and then in other advanced economies, big companies began slimming their workforces. This made a huge difference to people's experience at the workplace. In the 1960s workers had had an average of four different employers by the time they reached 65. Today they have had eight by the time they are 30. People's attitudes to security and risk also changed. If a job in a big organisation can so easily disappear, it seems less attractive. Better to create your own.

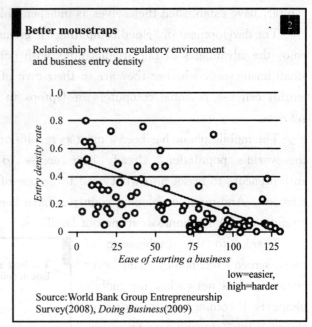

Better mousetraps

Relationship between regulatory environment and business entry density

Entry density rate

Ease of starting a business

low=easier,
high=harder

Source: World Bank Group Entrepreneurship Survey(2008), *Doing Business*(2009)

Yet another reason for the mainstreaming of entrepreneurship is that so many institutions have given it their support. Between 1999 and 2003 the number of endowed chairs in entrepreneurship in America grew from 237 to 406 and in the rest of the world from 271 to 536.

The media have also played a part. "Dragons' Den", a television programme featuring entrepreneurs pitching their ideas to businesspeople in order to attract venture capital, is shown in 12 countries. Even China's state-owned Central Television has a show about entrepreneurs pitching

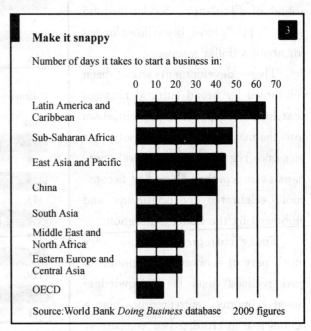

Make it snappy

Number of days it takes to start a business in:

- Latin America and Caribbean
- Sub-Saharan Africa
- East Asia and Pacific
- China
- South Asia
- Middle East and North Africa
- Eastern Europe and Central Asia
- OECD

Source: World Bank *Doing Business* database   2009 figures

ideas to try to win $1.3m in seed money.

The world's governments are now competing to see who can create the most pro-business environment. In 2003 the World Bank began to publish an annual report called *Doing Business* , rating countries for their business-friendliness by measuring things like business regulations, property rights and access to credit.

This "naming and shaming" caused countries to compete fiercely to improve their position in the World Bank's rankings. Since 2004 various countries have brought in more than 1,000 reforms. Most rich countries are working all the time to make it easier to start new businesses. Robert Litan, of the Kauffman Foundation, suggests that the World Bank may have done more good by compiling *Doing Business* than by lending much of the money that it has.

Ⅶ. **Answer the following questions.**

1. What drives entrepreneurship into its triumph?
2. How do the personal computer, the mobile phone and the internet change entrepreneurship?
3. What are the reasons for entrepreneurship becoming mainstream?
4. What do the world's governments do to promote entrepreneurship?

Keys

Key to Unit One

课文参考译文

拯救国际化银行

我们在过去一年学到的一个事实是：有些银行的确规模太大以至于不能倒闭。我们或许尚未发现一个更加令人担忧的事实，即有些银行规模太大以至于无法挽救。

美国财长蒂姆·盖特纳(Tim Geithner)这周上演了一出名誉恢复戏码——得益于变幻无常的股市。今天早晨，他将向国会作证，阐述了其有关改革监管以及在处理破产金融机构方面争取更大权力的计划。

关于财政部和美联储(Fed)如何能够做得更好——让雷曼兄弟(Lehman Brothers)优雅地倒下；在不必执拗于奖金合同的情况下，拯救美国国际集团(AIG)，盖特纳有自己睿智的见解。他希望美国政府在使用公共资金时，能够取得这些机构的控制权。

但美国政府没有这个能力：去年9月，美国政府不得不贷款850亿美元给AIG以维持其运营，而没有接管这家保险集团，同时美国政府也未能恰当地处理雷曼兄弟的问题。这一事实是盖特纳与国会出现矛盾的原因之一。

但这里也存在一个令人不安的想法。假如美国政府凭借自己的资产负债表和储备货币美元，获得了盖特纳和美联储主席本·伯南克(Ben Bernanke)所寻求的权力，结果会怎样？这会足以保证美国政府能够解决下一场AIG式的危机吗？不幸的是，答案是否定的。

这场危机及其发现——雷曼兄弟的英国分公司不受美联储的监管，AIG通过位于伦敦的法国银行分支机构安排了许多信贷衍生品交易——表明，这类机构让美国鞭长莫及。它们不仅拥有许多海外分支机构；而且已经编织了一个全球性的金融合同网络。

这加大了控制它们的难度，即便美国纳税人对于他们的钱正被用于偿还外国人的债务持乐观态度——但他们的政府并不这么认为。国有化可能不足以控制它们；我们需要国际化。

问题是，从这个角度而言，没有国际化这样的想法。拥有权力或财力，能够接管一家全球性金融机构、让其安全破产，并且在诸多国家的纳税人中间公平分配账单的跨境机构，并不存在。

盖特纳和伯南克联手追求的"决议机构"是以联邦存款保险公司(FDIC)为模板，该公司负责处理美国的破产银行。联邦存款保险公司拥有广泛的权力来接管银行、驱逐它们的管理者、把资产和债务移交给其他银行并承担任何亏损。

例如，上周，该公司就对科罗拉多斯普林斯的Colorado National Bank采取了这样的行动。该银行8 300万美元的存款和4家分支机构被强行移交给德克萨斯州阿玛里洛市的Herring Bank。美国联邦存款保险公司将会动用其保险基金，偿还Colorado National Bank 80%的亏损——约900万美元。美国所有的银行都会向这个基金缴纳保费。

比起我们去年秋见到的孤注一掷的临时做法，这种方法可能要好得多。它可以防止投行进入美国破产法第11章(Chapter 11)的破产程序，同时不必承担全部负债。

正如伯南克在上周二向众议院的一个委员会所指出的那样，它将允许政府撕毁那些可憎的合同，例如AIG保证发放的留任奖金(retention bonuses)；并让债权人及对手方承担部分亏损，例如AIG信用违约互换(CDS)的持有者。

但决议机构可能还不够。全球类似Colorado National Bank的银行都属于小而全的机构，这就提供了方便——一旦亏损得到解决，就会有现成的买家愿意接手。不过，雷曼和AIG都不属于那种规模小的国内机构。

以雷曼为例。去年9月15日，当其控股公司进入第11章破产程序时，盖特纳领导的纽约联邦储备银行(New York Fed)试图维持其投行部门的运营，从而令其能够实现有序破产。但纽约联邦储备银行失败了，其中的原因给了我们启示。

尽管纽约联邦储备银行为这家美国经纪公司的业务提供了支持，但它却发现事实上自己无法向这家公司的英国分公司提供融资。这家分公司过去一直依赖现已破产的控股公司的资金。在处理雷曼德国分行Lehman Bankhaus 的问题时，纽约联邦储备银行也遇到了障碍。决议机构或许可以派得上用场，因为政府本可以——并且在任何一家华尔街银行未来破产时大概都会——站在这家控股公司身后，通过该控股公司为其外国分支机构提供支持。不过，这无法保证政府能够触及作为这类机构的交易工具的所有海外实体。

即便它能够这样做，这里还存在一个政治问题。美国政府按面值偿还雷曼信用违约互换交易对手方债务的事实，正令国会感到越来越不安，这些对手包括以法国兴业银行（Société Générale）和德意志银行（Deutsche Bank）为首的外国银行。美国政府扮演了全球良好公民的角色，但这不会为它在国会加分。

如果你试图控制全球金融风险，那么明智的做法就是，不要按国别来区分对手方。不过，你要试着告诉那些必须贡献数十亿美元的纳税人这点。

一个理论上的解决方案是，建立一个全球性的金融权威机构——拥有类似于国际货币基金组织（IMF）的权力，能够救助一家跨国机构，并且能适当分配救助成本。不过，即便这在实际操作中行得通，在政治上却无法做到。

当某个国家掏钱援助另一个国家的银行时，或许可以找到另一种方法来分担这笔账单。我不是在危言耸听，但如果找不到这种方法，任何一个政府——不管它的国内权力有多大——都无法确保能够解决下一个 AIG 的问题。

国有化不是万能药

9 月中旬，当信贷危机环绕着华尔街的时候，我写了一个专栏建议美国前财长汉克·保尔森（Hank Paulson）不要纾困雷曼兄弟（Lehman Brothers）。他确实让这家投行倒闭了，而此后的一切大家都知道了，无需赘言。

回想起来，我还是认为政府应该让雷曼倒闭，但我错在没有领悟到这需要以一种有序的方式来进行。一旦私人部门接管的可能性完全没有了，政府必须出手干预以防止混乱。

现在我们又重新回到了起点，只不过这次是大型商业银行，而不是华尔街经纪商。

美英政府现在所面临的压力都不仅仅是纾困这些银行（它们已经尝试过），而是对它们实施国有化。这一紧张插曲之所以爆发，是由于苏格兰皇家银行（Royal Bank of Scotland）最近告诉投资者，其 2008 年业务面临 280 亿英镑（合 400 亿美元）的亏损。

英国零售银行的股价已经下跌得如此厉害——苏格兰皇家银行的市值只剩下大约 40 亿英镑，而巴克莱（Barclays）为 60 亿英镑——以至一些金融家和政界人士在呼吁英国政府结束这种不确定性，对它们实行国有化。

美国也出现了类似的呼吁，此前，花旗集团（Citigroup）和美国银行（Bank of America）披露了大额的资产减记，包括道富银行（State Street）在内的许多大型银行，似乎没有足够的股本可供安全渡过一场严重的衰退。对于这些机构而言，在股市或通过私募筹集它们所需要的普通股本已经变得极其困难。

与雷曼的情况不同，我不认为政府应该让作为经济基石的大型银行倒闭。如果英国政府不得不仿效爱尔兰政府对 Anglo Irish Bank 的处理，接管至少一家大型银行，那么就做吧。

但我并不认为哪个国家应该急于对银行实施国有化，除非迫不得已。

我支持任由雷曼倒闭的理由是，如果美国政府不断插手拯救投行，那么它的财政状况将会紧张，并且它可能会面临美元走软。

事实上，这些问题对英国的打击最为严重。去年 10 月份，英国首相戈登·布朗（Gordon Brown）因为在纾困银行方面做得比美国更彻底、投入更大而赢得了全世界的喝彩。而 3 个月后，布朗面临着银行业、英镑汇率和财政危机这三重威胁。

我们得到的教训是，尽管引人瞩目的干预在当时是令人满意的，但它们不一定能解决问题。国有化可能是需要的，但它不是万能药。

除了道德风险的观点，即放任危险性的风险承担会损害股东利益外，还有其他支持这一主张的理由。最近，威廉姆·比特(Willem Buiter)在他的 FT. com 博客上提出了一些观点；接着，约翰·麦克福(John McFall)和乔恩·摩尔顿(Jon Moulton)也在这个页面上给出了自己的观点。

或许最好的理由是，这为金融机构提供了明确的支持，而挣扎着的经济体需要这些机构继续放贷。正如比特指出的，目前的一个危险是，资产负债状况较差的私有银行"有足够的资金支撑，并能稍稍有所作为，"但它们害怕这么做。此外，如果一个政府觉得最终将不得不付诸国有化，那么它应该果断出手。上世纪90年代危机期间，日本直到1998年才把公共资金注入银行，而瑞典通过坚决要求银行减记自身的股本，然后调整它们的资本结构，获得了更好的效果。

不变的事实是，对于银行而言，政府是糟糕的所有者，任何了解德国政府所有的地方银行历史的人都可以证明。他们存在严重冲突的地方在于，尽管政客喜欢谴责银行家承担风险的行为，但为了让选民高兴，他们也会推动银行家自由放贷。

更具体地说，美国或英国银行完全由政府调整资本结构的成本，以及让它们的问题资产进入由政府控制的"坏银行"的保护成本，将会十分巨大。

尤其是美国，它无法像英国或瑞典一样，仅仅接管几家大型银行，就能放心地认为，它已经处理了银行业市场上的绝大部分问题。

Exercises

I. Answer the following questions.

1. Because the US government had to lend $85bn to AIG to keep it afloat last September rather than take over the insurance group, and also was unable to deal properly with Lehman Brothers, this is one reason why Mr. Geithner has been in trouble with Congress.

2. If you seek to limit global financial risk, it is sensible not to make any distinction between counterparties on the grounds of nationality.

3. The author's argument for letting Lehman go was that the US government, if it kept stepping in to rescue investment banks, would strain its finances and could face currency weakness.

4. A theoretical solution would be to have a global financial authority, with powers akin to the International Monetary Fund, that could salvage a global institution and apportion the costs appropriately.

5. The lesson is that, while dramatic interventions are satisfying at the time, they do not necessarily solve matters. Nationalisation could be needed, but it is not a panacea.

II. Paraphrase the difficult sentences or language points.

1. We have learnt the fact in the past year that some banks are so big that they should not go bankruptcy.

2. It is difficult to control them, even if American taxpayers were optimistic that their money were being used to pay the foreigners' debts, while their politicians are not so optimistic.

3. If you try to control financial risk around the world, it is wise not to distinguish the opponents according to their nationalities.

4. Nationalisation is not a cure-all, which cannot be used everywhere.

5. Once it is not possible for a private company to take over, the government should intervene to prevent chaos.

III. Choose the word or phrase that best explains the meaning of the underlined part from the text.

1. B 2. C 3. A 4. B 5. B 6. A 7. B 8. B 9. C 10. A

IV. Choose the best phrase or expression in the text from the following list to fit in each of the following blanks. Change the word form where necessary.

1. All in all 2. written off 3. go under 4. wind up 5. bailing out 6. has been taken over

7. impose…on… 8. complete with 9. akin to 10. has come up with

1. That makes it very hard to take control of them, even if American taxpayers were sanguine about their money being used to pay off foreign counterparties, which their politicians are not. Nationalisation may not be enough to corral them; it would require internationalisation.

2. If you seek to limit global financial risk, it is sensible not to make any distinction between counterparties on the grounds of nationality. Try telling that, however, to taxpayers who must contribute billions of dollars.

3. The lesson is that, while dramatic interventions are satisfying at the time, they do not necessarily solve matters. Nationalisation could be needed, but it is not a panacea.

4. No crors-border body exists with the authority or resources to take over a global financial institution, wind it down safely and divide the bill fairly among taxpayers of many countries.

5. The FDIC has extensive powers to seize banks, turf out their managers, hand over the assets and liabilities to other banks and absorb any losses.

6. The FDIC will pay 80 per cent of losses—some $9m—out of its insurance fund, to which us banks all pay levies.

7. Although the Fed propped up the US broker-dealer operations, it found that it could not efficiently fund the UK arm.

8. It was being a good global citizen, but that does not earn you points on Capitol Hill.

9. Perhaps another way can be found to split the bill when one country pays to prop up another's banks.

10. Both the UK and US governments face pressure not merely to bail out these banks, which they have already attempted, but to rationalize them.

Ⅵ. Translate the following into Chinese.

1. 关于财政部和美联储(Fed)如何能够做得更好——让雷曼兄弟(Lehman Brothers)优雅地倒下；在不必执拗于奖金合同的情况下，拯救美国国际集团(AIG)，盖特纳有自己睿智的见解。他希望美国政府在使用公共资金时，能够取得这些机构的控制权。

2. 这场危机及其发现——雷曼兄弟的英国分公司不受美联储的监管，AIG 通过位于伦敦的法国银行分支机构安排了许多信贷衍生品交易——表明，这类机构让美国鞭长莫及。它们不仅拥有许多海外分支机构；而且已经编织了一个全球性的金融合同网络。

Ⅶ. Answer the following questions.

1. Budget is the quantitative expressions of the objectives and the actions, stated in either physical or financial terms or both. Master budget is a comprehensive financial plan made up of various individual departmental and activity budgets. Operating budget is concerned with the income-generating activities of a firm: sales, production, and finished goods inventories.

2. Budget makes the management to plan for the future—to develop an all direction for the organization, foresee problems and develop future policies. It also conveys significant information about the resource capabilties of an organization, making better decision possible. It sets standards that can control the use of a company's resources and control and motivate employees. And budget also serves to communicate the plans of the organization to each employee and to coordinate their efforts.

3. A budget director is the person who works under the direction of the budget committee and is responsible for directing and coordinating the overall budgeting process. He is usually the controller or someone who reports to the controller.

4. The key features of the budget process is to direct and to coordinate the compilation of the budget.

Key to Unit Two

课文参考译文

后哥本哈根：我们必须另谋出路

哥本哈根气候峰会历时 12 天，期间抗议不断，与会者做尽姿态、说尽空话。为举办这次大象级的会议，人们大费周章，取得的成果却小如老鼠。相关方面在贝拉中心（Bella Centre）签署的抑制温室气体排放协议含糊其辞、软弱无力，既未规定切实责任、设定具有约束力的排放目标，也未要求任何一方采取具体行动。

那么，我们应该感到失望吗？事实上，不。人类导致的全球变暖并非是事实，我们也并非无需采取切实行动来应对。全球确实在变暖，我们的确需要行动起来。

但是，第 15 届联合国气候变化会议的可悲成果，仍应使我们怀抱希望。为什么呢？因为这次会议的失败或许正是唤醒世界的一记必要的警钟——泼到我们头上的冷水，或许终于促使我们正视现实，明白要抑制气候变化，什么会起作用，什么不会起作用。

自 1992 年里约"地球峰会"至今已有 17 年，应对全球变暖的努力始终遵循一个单一的思想，即唯一的解决方法就是大幅削减碳排放。如果有人贸然提议，在控制气候变化方面也许存在更有效的方法；或提议，试图迫使这个 80% 能源来自排放碳的化石燃料的世界骤然改弦易辙，不论从政治上还是从经济上来说，都是完全行不通的，此人就会被视为疯子、甚至是暗地里否认全球变暖之辈。应对全球变暖的里约-京都-哥本哈根路径显然毫无成效，对于这个明显令人不快的现实，人们宁愿不予理睬。

你可以把我视为一位荒唐的乐观主义者，但哥本哈根会议失败得如此之惨，不容我们对此不闻不问。虽然美国总统巴拉克·奥巴马（Barack Obama）大谈什么"空前的突破"，世界各国领导人真正做的，却是试图以一份三页长的会议公报，来掩盖他们之间的分歧。这份公报基本上是要求我们交叉手指祈祷，并尽量朝好的方面想。他们还不如承认自己无能为力、然后空手而回呢。减排策略的彻底失败从未显得如此醒目。

因此我心存希望，在全球变暖方面，政治领导人或许终于要面对以下事实：如果我们确实希望解决问题，我们就必须采取新的方法。承诺减少碳排放或许会使我们显得高尚，但其意义不过如此。假如我们确实希望让这个星球变凉，我们就需要技术上更高明、政治上更可行、经济上更有效的策略。

哥本哈根的一大教训是，世界既不愿、也无法骤然中止对化石燃料的依赖。问题在于，根本不存在人们负担得起的替代能源——这一点对中国、印度及其他发展中国家来说尤其如此。

记住，到 2050 年，全球能源需求预计将会翻倍。这意味着，假如我们希望减少（如果不是全然戒除）对化石燃料的使用，同时避免让全球经济陷入瘫痪，我们就必须把对绿色能源技术的依赖程度提高几个数量级。

麦基尔大学（McGill University）的伊莎贝尔·加利亚娜（Isabel Galiana）以及克里斯·格林（Chris Green）教授在 2009 年 7 月为哥本哈根共识中心（Copenhagen Consensus Centre）撰写的一篇论文中，阐述了非碳能源（包括核能、风能、太阳能和地热能）的现状，得出了一些令人不安的结论。他们发现，综合起来考虑，按照当前的发展速度，即便替代能源大幅增加，我们距到 2050 年保持碳排放稳定的目标也仍有一大半路要走，距到 2100 年保持碳排放稳定的目标则更为遥远。在可量测性或稳定性方面，技术届时肯定不会成熟。许多领域仍需要进行最基本的研发。我们甚至谈不上即将展开必要的技术革命。

为应对这一现实，哥本哈根协议做出一项含糊的承诺：发达国家最终每年将捐出 1 000 亿美元，用于帮助穷国应对气候变化。假如这些资金用于帮助穷国适应气候变化，那么这项承诺或许有些意义，因为这可能对人们的生活质量产生实质而即时的影响。但是，这并非这些资金的预期用途。根据协议文本，大部分资金（如果不是全部）将在"有意义的减排的背景下"使用。换句话说，资金将用于补贴削减碳排放的行为。

此举毫无意义,完全无助于改善当前困境——充其量可能在今后一个世纪内略微降低气温。

可要是我们把这些资金用在更好的地方呢?要是我们致力于降低绿色能源的成本,而非试图通过提高排放碳的燃料的成本,迫使全世界数 10 亿人口继续生活在贫困之中呢?就解决方法而言,降低绿色能源成本更加快捷、更有成效,所造成的痛苦也小得多。

目前,由于太阳能面板成本过高,只有既富裕又好心的西方人安装得起。但是,如果在今后 20 至 40 年内,我们能够使它们或其他绿色能源技术变得比化石燃料更便宜(没有理由认为我们做不到),我们就不用去迫使(或补贴)人们停止燃烧排放碳的燃料。每个人,包括中国人和印度人,届时都会转而使用更廉价、更清洁的替代能源——从而解决全球变暖问题。

那么,我们如何抵达"幸福的彼岸"呢?我们必须把绿色能源研发支出增加到现在的 50 倍。用全球年国内生产总值(GDP)的 0.2%(即 1 000 亿美元),我们有望取得必要的技术突破,降低绿色能源的成本,实现无碳未来。对发达国家和发展中国家的政府来说,这在政治上要比减少碳排放可行得多。

全球不计其数的人曾把希望寄托在哥本哈根上,会议的微小成果或许使他们深感失望。但是,这次峰会的失败或许是"塞翁失马"。过去 17 年里,我们一直本末倒置,假装我们能够在今日削减碳排放、在明日解决技术问题。如今,我们的领导人在从哥本哈根蹒跚而回时,或许会承认他们当前的做法存在深深的缺陷,并在随后描绘出一条更为明智的路线。

哥本哈根峰会能否成功?

哥本哈根气候变化峰会将无法达成目标。这要紧吗?既要紧也不要紧:说要紧,是因为采取行动的理由极其充分;说不要紧,是因为可能达成的协议将不足以解决问题。

我认为有必要采取果断行动的观点引起了争议。怀疑论者提出了两点反驳意见:首先,作为气候变化依据的科学存在高度不确定性;其次,成本大于收益。

但仅仅争辩科学具有不确定性是不够的。鉴于存在的风险,在听信怀疑论者之前,我们必须确信科学是错误的。等到我们发现它没有错,再要采取有效行动,可能就为时已晚了。我们只有一个地球,无法重复进行实验。

之所以要尽快改变这些趋势,是因为如果不这么做,抑制气温大幅升高的成本将变得极其高昂,甚至无法承受。IEA 指出,如果以把温室气体浓度控制在 450ppm 以下为目标,那么每推迟一年向所需的轨迹靠拢,就会使全球 10.5 万亿美元的估计成本再增加 5 000 亿美元。这些成本源于发电所需资本资产的超长寿命,以及甚至更长的大气中二氧化碳的寿命。

另一种情形截然不同:2030 年,与能源有关的排放量将仅为 264 亿吨,而非 402 亿吨——差距非常悬殊。欧洲气候基金会(European Climate Foundation)的一份简报显示,各国在哥本哈根会议前所作的承诺不足以填补这一差距。即使按照最乐观的看法,要把二氧化碳当量浓度控制在 450ppm 以下,目前各项提议距 2020 年所需的减排量还差三分之一左右。

因此,哥本哈根将仅仅是个开始。鉴于美国政府不能做出有约束力的承诺,而发展中国家不愿做出此类承诺,它或许连个开始都谈不上。不过,哥本哈根似乎标志着序幕已经拉开。人们已经达成共识:世界应当采取行动。同样达成共识的是,尽管口头表态不绝于耳,但迄今取得的实际进展寥寥。采取行动的时机就是眼下——如果不是在哥本哈根会议上,那就是在会后不久。

遗憾的是,这并不意味着我们将达成正确的共识。我们采取的政策必须尽可能有效且高效。这意味着什么?我想强调三条标准。

首先,我们需要适用于相应规划阶段的碳价格。这一价格不能永远保持不变,而是应该随着情况的改变而调整,但其稳定性必须远高于欧盟的许可证交易市场(见表格)。正因为此,在我看来,征税似乎比"限量及交易"更具吸引力。

其次,减排的发生地应与成本支付方相分离。我们需要在最能产生成效的地方实施减排。这就是为什么要把发展中国家纳入其中的原因所在。但减排成本应由富国承担。这不仅是因为它们有能力承担,也是因为它们是过去大部分排放量的产出者。

最后,我们需要在所有相关技术领域开发和应用创新成果。欧洲智库 Bruegel 的一份报告极具说服力地提出,仅仅提高碳排放价格,会巩固成熟技术的地位。我们还需对创新进行大规模补贴。

Exercises

Ⅰ. Answer the following questions.

1. In a paper for the Copenhagen Consensus Centre in July 2009, Isabel Galiana and Professor Chris Green of McGill University examined the state of non-carbon based energy today—including nuclear, wind, solar and geothermal energy—and came to some disconcerting conclusions. Based on present rates of progress, they found that, taken together, alternative energy sources could, if hugely scaled up, get us less than halfway towards a path of stable carbon emissions by 2050, and only a fraction of the way towards stabilisation by 2100. The technology will simply not be ready in terms of scalability or stability. In many cases, the most basic research and development is still required. We are not even close to getting the needed technological revolution started.

2. The three criteria are: First, we need prices for carbon that apply over relevant planning horizons. Second, where the abatement occurs must be separated from who pays for it. Abatement needs to happen where it is most efficient. Finally, we need to develop and apply innovations in all relevant technologies.

3. Tackling the risk of climate change is the most complex collective challenge humanity has ever confronted. Success requires costly and concerted action among many countries to deal with a distant threat, on behalf of people as yet unborn, under unavoidable uncertainty about the costs of not acting.

4. As vague as it is toothless, the accord on curbing greenhouse gas emissions that emerged from the Bella centre this weekend imposes no real obligations, sets no binding emissions targets and requires no specific actions by anyone.

5. The stark lesson of Copenhagen is that the world is neither willing nor able to go cold turkey when it comes to ending its addiction to fossil fuels.

Ⅱ. Paraphrase the difficult sentences or language points

1. People tried their best to hold this big-scale climate meeting, but at last the meeting achieved very little.

2. There are no substitute energy that can be bought cheaply, which is the problem for China, India and the rest of the developing world.

3. Mankind has faced the most complicated challenge, which is to deal with the risk caused by climate change.

4. It is very obvious that the carbon-cutting strategy has failed completely.

5. Well, call me an abnormal optimist, but Copenhagen's meeting is such a failure that we shouldn't ignore it.

Ⅲ. Choose the word or phrase that best explains the meaning of the underlined part from the text.

1. B 2. B 3. C 4. B 5. B 6. A 7. A 8. A 9. B 10. A

Ⅳ. Choose the best phrase or expression in the text from the following list to fit in each of the following blanks. Change the word form where necessary.

1. Thanks to 2. is heading for 3. Given 4. has committed … to 5. feasible to 6. range from … to
7. What if 8. at best 9. stirred up 10. accounts for

Ⅴ. Translate the following sentences into English.

1. Nonetheless, the dismal outcome of the 15th United Nations Climate Change Conference should make us hopeful. Why? Because its failure may be just the wake-up call the world has needed—the splash of cold water that may finally get us to face the facts about what works and what does not work to cure

climate change.

2. So I am hopeful that political leaders may finally be ready to face the truth about global warming—namely, that if we are serious about wanting to solve it, we need to adopt a new approach. Promising to cut carbon emissions may make us feel virtuous, but that is all it does. If we actually want to cool down the planet, we need policies that are technologically smarter, politically more feasible and economically more efficient.

3. Keep in mind that global energy demand is expected to double by 2050. What this means is that if we want to reduce (if not actually eliminate) our use of fossil fuels without totally crippling the world economy, we are going to have to increase our reliance on green energy technologies by several orders of magnitude.

4. Yet it is not enough to argue that the science is uncertain. Given the risks, we have to be quite sure the science is wrong before following the sceptics. By the time we know it is not, it is likely to be too late to act effectively. We cannot repeat experiments with just one planet.

5. Copenhagen then would only be a beginning. It is likely not even to be that, since the US administration is unable to make binding commitments and developing countries are unwilling to do so. Yet Copenhagen seems the end of the beginning. Something close to agreement exists that the world should act. There is, equally, agreement that, despite the rhetoric, little useful has been achieved so far. The time for action is now—if not at Copenhagen, then soon after.

6. Finally, we need to develop and apply innovations in all relevant technologies. A paper from the Bruegel think-tank argues, persuasively, that merely raising prices on carbon emissions would reinforce the position of established technologies. We need large-scale subsidies for innovation as well.

7. The elephanting gathering that was the Copenhagen climate summit has laboured mightily and brought forth… a mouse.

8. Well, call me a cock-eyed optimist, but Copenhagen's failure strikes me as being too abject to ignore.

9. The stark lesson of Copenhagen is that the world is neither willing nor able to go cold turkey when it comes to ending its addiction to fossil fuels.

10. The Copenhagen accord attempts to deal with this reality by offering a vague promise that developed nations will eventually contribute as much as $100bn a year to help poor countries cope with climate change.

Ⅵ. Translate the following into Chinese.

1. 哥本哈根气候峰会历时 12 天,期间抗议不断,与会者做尽姿态、说尽空话。为举办这次大象级的会议,人们大费周章,取得的成果却小如老鼠。相关方面在贝拉中心(Bella Centre)签署的抑制温室气体排放协议含糊其辞、软弱无力,既未规定切实责任、设定具有约束力的排放目标,也未要求任何一方采取具体行动。

2. 麦基尔大学(McGill University)的伊莎贝尔·加利亚娜(Isabel Galiana)以及克里斯·格林(Chris Green)教授在 2009 年 7 月为哥本哈根共识中心(Copenhagen Consensus Centre)撰写的一篇论文中,阐述了非碳能源(包括核能、风能、太阳能和地热能)的现状,得出了一些令人不安的结论。他们发现,综合起来考虑,按照当前的发展速度,即便替代能源大幅增加,我们距到 2050 年保持碳排放稳定的目标也仍有一大半路要走,距到 2100 年保持碳排放稳定的目标则更为遥远。

Ⅶ. Answer the following questions.

1. Barclays insurance services can protect the interests of you when you are self-employed or running your own business.

2. You are required by law to provide the employees with insurance cover against injury arising from their

employment.

3. Travel insurance.

4. The policies include: (a) new for old cover; (b) a choice of different levels of protection; (c) 24 hour helplines for domestic emergencies, glass replacement and legal advice; (d) options to cover your possessions away from home, and to include your buildings.

Key to Unit Three

课文参考译文

中国应加快人民币升值

许多支持或反对人民币加快升值的常见理由都是被误导的。加快人民币升值确实有利于中国,这不仅可以缓解国际压力,也有利于中国经济本身,使其以更快的步伐发展。在分析人民币升值的"真正"理由之前,首先应该讨论关于中国汇率问题的一些常见误解。

并非汇率操纵

让我们回顾一下中国的固定式或"准固定式"汇率体系的运作方式:中国央行,即中国人民银行每天发布汇率报价,并根据报价进行外汇交易。如果市场上美元过剩,无论是贸易顺差还是资本净流入导致,人民银行都将增发人民币购入美元;而如果美元供给不足,人民银行则卖出其美元储备弥补不足,从市场上回笼人民币。

近几年贸易顺差的扩大意味着,人民银行一直是美元的净购入者,平均每个月的净购入额接近 300 亿美元。到 2007 年 3 月,外汇储备总额已达 1.2 万亿美元。许多人因此指责中国有意低估人民币汇率,从而获得了超强的出口竞争力,自然导致巨额贸易顺差。但事实并非如此,在固定汇率体制下,一国央行必然要根据外汇市场情况履行自身职能。而从技术意义上说,美元的大幅流入仅仅是外汇市场在中国运行的结果。

事实上,明确中国的政策意图,有助于理解中国的固定汇率。首先,1997 年中国实行钉住汇率制,初衷并不是阻止人民币升值,而是避免人民币大跌。1995—1996 年,泡沫经济破裂给中国经济在国内外留下了沉重的坏账负担,利润大幅缩减,经济增长率降低至一位数。在此背景下,亚洲金融危机的爆发让许多投资者确信,人民币将是下一块倒下的骨牌,短期资本开始以空前的高速度流出中国。政府当局决定将人民币事实上钉住美元,这显然相当于人民币不贬值的承诺。而至 2003 年前任总理朱镕基离任时,他认为人民币固定汇率不仅是其任内的巨大成就,也是中国对全球经济稳定的巨大贡献之一。

第二,对于贸易顺差的猛增,中国政府和所有人一样不安。直到 2004 年年中,中国外贸仍然是逆差,认为人民币汇率存在结构性低估显然是无稽之谈。直到 2005 年年初,中国的贸易顺差才开始急剧上升,连创新高。无论中国政府还是大部分国外观察家,都对此大感意外。想一想中国政府的处境:2000 年左右的时候,人民币对美元汇率为 8:1,大多数经济学家都要求中国政府保持钉住汇率制,以免人民币贬值;六年后,汇率和当时大致相当,外国政策制定者们却在叫嚷,说人民币是世界上低估最严重的货币。

可以说,中国并没有操纵汇率。用"鞭策"来形容中国处境更确切,因为近年来的剧变令中国难以适应。

出口不会放缓

密切关注中国大陆经济的人会发现,近年来中国呈现出另一幅有趣景象。人民币对美元的升值速度在逐渐加快:2005 年升值 2%,2006 年为 4%,2007 年初以来的年增幅则为 6%。另一方面,随着农村单身青年劳动力的减少,中国农民工工资的年增幅已经由几年前的 3%—4%迅速提高到 10%—15%。

人民币升值加之劳动力成本上升的双刃剑,原本应该对玩具、服装、家具、家电、电子品等中国的传统出口部门造成沉重打击。但从企业盈利数据来看,轻工业的盈利水平稳如磐石,毫无承受压力的迹象。

为什么会这样？因为出口商把成本提高的压力转移给了国外的顾客。目前,不同国家的数据反映的价格趋势很少一致。但令人吃惊的事实之一是,中国内地、香港地区、美国、日本和欧洲的数据都无一例外地表明,过去3年之中,中国内地的出口价格已经开始上升。1995—2003年间,服装、玩具等传统制造业的美元价格年均下降3%—4%。但从2004年起,这些价格的走势发生了明显逆转,平均每年上涨3%—4%。电子品行业也出现了同样的变化。根据贸易伙伴国的数据,过去中国产电子品的美元价格通常每年下降6%—10%。而今,其价格已经不再下降。而中国的数据则表明,今年年初以来,价格已经已出现了大幅上升。

中国出口行业之所以能够避免成本上升造成的痛苦,原因在于其规模极大。参观过大陆工厂的人普遍认为,中国企业规模普遍很小,为了生存而以微薄的利润进行激烈竞争。对单个企业而言,情况或许如此。但总体看来,中国占据的市场份额已经非常庞大:美国玩具、鞋类等低端制品进口的70%—80%,服装进口的近40%,电子品进口的35%。这种情况下,中国厂商很容易转移其承受的国内成本压力。

当然,随着生产活动向越南、印度、印尼等成本更低的地区转移,工资上升和人民币升值最终会影响到中国传统低端制造业的终结,但这种转变非常缓慢。事实上,亚洲经济最惊人的趋势之一就在于,中国成本的提高让其亚洲邻国也获得了提高自身产品价格的"喘息之机"。

因此,至少几年之内,不要指望人民币升值能够减缓中国出口的强劲增长。充其量,其主要影响也只是抬高全球消费品价格。

美国就业不会减少

这并不是说,人民币升值无助于降低中国的贸易顺差。事实上,它会通过刺激进口来达到此目的。但是,颇有讽刺意味的是,如果人民币加快升值,在人民币固定汇率问题上声调最高的美国将是受益最小的国家。

一些数据有助于观察中美关系。从2004年上半年到2007年上半年的三年间,中国平均每个月的贸易顺差增加了近200亿美元。这种增加有多少来自于对美国的净出口呢? 其中新增的对美顺差仅为60亿美元,这个数字大致与美国在中国出口总额所占的比例相符。以名义美元来看,中国贸易顺差的增长大部分来自与其他国家之间的贸易。

另一个重要的问题是,即便是60亿美元的新增对美月度顺差之中,也有很大一部分其实间接来自中国的亚洲邻国。从1990年到2007年,美国对华贸易逆差从零增至GDP的2%,但显见的事实是,美国对整个亚洲的贸易逆差只增加了GDP的1.5%或更少。之所以如此,是因为今天美国进口的许多"中国制造"的产品原来是"韩国制造"或"台湾制造"。由于大批加工制造业由亚洲其他地区转移到了中国大陆,备受关注的美国的双边贸易逆差也人为地转移到了大陆。如果考虑到亚洲内部产业转移的影响,美国真正新增的贸易赤字主要来自亚洲之外的地区,包括欧佩克、欧洲、加拿大和墨西哥。

而且,没有充分证据表明,中国厂商突然侵占了美国的工作岗位。从1990年到2007年,制造业在美国非农业就业中所占的份额由16%降为10%。然而,1990年的份额也远低于1950年32%的份额。事实上,美国制造业所占的就业份额以直线方式平均每10年下降4%,在中国问题出现的前后一直保持着这样的速度。而且,中国市场份额增长最快的领域是传统的低端轻工业。而几十年前美国的这些行业就已经接近消失了,1990年其在美国总就业中所占的份额仅为1.7%。总而言之,如果说人民币加快升值对美国宏观经济会产生显著影响,那是不切实际的。

另一个重要事实在于,人民币的渐进升值并没有威胁中国国内的经济稳定。许多分析家认为,外汇储备迅速膨胀会推动国内流动性的增长,超出央行进行冲销操作的能力,最终使经济增长和资产价格出现严重的泡沫。

那中国为什么不这样做呢? 迄今为止,中国一直拒绝人民币的一次性大幅升值,或大大加宽人民币的升值速度,理由是这会导致经济动荡。说到严格意义上的货币升值,对中国这种观念我持有认同。如果人民币对美元汇率突然升值15%—20%,将会给那些以旧汇率设定合同价格,同时又缺少汇率对冲措施的出口商造成惨重损失。

因此,中国出口商表现优异的背景不仅是人民币对美元的缓慢升值,还包括其他亚洲货币更加迅速的升值,这实际上提高了中国的出口竞争力。而且,正如前文所说,与任何亚洲国家相比,中国大陆厂商向最终消费者转移成本压力的能力要强得多。

另一方面,一些著名经济学家认为,允许人民币浮动将使中国失去"货币锚"。但据我所知,中国从未真正拥有过"货币锚"。在开放的小型外贸型经济体中,汇率可以在稳定价格方面发挥很大作用。但中国是一个极其庞大的国内驱动型经济体,与其他亚洲国家相比,其外贸部门的相对规模要小得多。因此,在上世纪90年代,钉住美元的汇率制度并没有避免中国的大幅度通胀和通缩,今天也没有理由认为汇率挂钩会成为中国的货币锚。

最后,另一个反对人民币加快升值的隐射理由涉及投机压力。也就是说,如果人民币升值过快,投机资本将以"单向赌博"的方式大规模流入中国。理论上虽然如此,但从没有实际证据表明,人民币升值导致了任何大规模的资本流入。事实上,迄今为止,"热钱"资本流入中国的主要动力一直是中国资产市场的回报率。

2003—2005年间,人民币升值预期确实有助于吸引资本流入。但资本进入中国的真正动力还是上海房地产市场,当时上海豪华住宅的价格平均每年上涨70%—80%。相比之下,从2005年后期起,热钱开始流出中国。2006年后期,人民币的年升值速度加快到8%,却没有扭转热钱的外流势头。直到中国股市开始高涨,月回报率达到10%—20%,证券投资才过了6个月又一次进入中国。

鉴于逃避资本控制以及资本进出中国的实际交易成本,即使把人民币的年升值幅度提高到10%,中国政府也无需担忧。会这样吗?正如本文所说,中国还远未如此,但是我相信,人民币加快升值的利益将会逐渐稳定地表现出来。

Exercises

Ⅰ. Answer the following questions.

1. To keep the currency from collapsing and maintain mainland trade balance.

2. No. The main impact would simply be to raise prices for global consumers.

3. No, it won't gain anything for most of the real increase in the U. S. trade deficit comes from elsewhere, including the Organization of Petroleum Exporting Countries, Europe, Canada and Mexico. Another reason is that traditional low-end light industries disappeared in the U. S. decades ago.

4. No. Traditional low-end light industries where mainland penetration has increased the fastest were already decimated in the U. S. decades ago.

5. Fast appreciation would destabilize Chinese economy and cause speculative pressure.

Ⅱ. Paraphrase the difficult sentences or language points.

1. … in essence, central banks promise to meet the demand of the market readily…

2. The Chinese government's decision to construct an actual peg against the dollar was obviously established as a promise which aims at keeping the value of the yuan.

3. To sum up, even if the yuan is appreciated at a very high rate, American economy would not be influenced in a general sense.

4. On the basis of a nominal dollar or current dollar, most of China's net trade expansion has been achieved from the other countries.

5. During 2003—2005, the prediction of a coming appreciation of the yuan attracted money into China, but what really attracted the investors was the Shanghai property market, in which the price of luxury apartments increased by 70% to 80% a year.

Ⅲ. Choose the word or phrase that best explains the meaning of the underlined part from the text.

1. B 2. A 3. C 4. B 5. C 6. A 7. A 8. A 9. B 10. B

IV. Choose the best phrase or expression in the text from the following list to fit in each of the following blanks. Change the word form where necessary.

1. unprecedented　2. nominal　3. foreseen　4. overwhelm　5. volatile　6. looming　7. implore

8. bilateral　9. accounting for　10. careen

V. Translate the following sentences into English.

1. Impersonal manipulation of capital and industry greatly increased the numbers and importance of shareholders as a class.

2. Officers and tradesman are there to implore the gods to bless the voyage of the explorers.

3. Inflation means that nominal or money incomes per head is rising faster than real output per head.

4. Of course you'll want the lion's share of the profit as you've done most of the work.

5. Choices made today may be costly or impossible to reverse in the future.

6. The extraordinary election results confounded the government.

7. Dominoeffect is a cumulative effect produced when one event sets off a chain of similar events.

8. Despite high interest payments, some governments have not reduced other items of public expenditure in line with declining national income.

9. The agreement is explicit in saying the rent must be paid by the tenth of every month.

10. International marketing offers a way to counteract aggressive competition from foreign competitors at home.

VI. Translate the following into Chinese.

1. 在此背景下,亚洲金融危机的爆发让许多投资者确信,人民币将是下一块倒下的骨牌,短期资本开始以空前的高速度流出中国。政府当局决定将人民币事实上钉住美元,这显然相当于人民币不贬值的承诺。

2. 另一方面,一些著名经济学家认为,允许人民币浮动将使中国失去"货币锚"。但据我所知,中国从未真正拥有过"货币锚"。在开放的小型外贸型经济体中,汇率可以在稳定价格方面发挥很大作用。但中国是一个极其庞大的国内驱动型经济体,与其他亚洲国家相比,其外贸部门的相对规模要小得多。

VII. Answer the following questions.

1. It is due to the inefficiencies in the economy generated by high and rising levels of excess capacity and the continued heavy presence of the state sector in the current business cycle.

2. No. Because China's stock markets remain comparatively small in terms of capitalisation despite recent robust growth and only a quarter of shares in the Chinese market are liquid and available for trade.

3. It will bring additional imbalances with regard to China's severe environmental degradation and investment in heavy industry has resulted in lower employment generation, which has served to depress household spending. The lack of adequate social security nets and the widening wealth gap reinforces the trend.

4. The potential slowdown in external demand, and the need to maintain growth at high rates to absorb shocks generated by state sector restructuring combine to be the reasons why the authorities will not allow more appreciation in the yuan exchange rate.

Key to Unit Four

课文参考译文

石油美元的再循环

相比之前的价格涨势,最近石油输出国储存了更多的石油收入。很难辨明资金的具体流向。

许多美国政客和学者认为亚洲经济体,特别是中国的经常账户盈余是导致美国巨额经常账户赤字的原因。他们抱怨说,低估的货币和不公平的廉价劳动力削弱了美国的竞争力。实际上,从全球范围来看,经常账户盈余最多的国家已经不再是亚洲国家,而是石油输出国,高油价使他们大发横财。

今年,这些石油输出国将会通过出口石油获得 7 000 亿美元的收入。这些国家不但包括石油输出国组织的成员,还包括石油收入分居世界第一和第二的俄罗斯和挪威。国际货币组织估计,石油输出国的经常账户盈余可能会达 4 000 亿美元——是 2002 年的四倍还要多。以实际收入计算,这个数字几乎是 20 世纪 70 年代两次石油危机后的 1974 和 1980 年石油收入的二倍——当时俄罗斯的石油收入可以忽略不计。相比之下,今年中国和其他一些亚洲新兴经济体的经常账户盈余总计仅为 1880 亿美元。

相对于其经济规模,石油输出国的经常账户盈余远超中国。国际货币组织估计中国今年的盈余约占其国内生产总值的 6%,而在沙特阿拉伯这一比例高达 32%。中东石油出口国的平均盈余是 GDP 的 25%,俄罗斯可能为 13%,挪威 18%。

油价的升高意味着在石油出口国和进口国之间进行了一次大规模的收入再分配。以往的高油价持续时间短,但是这次产油国的额外收入看来较为持久。尽管作为行业基准的西德州中级原油每桶价格最近回落到 60 美元上下,期货市场依然预期油价将保持在高位运行。

令人羡慕的选择

所有这些石油美元的去向如何? 基本上不外乎花掉或储存。无论哪种情况,大量石油美元能够再循环到石油消费国,以缓冲高油价带给它们的冲击。如果石油出口国花掉这笔钱,它们会扩大进口,有助于维持全球的需求。但是,它们不可能花掉太多,相比较石油消费国,它们往往有更高的储蓄率:例如,阿联酋和科威特的储蓄率约为国内生产总值的 40%。因此,收入从石油消费国到输出国的转移会导致全球需求的放缓。

如果产油国将这份收入存起来,投资到全球资本市场,它们会为石油进口国的巨大经常账户赤字提供融资——实际上是将增加的石油收入重新借给了消费者。通过增加对外国金融资产的需求,它们追高了石油进口国的资产价格,降低了债券收益率,从而有助于维持这些国家的经济需求。

以往的经验证明,石油繁荣对石油出口国来说,既可是福也可是祸,这取决于能否明智地消费或储存额外的收入。过去的意外之财常常导致预算膨胀,而充足的资金导致了经济改革的延误。然而这一次,石油输出国花钱不如以前多,宁可维持更多的对外盈余、偿还债务和增加资产。在 1973 至 1976 年,石油输出国组织出口收入增长的 60% 被用于产品和服务的进口。在 1978 至 1981 年期间,这一比例上升到 75%。但是国际货币组织估计截止到 2005 年前二年的收入只有 40% 会被花掉。

俄罗斯政府明智地设立了"石油稳定基金",用于减少巨额外债。也就是说,俄罗斯比石油输出国组织成员更迫切地想花掉多余的钱。2002 年以来,俄罗斯出口收入增长中的约三分之二用于进口。一些分析家也怀疑,俄罗斯政府可能还会大量使用稳定基金,进行无节制的消费。然而,关注的重点在于,大笔现金涌入经济的同时,会延缓一些重要结构性改革的进行。

大多数中东政府比通常更加谨慎地对待它们的这份额外收入。国际货币基金组织中东和中亚事务部主任莫森·肯认为,这一地区的大多数政府正以每桶 30—40 美元为基础来制定明年的预算。据他估计,自 2002 年以来,这些政府平均只花费了额外石油收入的 30%;而 20 世纪 70 年代和 80 年代初,在油价迅速攀升后,75% 的额外收入被花费掉。这些国家的平均预算盈余从 2002 年占国内生产总值的 2% 增加到今年的接近15%。

矫枉过正的教训

石油输出国政府看来汲取了20世纪七八十年代的教训。第一,不要期望油价永远居高不下,以实际价格计算,从1981年到2000年,石油输出国组织年平均石油收入只是1980年的三分之一。第二,不要浪费额外收入。在以往油价高涨期间,产油国慷慨地将其石油美元花费在需要进口设备和熟练外国劳动力的耗资巨大的建筑项目上,而几乎没有创造本地就业或使其经济多元化。在最近公布的中东和中亚地区的《地区经济展望》中,国际货币基金组织建议这些国家政府优先考虑有助于经济持续增长和生活水平的提高方面的支出。

实际上,肯认为,与上世纪七十和八十年代相比,中东石油出口国有更大能力消费石油美金,因为这些国家的人口增长迅速,同时政府收入缩减那么多年之后,它们的基础设施也需要更新。高失业率意味着在增加教育和健康开支和鼓励私营经济用工方案等方面,有着较大的社会压力。

沙特阿拉伯是世界上人口增长最快的国家之一,其失业率约为20%。经过近20年的巨额预算赤字,到2000年为止,政府债务达到了GDP的百分之百。甚至到了今年,沙特阿拉伯的人均石油收入在实际金额上也比1980年少了约70%,部分原因在于人口增长了大约三倍。该国正在用一部分多余的金钱来偿还债务,政府最近也提高了公务员工资,涨幅为15%,这是20多年以来工资的第一次全面增长。

除了在健康、教育和基础设施方面增加开销,中东国家也有必要在石油生产和精炼石油产能方面进行投资,以缓解将来的供应短缺和平稳价格。国际能源机构本周警告说,未来20年中,石油价格还会攀升,除非这一地区的产油国比现在进行更大规模的投资。

不同寻常的是,国际货币基金组织还鼓励这些国家改变,目前节约的做法。通过扩大多方面的支出不仅有利于这些中东国家未来经济的发展,而且加大从世界其他国家的进口还将会改善全球经济的不平衡。这些做法有助于减轻高油价给世界经济带来的冲击。

到目前为止,大部分额外收入都被储存起来,而没有被花掉,那么它们到底去向何方?在20世纪70年代和80年代初,剩余的石油美元大部分存入了美国或欧洲的银行。这些银行向进口石油的发展中国家大量贷款,从而播下了拉美债务危机的种子。这一次,这些钱的去向不那么容易追踪,但更多的钱似乎被用于购买了外国的股票和债券,而不是存进了西方的银行。这一事实或许反映了这些国家越来越不愿意将钱存入外国银行,因为2001年911恐怖袭击之后,政府监管力度加大了。来自于国际清算银行(BIS)的数据表明,2002年和2003年,OPEC在BIS报告区的银行存款事实上在下降。自去年以来,存款有所增加,但速度很低。相反,俄罗斯在海外的银行存款增长得更快,中央银行的官方储备已经从2003年底的730亿美元增长到今年10月份的1 610亿美元。

俄罗斯人的投资,不管是投入银行存款、伦敦地产还是足球俱乐部,都相当惹人注意。而即使是国际货币基金组织和BIS的专家也发现很难追踪中东资金的流向,因为大量盈余不是作为官方储备持有的,而表现为政府的石油稳定与投资基金和国家石油公司的对外投资。中东石油出口国的官方储备(包括沙特阿拉伯货币局持有的外国净资产)今年已经增加了大约700亿美元,不足其经常账户盈余的30%。

追踪资金去向

令人迷惑不解的是,根据美国财政部公布的数据,石油输出国组织成员国持有美国政府债券的金额从今年1月份的670亿美元下降到8月份的540亿美元。但中东国家有可能通过伦敦市场购买美国证券。肯先生认为尽管目前石油输出国组织国家的大部分盈余收入用于购进以美元计价的资产,但这些美元资产越来越多地在美国境外被持有。还有很大份额流人到因不受管制而难以追踪的对冲基金和离岸金融机构中。

还有一部分石油美元流入了外国私人股权基金。一月份,迪拜国际资本公司买进了戴姆勒一克莱斯勒公司的10亿美元的股份。三月份,它又收购了主题公园运营商图沙兹集团。这个月,迪拜的国有港口运营管理公司,DP世界,开价30亿欧元(折合52亿美元)竞购英国最大的轮船集团铁行渣华公司(P&O)。

中东许多较小的私人投资者选择邻近的国家进行投资。20世纪70年代和80年代初,海湾地区几乎没有股票市场。这一次,大量资金涌向那里。沙特阿拉伯的股价自 2003 年以来已经涨了四倍,现在它的交易所是新兴股市中市值最大的。该地区的平均市盈率是 40,最近的股票上市认购已经超过几百倍。很多地方,尤其是迪拜,也出现了投机性的房地产繁荣,这个城市已经成为区域金融中心和休闲娱乐胜地。那里正在建设世界上最大的购物中心,这个国家的阿联酋航空公司(Emirates)实际上启动了空中客车 A380 的开发,它订购了 45 架以上这种超级客机,占总订单量的 1/3。

尽管缺乏可靠的数据,许多经济学家相信,很大一部分石油美元正在被用于购买美国政府的债券。假如是这样,资金通过债券市场的回流对世界经济产生的影响,将不同于上次石油繁荣中以银行为中介完成的资金回流。假如没有被消费的石油美元流入全球债券市场,它们就会降低债券收益,从而支撑石油进口国的消费开支。

Exercises

Ⅰ. Answer the following questions.

1. OPEC, Russia and Norway are substituting Asian economies to be the countries with the biggest current-account surpluses.

2. The oil exporters could import more from other countries and thus help to maintain global demand, finance oil importers' bigger current-account deficits and boost asset prices and push down bond yields in oil-importing countries. They do not intend to use their petrodollars to finance oil importers' deficits. Instead, oil exporters seem to be spending less, instead running larger external surpluses, repaying debts and building up assets.

3. Oil prices will not stay high for ever; windfall should be spent to create local jobs or to diversify economies. Because the thrifty spending of petrodollars hampers the overall development of world economy, while increased spending will allow Middle East countries to orderly narrow global imbalances and cushion the world economy against the negative impact of rising oil prices.

4. The bulk of OPEC's surplus revenues has so far gone into dollar-denominated assets held outside the United States. A big chunk is also going into hedge funds and offshore financial institutions. There has also been a flood of petrodollars into private equity abroad.

5. Saudi Arabia now has the largest capitalisation of any emerging stock market. Dubai has become a regional financial centre and leisure playground. The world's biggest shopping mall is being built there and Emirates orders no fewer than 45 of the super-jumbos.

Ⅱ. Paraphrase the difficult sentences or language points.

1. Actually, if we consider the world as a whole, oil exporters have substituted Asia to be the group of countries with the biggest current-account surpluses, which are owing to high prices of oil with the outcome of impressive wealth.

2. It is very usual that the large profits of the past are lavished without the consideration of budget, while the profusion has postponed economic reforms.

3. Several critics are also doubtful that the government may spend the stabilisation fund recklessly and extravagantly.

4. The International Energy Agency warned this week that oil prices would keep rising in the future twenty years if the oil producers of this region do not invest considerably more than they intend now.

5. Mr. Khan holds the view that although most of OPEC's spare revenues have been invested in the assets denominated in the form of dollars, more and more assets are owned by the investors outside the United States.

Ⅲ. Choose the word or phrase that best explains the meaning of the underlined part from the text.

1. B   2. A   3. A   4. C   5. C   6. B   7. C   8. A   9. B   10. C

Ⅳ. **Choose the best phrase or expression in the text from the following list to fit in each of the following blanks. Change the word form where necessary.**

1. in turn　2. adjust to　3. as much as　4. in contrast with　5. point at　6. take to heart　7. has built up　8. as a whole　9. so far　10. pushed…down

Ⅴ. **Translate the following sentences into English.**

1. We have learned that if anything could undermine our corporate reputation we must share it with top management quickly.

2. It was the policy of the good old gentlemen to make his children feel that home was the happiest place in the world; and I value this delicious home feeling as one of the choicest gifts a parent can bestow.

3. Iraqi officials say they have postponed a key national conference that was scheduled to start on Saturday.

4. The scientist is doing experiments no one has so far attempted.

5. Optimism assumes, or attempts to prove, that the universe exists to please us, and pessimism that it exists to displease us.

6. Russia has tightened restrictions on the technology and equipment it supplies for Iran's nuclear energy program but would be reluctant to give up the lucrative contracts.

7. China has appreciated the RMB over 20 per cent against the dollar since 2005.

8. Wild plants and animals are increasingly diversifying due to changes in ecosystems in which they live for thousands of years.

9. China would account for 50 per cent of the growth in carbon dioxide emissions in the next 20 years and produce 60 per cent more greenhouse gases than the US by 2020, the special envoy for climate change said.

10. Sales have dwindled as the cost of petrol in the U. S. and abroad has soared.

Ⅵ. **Translate the following into Chinese.**

1. 以往的经验证明,石油繁荣对石油出口国来说,既可是福也可是祸,这取决于能否明智地消费或储存额外的收入。过去的意外之财常常导致预算膨胀,而充足的资金导致了经济改革的延误。

2. 尽管缺乏可靠的数据,许多经济学家相信,很大一部分石油美元正在被用于购买美国政府的债券。假如是这样,资金通过债券市场的回流对世界经济产生的影响,将不同于上次石油繁荣中以银行为中介完成的资金回流。

Ⅶ. **Answer the following questions.**

1. Because market saturation and environmental policies move the US and Europe away from oil and Asian nations, such as India and particularly China, are taking their place.

2. American politicians continued to pursue energy legislation that would put a cap-and-trade system in place for carbon emissions. In Europe, the economic slump, combined with high petrol taxes, biofuels and emissions targets, pushed demand into reverse last year.

3. No, because of the fungible nature of oil, it will limit the extent to which this economic shift eastward translates into a geopolitical one.

4. Opec would eventually have to discuss lowering other members' quotas to make room for Iraq.

课文参考译文

亚洲奇迹与现代增长理论

在过去35年间韩国、台湾地区、新加坡、香港地区的经济从技术落后、贫穷转为现代化、富裕的经济。每个国家的个人平均收入在此期间都增长了四倍多。从19世纪开始，英国、美国、法国和德国花了大约80年的时间达到这种增长，而日本从1952年到1973年的增长要快得多。如今每个经济体都有大量公司生产技术复杂的产品，有效地与美国、日本和欧洲的对手竞争。这些国家的增长情况大大超过了20世纪60年代具有类似生产力和收入水平的所有其他国家的成绩。仅在这种基础上"他们如何做到这点的"就具有极大的科学和政策重要性。

1997、1998年的危机也许使"亚洲奇迹"蒙上一层阴影。然而他们的人力、组织、和有形资本保持完整，韩国和台湾与购买力对等的GNP比类似国家，如加纳和墨西哥1960年时的情况要高许多。重要的是不要忘记他们从贫穷、经济技术落后到相对富裕、经济技术现代化只用了不到40年的时间，这的确是一个奇迹。这篇论文认为对现代技术的吸收或同化是这项进程关键的因素。

1. 政策环境

经过短暂的进口代入工业化后，韩国、台湾地区、新加坡转向更自由的贸易政策，而香港一直是自由贸易转口港。韩国和台湾地区提供了大量出口激励，同时逐渐降低了贸易壁垒。当国内市场被赋予保护时，特别在韩国，这就与出口成绩紧密联系起来。给予低息贷款也很有可能帮助公司达到出口目标，在韩国尤其如此。作为关税待遇回扣体制的结果，公司能够以国际价格获得为生产出口产品所需的投入。有补贴的借款对出口成功也有关系。因此，每个公司有强大的动机提高效率进行出口，而不是在国内市场寻求纯利。一个相对稳定的宏观经济环境以与许多发展中国家有关的有限的通货膨胀为特点，这提供了整体的大背景。真正的有效汇率很少提高，而这样的情况很快得到纠正。生产商因此能够专注提高生产力，而不是对付快速变化的投入产出相对价格。在这种情况下，谈到的这些国家在30到35年内个人平均所得增长了5％或更多。政策环境明显是这些国家成功的重要因素。

2. 亚洲增长的同化理论

在过去几十年有很多观点被提出来试着解释"亚洲奇迹"。其中一个观点我们称为"同化"理论，它强调创业精神、革新、学习，这些都受到政策体制的鼓励，这些经济体在掌握从更先进国家吸收的新技术前必须经过这些步骤；它还认为对人工和有形资本的投资是同化过程必要却远远不够的一部分。另一种强调有形和人力资本积累的理论我们称为"积累理论"。

同化理论注意到20世纪70、80年代新工业国家逐渐掌握的技术是他们在60年代时还完全没有经验的。除此之外，产品比例急剧变化，如在表1里所示的台湾产品。比如，1960年时台湾实际上没有任何电子产品，但到1990年电子产品大约占生产出口的21％。学习使用新技术、在新领域有效发挥其功用，要求发展新技术、新的经济行为组织方式，熟悉新市场并有竞争力。要完成这些远不仅是一种常规，而涉及冒险的创业精神和良好的管理。亚洲奇迹之所以神奇在于这些国家和地区做得非常成功，而其他国家和地区却大为不如。可以肯定，采用发达国家的技术在有别的要求的同时，需要对有形资本和人力资本进行极大投资，新工业国家完成了这些高投资。然而说这些投资是要求的全部，实在不足以描述这项成就的范围。

表1　有形产品水平的变化精选的工业产品台湾地区 1960—1990

产品	1960	1990
人造纤维——百万吨	1,762	1,785,731

产　品	1960	1990
聚氯乙烯——百万吨	3,418	920,954
钢条——百万吨	200,528	11,071,999
机器工具	0	755,597
缝纫机	61,817	2,514,727
电　扇	203,843	15,217,438
电视机	0	3,703,000
摩托车	0	1,055,297
电　话	0	13,992,431
收音机	0	5,892,881
录音机	0	8,124,253
电子计算器	0	44,843,192
集成电路(1,000)	0	2,676,865
电子表	0	5,115,695
造船(吨)	27,051	1,211,607

来源：台湾地区数据表，经济计划和发展委员会1992，台北，表5-6c。

仅强调投资的看法认为任何时候的技术知识状况在很大程度上体现在机器上，并用蓝图和相关文献整理成系统，一个公司要采用对它而言却不是对世界而言的新技术，主要需要获得设备和蓝图。然而人们需要知道的如何利用技术的知识仅有很小一部分被整理为机器使用说明、教材和蓝图，许多都是依惯例而行的，操作和使用与读书学习对掌握新技术一样重要。大量实例研究记录了亚洲国家上百间公司类似的情况。所有研究得到了同一结论，霍布德的话可以说明它。

东亚的后来者并没有从技术的一年跳到另一年。相反，证据说明这些公司忙于一个痛苦而积累的技术学习过程：这是埋头苦干而非蛙式前进。通往先进电子信息技术的道路是一个漫长困难的学习过程，为生产出口商品所激励。

这样的学习以及最终操作进口设备的高水平生产力使现代化的部分逐渐增加其在产量、资金、劳动力方面的份额。现代部分扩展，生产性不强的其他部分相对规模收缩，带来全国生产力水平的上升。这种变化是以下介绍的模型的主要特点。

新工业国家快速提高的教育水平是经常为人所关注的现象。提高的人力资本可以被简单看作质量或劳动力有效性的提高，对传统的生产功能增加了第三种因素。对快速提高的教育成就效果的另一种看法是认为它在实现新机会和学习新东西方面提供了相对优势，特别是这些国家不断产生了受过良好训练的领导者、经理人、工程师和应用科学家。这实现了对新产品区域和新技术更早的发现，并使转化成它们的过程更为有效。因此教育对实现台湾的部分结构变化非常关键。

3. 为什么这个问题很重要？

同化理论强调学习、控制风险、掌握对本国而言，即使不是对世界而言比较新颖的技术和其他做法。"使用投入"只是故事的一部分，但重点是革新与学习，而非使用。在这种观点下，如果人们只是使用，而不革新与学习,就不会有发展。我们的观点是认为新工业国家的成绩并非大量依靠生产作用,而对此的理解必须涉及以最基本方式进行的"学习"。在政策体制方面还有许多基本因素:财政的、金融的、汇率政策,它们使出口生产非常吸引人,并刺激了储蓄与投资、对人工资本的大量投资、让公司管理者警觉的竞争。

但仅使宏观经济环境变得良好并不能保证有效的经济发展。政策导向需要保证潜在的企业领导者既有能力又愿意冒险接近任何管理企业需要的事物。由于无法预先判断胜者和败者,企业家应该得到鼓励去尝试、得到成功的报酬、但对失败绝不纵容。而同时由于学习有效地在世界范围内开展现代实践需要时间和努力,政策环境需要培养学习。成功的亚洲新工业国家直到最近才成功,尽管是以不同的方式。

最重要的是,我们认为重要性在于对公司性质和学习过程的认识。回到我们早先的讨论,当一个公司"选择"做些对它而言,以及对它位于的社会而言都是崭新的东西时,这涉及冒险,如果成功地话,需要有效的学习。相应地,学习会在不同的层次上展开:个体的工人、工人群体、当局、公司和行业。

Exercises

Ⅰ. Answer the following questions.

1. What makes the Asian miracle miraculous is that these countries made progress so well, while other countries were much less successful. For instance, over the past thirty-five years Korea, Taiwan, Singapore, and Hong Kong, have transformed themselves from technologically backward and poor, to relatively modern and affluent economies. Each has experienced more than a four fold increase of per capita income over the period. It took the United Kingdom, the United States, France and Germany eighty years or more, beginning in the 19th century to achieve such growth. The growth performance of these countries has vastly exceeded those of virtually all other economies that had comparable productivity and income levels in 1960.

2. These include liberal trade policies, substantial export incentives, low trade barriers, low interest loans, a tariff rebate system, subsidized credit, and limited inflation.

3. Assimilation theories stress the entrepreneurship, innovation, and learning, all encouraged by the policy regime.

4. The levels include that of individual workers and teams of them, that of establishments and firms, and the level of an industry.

Ⅱ. Paraphrase the difficult sentences or language points

1. We have to remember that it only took them forty years to change from poor and economically backward countries to relative rich and modern countries, which has been a great miracle.

2. The provision of loans with low interest was also dependent upon firms which have achieved their export aims, especially in Korea.

3. The East Asian countries that have arrived late did not progress by large jumps from one period of technology to another.

4. The sector expands and the relative size of less productive sectors contracts, yielding a growing level of national productivity.

5. Since it is impossible to judge winners and losers in advance, entrepreneurs should be encouraged to try, success rewarded, and failure not coddled.

Ⅲ. Choose the word or phrase that best explains the meaning of the underlined part from the text.

1. B   2. C   3. A   4. C   5. B   6. C   7. A   8. C   9. A   10. C

Ⅳ. Choose the best phrase or expression in the text from the following list to fit in each of the following blanks. Change the word form where necessary.

1. account for   2. in turn   3. cope with   4. been engaged in   5. far from   6. in terms of   7. A number of   8. in question   9. in particular   10. put forth

Ⅴ. Translate the following sentences into English.

1. Each has experienced more than a four fold increase of per capita income over the period.

2. On these grounds alone the question of "how they did it" obviously is of enormous scientific and policy importance.

3. Korea and Taiwan area provided substantial export incentives while gradually lowering trade barriers.

4. Hence individual firms had strong incentives to improve efficiency to enable them to export rather than to engage in rent seeking in the domestic market.

5. The assimilationist view notes that the technologies that the newly industrialized countries(nics) came progressively to master during the 1970's and 1980's were ones with which, in 1960, they had no experience at all.

6. To do this was far from a routine matter, but involved risk taking entrepreneurship as well as good management.

7. What makes the Asian miracle miraculous is that these countries did these things so well, while other countries were much less successful.

8. The modern sector expands and the relative size of less productive sectors contracts, yielding a growing level of national productivity.

9. Thus education was critical to realizing the change in the sectoral structure in Taiwan.

10. The assimilation account stresses learning about, risking operating, and coming to master, technologies and other practices that are new to the country, if not to the world.

Ⅵ. Translate the following into Chinese.

1. 1997、1998 年的危机也许使"亚洲奇迹"蒙上一层阴影。然而他们的人力、组织、和有形资本保持完整，韩国和台湾地区与购买力对等的 GNP 比类似国家，如加纳和墨西哥 1960 年时的情况要高许多。重要的是不要忘记他们从贫穷、经济技术落后到相对富裕、经济技术现代化只用了不到 40 年的时间，这的确是一个奇迹。

2. 由于无法预先判断胜者和败者，应该鼓励企业家去尝试、获取成功报酬、但绝不纵容失败。而同时由于在世界范围内学习有效地开展现代实践需要时间和精力，政策环境需要培养学习。

Ⅶ. Answer the following questions.

1. Mr. Wong was fired in America and hired again in Hong Kong, which indicates that Asia has already emerged more forcefully from recession than the United States and Europe.

2. Economists say that any early signs of job growth are a prerequisite for a more solid-based recovery.

3. While unemployment continues to rise in much of Europe and is expected to top 10 percent in the United States before any improvement materializes, rates in Asia have remained relatively low: 5.4 percent in Hong Kong and 3.3. percent in Singapore.

4. It is still very much an employers' market.

Key to Unit Six

课文参考译文

营销效率的标准

要试图分析营销效率，需要记住两个观点。这种分析可以来自个体企业家或某阶层的商人的角度。这种看法常被称为个人观点。哈佛大学和西北大学商业研究所进行的这类调查就属于这类，这也是美国市场局所致力的项目，一些大型企业贸易组织的商业研究所进行的活动也是这类。其他由调查人进行的分析对增加个体公司或某阶层个体商业组织的营利并不感兴趣。他们采用的是我们称为社会或公共的观点,这里我们也找不到更好的称谓。他们的目标是研究营销的社会重要性。他们的目标除了科学地寻找真理之外,就是研究如何进行营销,以提高整个社会的经济状况。对他们而言,营销是将商品从生产者转向消费者的宏大机制。有时这个机制的功能不够完善,过程费用很高。因此,就需要对此进行研究,来决定是否可以使其更有效、更经济地运行。

采取后一种观点的人进行的具体研究方式,甚至他们当前的目标往往与那些有兴趣的个体、或作为某一大类企业家代表的人相一致。然而那些采取个体立场的人感兴趣,是因为他们追求一种增加个体利润的手段,后者对个人成功有兴趣仅限于它趋向发展一种更有效、更经济的分配组织。在以下讨论中需要记住这点。在最后的分析中,这将那些有个性化倾向的人带到了消费者角度。对营销的社会目的来说,如同生产的目的一样,是尽量有效、经济地满足消费者的需要。因此,现在我们通过从消费者角度看营销的调查者视角来分析营销效率的标准。

那么,什么是决定市场组织、组成市场组织的个体单位有效性的标准呢?首先,必须考虑提供的分配服务的有效性。其次,分配服务的成本,该成本包括实际发生的金钱成本加上涉及营销人赚取的任何利润,无论他们是生产者、消费者、中间人或经销商。最后,必须考虑这个成本以及执行这项服务的种种方法对生产和消费产生的效果。换言之,要决定我们的市场组织是否有效,我们必须回答以下问题:这种体系能满足我们的需要吗?我们为这项服务是否多付了钱,即使这样服务做得很好?我们的营销分配体系对生产和消费起到了什么作用?如果这个体系有效却花费高,它就是没有效率的。如果它便宜却达不到效果,也是没有效率的。即使设计的机制导致了对商品有效经济的分配,却对生产或消费产生了不良影响,它也是没有效率的。

很明显前两个标准,即服务与成本,往往应该作为一个问题来研究,虽然某个调查者的重点也许放在服务、实际的金钱成本、贸易、服务中涉及的投机利润方面。最后的标准,即市场组织对生产和消费的效果这点,涉及一些最有趣、最令人迷惑的看法。只有当伟大的战争扩大了它们的难度,需要立即得到解决时,商人和经济学者才会学着考虑这些看法。价格制定者尤其需要面对这些问题。

我们碰到的大部分问题,几乎都提出了关于技术效率的一些大问题。其中一组问题围绕涉及运输和储藏的纯技术成分。这些问题包括船运和仓库设备的有效性、机械设备和市场的实际布局。劣质的乡村路、有限的火车设施、拥挤的终点站、计划不佳的批发市场带来的困难造成了这样的问题。这是我们在面对农产品市场时的大问题之一。我们如何保持在广大地区通过将需要和供应的力量集中在中心市场而得来的优势,同时去掉市场设备拥挤造成的劣势?这些设备来源于这些市场强力促成了供应大量商品的趋势。

另一组问题关于商品的所有权从生产者转向消费者的方法。这里存在一些最重要的问题。其中包括与市场信息服务相关的效率问题,我们正是依靠它保持供需的平衡;还包括联系生产与营销不同因素的价格系统的充分性以及交换双方法律保护的相关问题、涉及买卖的现代方式中产生的巨大成本问题,这包括标准化成本、检验和分级、商谈成本、需要创造的大量成本。这里,还围绕来自于存在必要的营销风险和营销财务带来的问题。

这两组问题关于我们市场机制的技术效率,一个来自于设备的纯机械效率,另一个源于商谈系统的贸易效率,它们与基于服务和成本的效率标准直接相关。

更难分析却同样重要的是另一组问题,它涉及现有的机械和贸易市场机制对生产和消费的反应。这组问题包括使用标准分级的效果、这时它带来改进的产品和生产者更高的稳定收入。这里也许要考虑到当市场组织保证生产者拿到他认为在最终售价中的"合理分红"时,这种情况对生产的影响。这里还有市场竞争对生产和消费产生结果的问题,也有铁路费结构、基点体系、印花费、商品费以及在生产值、重量、距离、其他承运人和其他市场竞争中妥协基础上的各种费用这些因素产生的效果的问题。同样,也可以考虑我们的财务及仓储方式对易坏和季节性商品生产产生的效果,以及对大市场区域的反应,这些区域增加了大型、专业产品的数目。

转向消费，我们通过调查发现现代的分配方式使消费者拥有大量不同的商品，而现代销售方式的趋势是在消费者心中创造对多样性、质量、风格和季节性商品的需求。

对现代营销的大部分批评直接或间接指向我们现有的竞争机制。即使运输效率和中心市场区域拥挤这样的重要问题，也与私人财产体系中的竞争条件紧密联系。大多数提出的补救办法和改革建议摒弃我们现在的竞争体系，或者建议政府加强现有的控制形式，或者建议生产商和消费者通过在本阶层成员间形成合作或合并，引入或增强控制力。

经济学家总的来说认为在竞争体制下，比起在其他任何已知或提议的机制下，经济进步会更大。简言之，他们认为最好的人、最好的过程和政策得到发展，被需要的商品和服务被最有效和最经济地生产出来。放至营销上，这就意味着最有效的公司会存活，最好的分配渠道和最好的销售方式会获胜，被要求的商品在数量、种类和质量上都被合理地投入市场。最后，关于价格和成本，竞争会降低价格接近成本，包括合理（社会上必要的）利润，但这种价格又会保证必要的生产。这种模式完全没有得到实现，特别是在如今情况快速变化的情况下，对生产和营销的解决办法在发展出来时便已经常过时。其结果是，如今通过价格来进行的选择过程往往缓慢昂贵。用竞争来清除低效的生产商、分配商和他们的作法非常慢。但现有体制的倡导者尽管认识到这点，却认为这是至今为止发明的关于生产和分配的最佳制度，并且认为许多提议的治疗方法，如社会主义、通过生产商或农学家、甚至消费者联合控制某种商品的生产，都会带来比竞争的浪费更大的危害。

然而长期以来许多调查者认为古典经济学家心中的竞争机制必须被代替或抛弃。但我们还没认为需要严肃考虑代替被抛弃机制这一体系。但今天也许有一种主导的情绪，认为我们也许可以依靠竞争保持、促进个人即个体企业家的效率，但还需要在个人行为之间建立联系，特别是在某种产品的生产商或消费者之间建立联系，这样才能提高整体效率。一位著名调查者之前曾说："个人或个体企业内部的努力是仔细计划的，但它们之间的联系却是无计划的。"

人们提出可以使用的两种行为类型：政府支持，如通过预测收成，以及个人间的合作，如联合行动、或消费者和生产者的合作。两种类型都有益于：

1. 提高市场信息。
2. 按市场需求情况控制或增加生产。
3. 增加中心市场的效率。
4. 提高交通速度和效率。
5. 提高产品的标准化和分级。
6. 去掉不必要的中间商。
7. 控制过度利润。

Exercises

Ⅰ. Answer the following questions.

1. People with the individual perspective are interested because they seek a means to increase individual profits, while those with the public perspective are interested in individual success only in so far as it tends to the development of a more effective and a more economical distributive organization.

2. First among these must be considered the effectiveness with which the distributive service is rendered; then, the cost at which this service is performed. And, finally, there must be considered the effect which this cost and these methods of performing this service have upon production and consumption.

3. Most of the criticism of modern marketing propose to eliminate our present competitive system, or they involve proposals leading to an increase in existing forms of control on the part of the government, or to an introduction or enlargement of the control exercised by producers and consumers through some form of cooperation or combination among the members of these classes.

4. According to the author, this ideal comes very far from being realized, particularly when conditions are

changing so rapidly that attempted solutions of problems of production and marketing are often out of date when they are evolved. In consequence, the process of selection when working through price is for times like the present slow and expensive. For competition is slow to weed out the inefficient producers and distributors, and their methods.

Ⅱ. Paraphrase the difficult sentences or language points

1. The social aim of marketing which is the same as that of production is to meet the demands of customers as effectively and economically as possible.

2. Another group of problems is about how the ownership of goods is shifted from producer to consumer.

3. Most criticism of modern marketing is directly or indirectly related to our competitive system that is now applied.

4. Generally economists believe that economic progress is at its best under a competition system.

5. For a long time we have understood that many investigators assume the competitive regime held by classical economists is and must be added or deserted.

Ⅲ. Choose the word or phrase that best explains the meaning of the underlined part from the text.

1. B 2. C 3. A 4. C 5. A 6. B 7. C 8. A 9. B 10. C

Ⅳ. Choose the best phrase or expression in the text from the following list to fit in each of the following blanks. Change the word form where necessary.

1. coincide with 2. in use 3. at times 4. weeded out 5. In so far as 6. be composed of 7. even though 8. avail to 9. In other words 10. a host of

Ⅴ. Translate the following sentences into English.

1. Their aim is to study the social significance of the marketing.

2. To such, marketing appears as a great mechanism for bringing goods from producer to consumer.

3. What are the criteria for determining the efficiency of our market organization, and of the particular institutions of which it is composed?

4. What effect does our system of market distribution have upon production and consumption?

5. It is evident that the first two criteria, service and cost, must usually be studied as one problem.

6. The difficulties caused by poor country roads, limited railway facilities, congested terminals, and ill-planned wholesale market areas raise such problems.

7. Two types of activity are suggested and in use: governmental assistance, such as is rendered through the crop estimates, and private cooperation as expressed in the combination movement and in consumer and producer cooperation.

8. Most of the criticism of modern marketing is really pointed directly or indirectly at our competitive regime.

9. Improve the physical efficiency of central markets.

10. Bring about the elimination of unnecessary middlemen.

Ⅵ. Translate the following into Chinese.

1. 采取后一种观点的人进行的具体研究方式,甚至他们当前的目标往往与那些有兴趣的个体、或作为某一大类企业家代表的人相一致。然而那些采取个体立场的人感兴趣,是因为他们追求一种增加个体利润的手段,后者对个人成功有兴趣仅限于它趋向发展一种更有效、更经济的分配组织。

2. 但今天也许有一种主导的情绪,认为我们也许可以依靠竞争保持、促进个人即个体企业家的效率,但还需要在个人行为之间建立联系,特别是在某种产品的生产商或消费者之间建立联系,这样才能提高整体效率。一位著名调查者之前曾说:"个人或个体企业内部的努力是仔细计划的,但它们之间的联系却是无计划的。"

1. Billions of text messages are sent and received every day. That is more than the number of cellphone calls. SMS is still a relatively uncluttered and spam-free marketing channel.

2. If they hired spammers to do marketing, the practice would expose them to stiffened penalties for text spam, and the vast majority of the messages would never even get through, or through for long, before the cellphone carriers cut them off.

3. Businesses can think about the resources they already have at their disposal. Besides, they can offer text coupons, use a combination of on-site signs, end-of-aisle displays at local stores, and TV advertising.

4. As people's mobile numbers may be one of the most guarded numbers they have, businessmen have to change their ideas of intentions of messages. By offering them free stuff, businessmen can hope for further gains.

Key to Unit Seven

课文参考译文

不思悔改的巧克力制造商

世界头号食品公司将宝压在健康营养产品的新兴阶层以促进公司壮大。然而,危机四伏。

这是一种厨房与实验室的新奇结合。从一间屋里飘散出制作者将巧克力微微加热并搅动而散发出的又苦又甜的香味。而在拐角处,则全是有关科学的。两排小隔间里容纳着实验对象,他们嗅闻、品尝小盒中的食物,并根据甜、苦等标准给每一盒打分,从而绘成复杂的风味图表。

这就是一墙之隔的雀巢110年巧克力工厂的科学之道。正是在这些实验室里,些许艺术与身价2500万瑞士法郎的技术相结合,研发出了新的巧克力配方。与此同时,在位于洛桑的雀巢的另一家研发中心,研究者们一直在把巧克力当做药物来分析,而不是食品。

在这种研究上投入资金似乎是败家之举,尤其是在经济萧条时期。然而,这是雀巢的未来成长战略的缩影。董事长 Peter Brabeck-Letmathe 和首席执行官 Paul Bulcke 希望把公司从食品企业转变为世界领先的保健、营养和"健康"公司。人们很容易将此举理解为一种单纯的营销噱头(努力让人们对于吃本不应该吃的食品感觉更好些)。然而,在雀巢向保健、营养转型的背后有着充分的商业逻辑。

功能性食品的销售额在大部分情况下增速远远快于整体的食品销售。"功能性食品"即经制造商刻意修改和改进从而提供所宣称的健康益处的食品。

进一步着眼未来,雀巢看到"个性化"营养概念的潜力巨大。正如医药公司长久以来一直在谈论的研制顾及到个体间基因差异的药物,雀巢打算在食物上采取同样做法。这就是该公司在代谢学和蛋白质组学的新生领域投资的原因,其目的在于通过这些研究,雀巢能够为特定人群提供特定的食物、节食食品、器具甚至是服务。

转向新型食品

雀巢希望通过这次的重心向保健和营养方向转型能够把公司从一个售卖利润低的、商品化的食品公司转型为高利润产品和服务的供应商。雀巢需要新的增长点。瓶装水的销量目前占整个业务的10%,但是由于经济衰退其在发达国家的销量正在下降。销售额也可能会回升,但是分析人士担心由于瓶装水现在被环保组织紧紧盯上了,可能会重蹈裘皮贸易的覆辙。

似乎雀巢其他产品的市场份额也在下降,虽然公司高管对此予以否认。人们对雀巢前景的担忧在其股价上便可见一斑:股票交易时的盈利率低于其主要欧洲竞争对手数倍。原因之一是投资者担心明年雀巢可能投资比目前利润更低的业务。

投资者还担心雀巢已经变得过于巨大而笨重不堪。该公司目前有 30 条生产线,其中包括雀巢咖啡、Nesquik 牛奶、Purina 宠物食品。近年来,消费者开始减少消费,购买价格更加低廉,无品牌的食品。这可能导致大品牌的价值悄然缩水。所以雀巢指望在产品中添加更健康的成分能够帮助该公司在发达国家的销量能够再次上升,同时赢得新兴市场消费者的青睐。

2008 年雀巢的功能食品的增长率为 20%。10 月 22 日雀巢公司宣布从经济危机开始到 2009 年 9 月该公司所有食品和饮料产品线的实际增长率(除去价格变动和货币运动)为 0.7%,而功能食品仍然实现了 4% 的增长率。其他公司也从这一趋势中受益。法国乳品和酸奶公司达能于 9 月 23 日发布的结果显示含有能够增强免疫力或缓解便秘的益生菌的酸奶最畅销。甚至连医药公司都盯上了这块新市场。法国医药公司赛诺菲-安万特的总裁三月份曾表示意欲收购食品和营养企业以作为促进公司增长的途径之一。

然而,鲜有公司效仿雀巢大量投资于研发专用于改善健康的食品。尽管如此,Brabeck-Letmathe 先生重新打造公司的庞大计划也存在着诸多危险。为了一个可能不会成型的市场,投资于一个耗资巨大和周期长的研究是否有意义?另一个风险是雀巢对保健功效的极力宣传说服不了满怀疑虑的公众,反而招致公众或激进分子的强烈反对。还有一个风险在于新战略可能损害该公司业已成功的传统品牌,例如雀巢咖啡,这个牌子耗费了数十年才树立起来。

利润还是危险?

首先是研究费用。如果雀巢满足于和卡夫(世界第二大食品公司)在产品销售领域的竞争,则该公司在研发上的开支将很难被证明是合理的。但是早在十年前 Brabeck-Letmathe 先生就意识到食品行业的利润日益下降,正成为商品化的苦差,可供颠覆性创新的空间很小。所以,他开始推动雀巢研发利润丰厚的功能食品,并相应增加相关投入。

曾任医药公司执行官,现任雀巢营养业务负责人的 Richard Laube 对大约 75 个研究项目的"渠道"进行了描述。考虑到开发这些新产品的时间,从医药行业借用专业术语似无不妥。与快速消费品的研发周期通常只有 1 至 2 年不同,雀巢的营养渠道中的产品可能需要 4 至 6 年来研发。

Laube 先生承认追求功能性食品意味着研发费用必然增加,尤其是因为欧美两边的管理者都更严格地对待对功能性食品。美国食品药品管理局 10 月份发出警告,该组织正在检查食品公司声称的保健功效是否属实,并计划很快宣布更加严格的指导方针。欧洲委员会已经先行一步,制订了严格条例规范营养功效的宣称并正在对允许做出的关于健康的功效的宣称加紧限制。想要宣称与疾病有关的功效的公司将必须要出示可靠的科学证据以证明宣称的功效。

如果消费者愿意(消费者似乎愿意)花更多钱购买具有健康功效的产品,则之前的努力是值得的。Laube 先生认为这种长期研究的另一个好处是趋向于产出比对消费者产品进行微小的、暂时的改进带来的红利更长期的创新科技。他指的是用于雀巢 PowerBar 系列和低过敏性婴儿食品的乳清蛋白。在以上两种情况下,消费者在产品进入市场 10 年之后仍然愿意继续花费高额费用购买这些产品。

雀巢惯常打持久战。以 Nespresso(一种速溶的蒸馏咖啡,由咖啡机用一个咖啡胶囊制成)为例,这项技术始于 1970 年并于 1976 年申请了第一个专利。而开始销售这种 Nespresso 咖啡胶囊和咖啡机器又花费了十年时间。此后,这项业务一直处于亏损状态长达 10 年之久,然而现在却是雀巢增长速度最快的产品之一。"这一过程相当缓慢,20 年的坚持使得我们最终才能看到成果。"Bulcke 先生如是说。

功能性食品更严格的监管前景,实际上,对于雀巢是有利的。因为鲜有竞争对手有如此雄厚的经济实力投资这种研究。而雀巢这家瑞士公司最后很可能占据市场高位,只要其能生产出带有真实功效的食品,让消费者乐意购买即可。

雀巢战略的另一个潜在风险是过度扩张的危险,源于两个致命的弱势:一个是公司过往丑闻造成不良影响。其中包括在穷国销售奶粉导致当地居民联合抵制,造成的影响颇著。另一个是食品产业经历过的民众对转基因作物的抵触。

Laube 先生在描述公司在发展中国家的作为遗留的不信任时悲叹道:"母乳喂养是最好的。我们每天都在宣传这个,但是没人相信我们。"雀巢创始人研制的招牌母乳替代奶粉并非意欲替代母乳。母乳替代奶粉只是用于喂养那些不能得到安全母乳喂养的新生儿。这并非雀巢的宣传噱头。但是在非洲和其他地方，雀巢推销奶粉的力度过大，奶粉实际上不当地取代了母乳的地位。雀巢强调它已经改邪归正了。

雀巢在发展中国家的深厚基础源自几十年前。这使得该公司在开发增长点时，在起跑线上就领先于大多数发达国家的竞争对手。雀巢早期融入全球化并非计划使然，而是出于巧合：恰巧在一个小国家并售卖流通性很高的商品。早在1919年，雀巢浓缩奶消耗了本国农民生产的所有牛奶。迫于情势，雀巢在澳大利亚、英格兰、德国、挪威建立了分厂。

今日雀巢在其国内市场的销售额只占总额的不到2%，而卡夫则为60%。强制的全球化早早教会了雀巢研制独特口味方可行销世界的道理。其他竞争对手对此则后知后觉。然而，奶粉丑闻的影响犹在，所以雀巢在贫穷国家的各种行动都受到严密的监督，享受如此"殊荣"的企业寥寥无几。这就意味着任何重塑公司"健康"形象的重大举动都会受到质疑，在新兴市场尤其如此。

这次雀巢的策略是与世界各地的健康权威紧密合作，目的是沿用咖啡适应各地市场的方式将"健康"本地化。例如，雀巢正在努力将微量元素加入普通的食品当中。雀巢曾认为婴儿谷物产品的市场很小，但是现在的研究人员却把这种产品当做为婴儿补充益生菌和维生素的"载体"，同时也在开发面向极贫困人群的价格低廉，营养丰富一次性包装食品。这是另一个雀巢过去不曾涉足的市场。

那也许能够帮助贫穷世界，欧洲人对转基因食物的过度热情会妨碍雀巢保健食品的发展。雀巢正在小心前行。位于洛桑的雀巢总研究中心的负责人Peter van Bladeren坚持认为功能性产品将只通过增加健康成分以改善自然："没有奇怪的东西"。研究公司Sanford Bernstein的Eric Scher表示：必须出具确凿的证据才能达到监管者的要求，这样应当可以令消费者放心。

扩张品牌

最后，雀巢的新战略可能会损害耗费数十年树立起来的畅销品牌。这有可能以几种方式呈现。如果雀巢的功能性食品有几项未能通过监管者审核，或者更糟，被证明对人体有害而不是有益。如果真是如此，消费者会抵制雀巢旗下的所有产品，甚至完全非功能性的产品也不能幸免。

这又指向另一个潜在的障碍。如果一个以推销放纵著称的公司将自己重塑为推销健康的公司，消费者就不会收到好坏混合的信息吗？Bulcke先生坚持认为毫无自相矛盾之处，在开发新产品的过程中口味总是将取代营养功效占据优先地位。毕竟，汽车制造商只要能够研制出温室气体排放量低却不影响表现的轿车就不会认为在推广新车的时候会遇到问题。

Brabeck-Letmath先生坚信雀巢所有品牌的产品都可以通过调整融入健康战略。他坚持认为"如果每个产品的标准越来越健康，你就没必要调整。"每个产品都必须经过他所谓的"六十、四十、加"分析：必须至少有60%的人在品尝之后偏爱这款产品，而非竞争对手的产品或是这款产品正在取代的产品，而且这款产品必须更加富有营养。

然而，批评家怀疑雀巢是否能够总体上实现其雄心勃勃宣扬的保健和健康许诺。

Exercises

Ⅰ. **Answer the following questions.**

1. The strategy is to transform the food company into the world's leading health, nutrition and "wellness" firm.

2. Sales of functional foods are, in many cases, growing far more quickly than foods sales as a whole. Also, looking further ahead, Nestlé sees great potential in the idea of "personalized" nutrition.

3. Whether it makes sense to invest in costly, long-term research for a market that may not materialize; another risk is that a sceptical public will not be convinced by Nestlé's grand health claims, prompting a backlash from the public or activists; there is also a danger that the new strategy might damage the firm's blockbuster legacy brands.

4. The coincidence of being based in a small country and selling a highly tradable commodity.

5. To prove that Nestlé is used to playing a long game. It took 20 years for Nespresso to become a highly

profitable product of Nestlé.

II. Paraphrase the difficult sentences or language points

1. experimental subjects 2. Even pharmaceutical companies are looking at this new market with interest.
3. prove they are true 4. started to be successful/popular 5. substantial financial resources 6. stopped doing things that caused trouble and improved its behaviour 7. an initial advantage 8. refrain from
9. become hostile to 10. (considered) as a whole

III. Choose the word or phrase that best explains the meaning of the underlined part from the text.

1. B 2. C 3. A 4. C 5. B 6. C 7. A 8. A 9. C 10. B

IV. Choose the best phrase or expression in the text from the following list to fit in each of the following blanks. Change the word form where necessary.

1. eke out 2. incorporate into 3. muse about 4. turn against 5. take off 6. Give a head start
7. end up 8. take account of 9. After all 10. in many cases

V. Translate the following into English.

1. This shift in emphasis towards health and nutrition will, Nestlé hopes, transform it from a purveyor of low-margin, commoditised foodstuffs into a provider of high-margin products and services.

2. It is tempting to dismiss this as a mere marketing stunt—an effort to make people feel better about eating things they really shouldn't.

3. Analysts fret that bottled water, which is now firmly in the sights of environmental groups, may go the way of the fur trade.

4. Scepticism about Nestlé's prospects can also been seen in its share price: its shares trade at a lower multiple of earnings than those of its main European competitors.

5. Another risk is that a sceptical public will not be convinced by Nestlé's grand health claims, prompting a backlash from the public or activists.

6. But Mr Brabeck-Letmathe saw a decade ago that the food industry was becoming a commoditised grind with diminishing margins and little scope for disruptive innovation.

7. The tighter regulatory outlook for functional foods could, in fact, benefit Nestlé because few of its rivals have the deep pockets necessary to invest in such research.

8. Nestlé's early embrace of globalisation had less to do with planning than with the coincidence of being based in a small country and selling a highly tradable commodity.

9. Nestlé's strategy this time round is to work more closely with health authorities across the world. Its aim is to localise "wellness" in much the way it has adapted its coffees to various markets.

10. If some of the firm's functional foods fail to pass muster with the regulators or, worse, turn out to cause harm rather than do good, then consumers could turn against all its products, even those that make no health claims at all.

VI. Translate the following into Chinese.

1. 如果消费者愿意（消费者似乎愿意）花更多钱购买具有健康功效的产品,则之前的努力是值得的。Laube 先生认为这种长期研究的另一个好处是趋向于产出比对消费者产品进行微小的、暂时的改进带来的红利更长期的创新科技。他指的是用于雀巢 PowerBar 系列和低过敏性婴儿食品的乳清蛋白。在以上两种情况下,消费者在产品进入市场 10 年之后仍然愿意继续花费高额费用购买这些产品。

2. 这又指向另一个潜在的障碍。如果一个以推销放纵著称的公司将自己重塑为推销健康的公司,消费者就不会收到好坏混合的信息吗？Bulcke 先生坚持认为毫无自相矛盾之处,在开发新产品的过程中口味总是将取代营养功效占据优先地位。毕竟,汽车制造商只要能够研制出温室气体排放量低却不影响表现的轿车就不会认为在推广新车的时候会遇到问题。

VII. Answer the following questions.

1. The company's track record is pretty impressive. Since 2000，Inditex tripled its sales and profits as it has doubled the number of stores of its eight brands. Inditex has transformed itself into Europe's leading apparel retailer over the past five years

2. As Zara ventures deeper into far-flung territories，it risks losing its speed advantage. With more outlets in Asia and the U. S. ，replenishing stores twice a week — as Zara does now — will be increasingly complex and expensive. As Professor Pankaj Ghemawat pointed out，as long as Zara has one production and distribution base，its model is somewhat limited. The further away from Spain they move，the less competitive they will be.

3. Zara has succeeded by breaking every rule in retailing：
   1）Running out of best-selling items is a disaster；
   2）Setting trends；
   3）Collaborations with big-name designers and multimillion-dollar advertising campaigns.

4. Fashion faux pas means fashion mistakes.
   Committing fewer fashion faux pas means Zara sells more at full price，and when it discounts，it doesn't go as deep.

Key to Unit Eight

课文参考译文

新闻产业狂风过后

这不仅仅是报纸：如今新闻界的大部分产业都处在下坡路，但新闻本身，依然蓬勃发展。

报纸业还是在劫难逃，其中最明显的标志就是：过去一贯为他们所评论的政客们，如今却开始为其感到惋惜。上个月，众议院委员会和参议院委员会分别举行了听证会。约翰·克里，一名来自马萨诸塞州的初级参议员，称报业为"一个濒发可危的物种"。

事实也确实如此。根据美国新闻编辑协会数据显示，过去两年里，美国新闻业的就业率下降了15％。咨询公司OC&C的保罗·兹韦伦勃格估计从2008年初起，有近70家英国当地报纸倒闭。这种紧张不仅局限于英语国家：法国报纸只有在通过争取获得更多政府补助（之前，他们已经获得了高额的政府补助）来避免遭遇同样的命运。

广播电视新闻如今也面临同样的困境。观众被其他产业瓜分和侵蚀了：对比上世纪九十年代，有30％的美国人通过三大传统广播电视网（ABC，CBS及NBC）收看晚间新闻，如今的比例下降到了16％左右。英国最大一家商业广播电视台—ITV，如今正申请免除其报道当地新闻的职责。

但新闻产业如今面临的困境并不预示着新闻的终结。随着新闻业一些较大分支的萎缩，新枝正在萌发。结果是一种更小巧、更薄利但同时更高效、更新颖的商业。

更深但没有更广

这不单纯是人们从一种媒介转换到另一种媒介的问题。几乎每一个上网看新闻的人一般也会通过电视或报纸看新闻。科技使博识的人更加通晓天下事，但并没有使关注新闻的人群范围有所扩大。

那些关注新闻的人通过一种不同以往的方式获取新闻。摒弃了辛苦地阅读早报或收听晚间播报，他们越来越多地在他们想要的时候寻求他们想要的信息。花费更少。《华尔街日报》的主编罗伯特·汤马斯，说到有些人将在线新闻视为"一种只需向网络提供商交费，就能无限享用的自助餐"。

当今趋势下的主要牺牲者，并不是报纸行业，而是传统的新闻包。翻开任何一份主流都市报纸，或看一下它的网站，你都会有相同的发现：当地的、国内的、国际的、商务的、体育的各种新闻混杂在一起；还有天气预报；各种展出及分类广告；当然也少不了社论、读者来信和纵横字谜。

无论是过去的广播电台，还是后来的网络开拓者像 AOL. com 和 MSN. com，都效法过这种捆绑式新闻包。这种新闻包如同一个老式的百货商场一样运作。它在单个地点提供许多精选的质量有保证的有用信息。而如今，捆绑式新闻包所处的命运也正如这种老式的百货商场：部分顾客被折扣连锁店所吸引，而另外一些顾客则转向了精品店。

新闻世界中的沃尔玛是在线门户网站如雅虎新闻和谷歌新闻，他们收集了数以万计的新闻故事。有些是从通讯社如路透社、美联社获得许可转载的，但大部分都仅仅只包括一个标题、一句话或一个链接，点击链接到报纸或电视网站上可以阅读全文。搜索网站通过使得读者穿过重重广告来赚钱，这些广告可能是根据读者可能的兴趣而订制的。

尽管他们看上去非常便捷，但这些新闻仓库却让人感到不人性化。因而另一种搜索网站诞生了，它提供精选的新闻及评论。其中一些兼收并蓄，像每日野兽、德拉吉报道这样的精品搜索网站开创者。其他的则更专门化，如德国文化网站—Perlentaucher。这些网站中最成功的同时也是那些最近想尝试自己创立网站的失业记者们的范例的网站，当属《哈分特邮报》。

正如大家所知的，《哈分特邮报》只有四个记者，总共职员也只有约 60 人。那里大部分的新闻都是二手的，但它以拥有约 3 000 名无需支付佣金的博主（大多是左翼的）。这个网站感觉上是大学公共休息室和比弗利山酒店的混合体（人们对《哈分特邮报》的看法，很大程度上决定于他们是否认为此视角有吸引力）。《哈分特邮报》的经营者 Arianna Huffington，称其为"围绕新闻的社区"。

老式新闻的从业者越来越抱怨搜索网站是"寄生虫"，靠他们的劳动牟利。某种意义上来说，他们是寄生虫，但寄生虫也可以是有用的。由于现在新闻的质量得不到保证，所以对于新闻故事的筛选变得愈加至关重要。而搜索网站可以带领读者，从而带领广告到达拥有第一手新闻资料的网站。另一家市场研究公司 Hitwise 估计，三月份中，22% 对新闻网站的访问来自于像谷歌这样的搜索引擎，而 21% 来自于其他新闻站点。

搜索网站的兴起揭露了新闻产业的一个令人苦恼的事实。从前，新闻记者们遵循着一套标准的新闻报道程序：即记者撰写一篇新闻稿后，先发表在广播或报刊上，然后再独家刊登到一个网站上。如今，这套系统变得效率低下。在更广泛地散布新闻的边际成本接近于零，但从中产生的边际收益是可观的。

传播新闻产生的潜在利润帮助解释为什么一些知名的新闻机构正开始效仿搜索网站。新闻公司开设了一个名为 Fox Nation 的网站，将新闻中与右翼人士的评论混合在一起，意在打造一个保守版的《哈分特邮报》。事实上，《一周》是美英两国新闻出版的伟大成功之一，它就相当于把搜索引擎搬到了报纸上。

层层计费

综合新闻很可能在网络上保持免费。相似新闻故事重复的太多了，人们对挖掘隐私的愿望太过强烈，且搜索网站轻易就可以找出免费的新闻报道。然而已经变得显而易见的是仅靠在线广告不能支撑好的原创新闻了。

直到前一阵，依然有一些纸质新闻报刊的主管认为广告收入会随着他们的观众群的转移，而从纸质报刊转向网络。但从 2008 年二季度开始，网络广告收入开始下降。一些网络广告收入转向了搜索网站，如谷歌，同时，过剩的广告资源也压制了广告价格。这直接导致各位主管们虎视眈眈的将目光投向了少数不惧向读者们收费的网站。

其中之一就是《金融时报》，其规定：想每月阅读三篇以上，需要注册；想每月阅读十篇以上需要缴费。有约 100 万人注册，其中有 10.9 万人缴了费。通过比较宽容地对待偶然阅读《金融时报》的读者，《金融时报》在被其首席执行官 John Ridding 称作是网络"巨型旗舰"的谷歌和雅虎上保留一席之地。而这些可将网络人流带到《金融时报》的网站。注册用户会收到有针对性的广告，做这种广告的利润更大。这是一种融合订阅模式和由广告支撑的模式的尝试。

《华尔街日报》采用高明的方式与《金融时报》殊途同归。与从特定类型读者群收费的方式不同的是，《华尔街日报》采用从特定类型新闻内容收费的方式。本周早些时候，关于猪流感的新闻、对最新的《星际

《旅行》电影的点评及即将削减汽车销售商的报道都是免费获取的。但有些报道是要收费的,比如说:关于Cigna集团的养老金计划,洛克希德·马丁的季度游说演讲花销和对一灌装公司的诉讼案,称其董事会不作为的相关报道。简言之,有趣的文章都是免费的,枯燥、晦涩的新闻需要出钱才能看。

这样做的思路是具有广泛吸引力的文章可以吸引读者进站浏览,这样网站就可以通过广告或者《华尔街日报》中更多的可供选择的新闻故事来吸引读者。大部分的人都对费城一家人寿保险公司的养老金问题不关心。但那些少数对此非常感兴趣的人则是对此非常感兴趣,以至于他们就为这篇新闻支付一个月的订阅费。而那些订阅了网上新闻报的人们,可能又会被说服继续花钱看更有价值的新闻。《华尔街日报》也正在探索针对单篇文章的"微型付费"模式。

看起来不仅只有金融类新闻人们才愿意付费阅览。ESPN,一个有线体育频道,在其官网上也建立了几道收费关卡。他们保护起那些只有最狂热的体育迷才想去了解的新闻,遵循着《华尔街日报》的格言:读者愿意付费阅览的意愿与这篇文章的潜在读者群大小成反比关系。有利可图的新闻细分市场的数量可能会随着竞争对手关闭办事处或是彻底倒闭而增加。

相对于新科技而言,免费和付费阅读方式的有机结合或许是报纸杂志更好的出路。而对于被一些人誉为潜在的拯救者的便携新闻浏览器—Kindle DX,也只能帮忙做到从网络(网上的新闻大部分是免费的)吸引读者的程度。如今,便携式阅读器似乎正在做着其他的事。Outsell研究公司的肯博士认为Kindle对那些习惯于看纸质报纸杂志,在婴儿潮时期出生的人来说,较有吸引力。年轻一代更偏爱用iPhone和搜索网站获取新闻信息。

最高评论

如今的有线电视业,另一种细分产品正大把捞钱。右翼的福克斯新闻频道已成为至今最受欢迎的新闻的专业提供者。这并不奇怪。该电台的新闻节目和舆论节目质量都非常之高,而共和党的衰落使得保守人士开始寻求发表自己的言论。更令人吃惊的是,在黄金时段,左翼的MSNBC吸引的年龄在25—54岁之间的观众,竟超过了远比其声名显赫的CNN。

福克斯及MSNBC公司提供了各种混杂的新闻、专访及偶尔的热烈评论。其目的在于使读者在一天里获取的各种各样杂乱的信息变得完善并有意义。读者知道他们正得到什么;的确,他们评价说有线电视节目比报纸更可靠。摒弃了党派之间的相互指责,MSNBC的首席执行官格里芬先生道出了这个有线电视新闻产业共同的口号:"我们目的不是为了迎合所有人。"

Hot talk在现阶段可能会备受关注因为如今美国正处政治两极化的状态。大选之夜,更沉稳的CNN赢得了有线电视的最高收视率,并很可能在2012年再次成为赢家。然而,正如新闻产业中很多情况一样,回归常态是不太可能发生的。新闻市场很可能持续不稳定,政治,经济,甚至于体育等不同的领域的"收视之冠"也将不尽相同。

就以美国一家名为Real Clear Politics的政治新闻网为例,它集合各种新闻、评论以及民意调查。在去年总统竞举中,它成为了重要的新闻发布站点。根据comScore公司的数据显示:最高峰时,即就在大选前,它的月净访问量达到了140万人次。那之后它的访问量一下子下跌了75%,这样的起伏波动,对于像报纸、杂志及电视节目这样高固定成本的媒介而言,是毁灭性的。

不久以前,新闻业曾是个高利润率的行业。然而为了生存,新闻不能总处于高赢利状态。即使是在利润下降的状态,主流的报纸依然可以吸引到那些寻求政治或经济影响力的富人们,以及那些坚信无论如何总是有钱可赚的人。鲁伯特·默多克对油印墨水的喜爱常常令华尔街分析师们感到不解。就在上个月,传媒大亨大卫·格芬被报道试图购买《纽约时报》母公司的一部分股份。

不太知名的新闻机构也有贵人相助。圣地亚哥的一家小型的、不完整的新闻网站一开始大部分的赞助都来自于当地一位商人。《圣地亚哥之声》关注于水资源,犯罪及医疗保健等的事实真相问题,这些问题在当地报纸上曾是被大量报道的。

数码相机的广泛流传也使普通群众能直接制作新闻图片和报道。这样的活动最先是由新闻巨头如CNN发起的,他们视群众记者为内容和浏览量的一种资源。加拿大一家大型新闻采集公司NowPublic的总裁莱昂纳多·布罗迪笑称,他相信总有一天,业余新闻工作者将把专业记者们从纷杂的报道中解救出来,而专注于新闻分析工作。

如今对记者们来说,相比群众,他们更感到了来自政府的竞争。在英国,当地政府创办了简报,其中也包括了广告。现任美国的总统,经证明,也是一位格外多产的群众记者,那些在去年向奥巴马竞选团队提供邮箱的人们,至今还能不时收到他们发送的公函。而白宫在 YouTube 上面上传的视频比新闻网制作的视频还要精良。

昔日曾经辉煌的报纸行业及新闻节目如今的衰落并非不用付出代价的。这衰落意味着一种公民的识别力的终结。这种识别力曾是构建在对于什么是重要的和什么是不重要的问题的广泛的一致的基础上的。

Exercises

Ⅰ. **Answer the following questions.**

1. They are ABC, CBS and NBC.

2. The Wal-Marts of the news world are online portals like Yahoo! and Google News. They make money by funnelling readers past advertisements, which may be tailored to their presumed interests. Their main drawback is being impersonal.

3. The website feels like a cross between a university common room and a Beverly Hills restaurant. It is a "community around news".

4. Aggregators are useful in that they do the increasingly vital job of sifting news stories, and they drive readers, hence advertising, to original-news websites.

5. The Financial Times charges certain types of user, whereas the Wall Street Journal charges for certain types of news.

Ⅱ. **Paraphrase the difficult sentences or language points**

1. be exempted from

2. help yourself to as much food as you wish to eat

3. pass through

4. a mixture of

5. It is partly right to say they are parasites.

6. searching for and discovering

7. Be gentle on

8. making a lot of money

9. everything that every person wants

10. baron

Ⅲ. **Choose the word or phrase that best explains the meaning of the underlined part from the text.**

1. C   2. B   3. A   4. C   5. C   6. B   7. B   8. A   9. C   10. C

Ⅳ. **Choose the best phrase or expression in the text from the following list to fit in each of the following blanks. Change the word form where necessary.**

1. so much so that   2. nitty-gritty   3. in case   4. clean up   5. in effect   6. a cross between   7. in a sense   8. seeking a voice   9. adhere to   10. plod through

Ⅴ. **Translate the following into English.**

1. Perhaps the surest sign that newspapers are doomed is that politicians, so often their targets, are beginning to feel sorry for them.

2. Technology has enabled well-informed people to become even better informed but has not broadened the audience for news.

3. Robert Thomson, editor-in-chief of the Wall Street Journal, says many have come to view online news as "an all-you-can-eat buffet for which you pay a cable company the only charge."

4. The most successful of the lot, and the template for many newly unemployed journalists who have tried to launch websites of their own, is the Huffington Post.

5. As the quality of journalism becomes more erratic, the job of sifting stories is increasingly vital.

6. One is the Financial Times (part-owner of The Economist) which demands registration of anybody wishing to view more than three articles per month and payment from anybody wanting to see more than ten.

7. Newspapers and magazines are more likely to be rescued by a careful combination of free and paid-for content than by new technology.

8. Portable news readers such as the Kindle DX, which some have hailed as potential saviours, will help only to the extent that they lure readers from the web, where news is mostly free.

9. For newspapers, magazines and television programmes, with their high fixed costs, such fluctuations would be ruinous.

10. Leonard Brody, the head of NowPublic, a large Canadian news-gatherer, believes that amateurs will eventually liberate journalists from the tedious business of reporting, leaving them free to concentrate on analysis.

Ⅵ. Translate the following into Chinese.

1. 无论是过去的广播电台,还是后来的网络开拓者像 AOL.com 和 MSN.com,都效法过这种捆绑式新闻包。这种新闻包如同一个老式的百货商场一样运作。它在单个地点提供许多精选的质量有保证的有用信息。而如今,捆绑式新闻包所处的命运也正如这种老式的百货商场:部分顾客被折扣连锁店所吸引,而另外一些顾客则转向了精品店。

2. 看起来不仅只有金融类新闻人们才愿意付费阅览。ESPN,一个有线体育频道,在其官网上也建立了几道收费关卡。他们保护起那些只有最狂热的体育迷才想去了解的新闻,遵循着《华尔街日报》的格言:读者愿意付费阅览的意愿与这篇文章的潜在读者群大小成反比关系。有利可图的新闻细分市场的数量可能会随着竞争对手关闭办事处或是彻底倒闭而增加。

Ⅶ. Answer the following questions.

1. Different reactions from her friends and those online strangers towards a blog entry about a banjo which was supposed to be a joke.

2. Like Ms Trott, Vox is unpretentious and accessible. Also like Ms Trott, Vox celebrates the frivolous and mundane.

3. It is intimate. For every item on Vox—a text paragraph, a photo, a link—bloggers can determine if it is to be public or private and, if it is private, exactly who can see it.

4. Something to have because it is fashionable, without caring much about it. This metaphor is used to show the contrast between different attitudes held by large internet companies and Ms Trott and her husband.

Key to Unit Nine

课文参考译文

经济低谷,激发你的客户

毫无疑问,这是个商业客户销售的艰难时期:预算准备金没有了。更糟糕的是,你的客户关系也失去了以往的作用。由于可支配的资金减少，客户方的采购提案要由更高的人员来批准，你之前打交道的那些经理们不再是决策者。

自 2001 年网络泡沫破灭以来，我们做了大量的研究和咨询工作，发现了有些公司如何能在经济衰退中存活下来甚至从中赢利的秘密。面对客户程式化的回答"对不起，我们没有这方面的预算"，有些销售商，通过运用我们所称的激发式销售方法，说服客户相信他们提供的解决方案不仅好，而且必不可少。

激发式销售超越了传统的咨询式或解决方案式销售，后两种销售方法是通过销售商的销售团队与客户方经理的问答式对话，弄清客户目前所关心的问题；同时，激发式销售也与现在最常用的产品式销售大为不同，后者只是泛泛介绍产品的特性、功能和效果。激发式销售帮助客户从一个崭新的视角去认识它所面临的竞争挑战，使解决具体的棘手问题显得十分紧迫。对于许多发现传统销售方式已失灵的公司来说，激发式销售的时代已经到来。

学会激发式销售

激发式销售背后的理念是：即使客户自由支配的资金似乎已经用完，销售商也应该帮助客户找到投资资金。

激发式销售的最佳方式是：销售商首先确定在目前的商业环境下哪个流程对客户至为重要，接着就该流程如何被破坏以及它所意味的代价形成令人信服的观点，然后将这一问题与自己提供的解决方案联系起来。这种方法对客户的思维具有挑战性：它没有迎合客户对自身前景的普遍看法，而是提供了一个崭新的视角。解决方案式销售的销售人员会聆听客户清晰阐述的"痛处"，但是激发式销售是在指出客户正在经受但还未言明的问题时最有效的。

当然，要提出一个能让潜在客户觉得新颖独到而又颇有裨益的激发性观点，并非易事。但是这也并非不切实际。在销售产品和提供售后支持的产品过程中，那些曾经成功满足客户需求的销售商已同业内其他公司有过交往，自然会产生不同的视角，来看待客户仅从内部看到的问题。而且，他们也不会像客户公司的经理那样，身陷所在环境而难以对现状提出挑战。在经济普遍动荡时期，人们就更不愿招惹是非。当你的客户公司的职员因为过于担心自己的工作而不能提出任何有创见的或发人深省的想法时，销售商提供的新视角就像呼吸所需的新鲜空气一样更容易被理解和接受。

要开始激发式销售时，你必须做好三件事：一是确定一个能够引起目标客户前台执行主管高度共鸣的问题；二是就该问题形成一个激发性观点；三是向客户公司中能够采取预期行动的决策者阐述这一观点。下面我们来分别解释上述每个步骤。

确定关键问题　对于任何一个潜在客户或现有客户，你的销售和营销团队都可以就有关整个行业和某一公司的问题，列出一份长长的清单，而单子上的问题都可以用更好的方式来解决。关键是要找出影响最深的问题，这一问题即使在经济衰退时期也必须设法筹集资金解决。你可以从以下三个方面来思考问题：

- 这个问题是否符合让客户公司 CEO"彻夜难眠"的标准？
- 这个问题在现有的流程、系统或服务中是否被疏忽、置之不理或者没有有效解决？
- 对于这一问题，你是不是个可靠的建议人？

开始寻找这类关键问题的一个非常好的方法是注意证券分析师最近对目标公司或者其所在的整个行业的观察分析。当分析师指出某个问题时，你可以推测目标公司的投资者正向管理层施压以解决这个问题，那么他们就会听取解决这个问题的提议。

形成激发性观点　在确定了深度关切的问题之后，你需要就这个问题给出独创性的观点。否则，没有哪位高管会抽时间给你。这似乎取决于你头脑中不可预知也无法控制的灵光一现。但实际上，这一观点是可以采取系统的办法来形成的。

首先，重新与客户、合伙人和行业分析师一起针对整个行业面临的挑战建立全面理解。通过这项工作，得出一个激发性观点，以帮助客户认识到这一问题，并将他们自身的处境与同行进行比较，提高整个高管层对该问题紧迫性的认识。最后，做出一个多期计划，像交通地图一样说明他们如何能采用你的方法来解决问题。

向客户阐述你的观点　宣传这些精明的想法必须适当。我们提出"激发"一词，并不意味着鼓励对客户不尊重的行为。你的陈述要明确挑战，并表明你知道客户公司针对这一问题目前采取的办法。你的目的是打破高管的心理平衡，使他认识到现状难以维持，但又不让他产生防卫心理。你要给出充分的论据，坦率地指出具体问题和解决办法，以使焦点始终放在高管所负责的经营业绩上。

激发式销售依靠的是你与你精心选择的客户公司某位业务高管之间的一次重要会谈，在会谈中你要清晰地阐述你的观点。不要忘记事先演练一下如何向这位高管阐述观点，并且预测会谈可能朝哪些方向发展。激发式销售既要保持问题的激发性，又要表现出对客户解决这些问题时所遇到的挑战的同情，所以销售商培训课程上的模拟推销的一个关键目标就是在这二者之间找到合适的平衡点。销售团队还可以借客户公司内级别较低的支持者或者是对客户公司十分熟悉的第三方，来尝试激发式销售。如果你有这样的机会，抓住它；然后，你的支持者有能力会为你和高管人员的会谈做好安排，或者必要时的介绍。考虑到风险和收益，为这类会谈的演练投入时间和精力是非常值得的。在你争取到的与客户方高管会谈的有限时间里，你需要阐明自己对相关问题的看法，了解高管对该问题紧迫性的认识，解释这些和你们公司业务的关系，并获准进行诊断性研究。

证明你的观点

由于诊断性研究对客户是有价值的，销售商可以选择对此收费。诊断性研究承诺提供有价值的信息——一份关于客户公司弱点和能用于处理相关问题的资源的报告，没有任何附带条件。

对你来说，诊断性研究的价值，已远远超出了区区数小时收费的价值。它表明客户公司需要并且欢迎你与其关键人员进行一系列访谈，并在客户公司的帮助下获取重要数据。当然，该研究的目标是进行的深入分析，为你的提议提供所需的数据支持。如果你决心赢得后续业务，你就应该利用诊断性研究，与客户公司采购流程中的每一位重要人员建立联系；弄清谁是你的关键支持者，谁可能会诬蔑你的观点；找出任何必须战胜的竞争对手，并掌握客户公司内部可能与你的观点不相融或者相对抗的任何动向。

如果要成功，你就需要依靠你与客户公司一线人员交谈得来的明白无疑的事实，投入大量精力改变现状，并获得客户公司某位高管的全力支持。

根据诊断性研究可分三个阶段制订销售提案。第一阶段：你们公司马上能够提供什么——通常主要是一些服务；第二阶段：你们公司在当年能够提供什么——通常是在现有产品或服务的基础上为客户量身定制的解决方案；第三阶段：为了完全解决问题，客户目前或今后一段时间内其他所有需要。

不要急切地提交提案。只要你仍然在设计解决方案，你就有权回到客户公司获取更多信息——而这每一次接触都为你提供了更多销售的机会。设法推迟提交建议，直到你有信心你已经赢得了交易。

找对人

到目前位为止，我们的讨论中反复提到客户公司的业务高管。只有客户公司中的资源所有者——一般是指对公司盈亏负责的高管——才能重新分配资源，为购买销售商的产品或服务设立预算。但是这类高管通常有精心设计的防护机制来避开推销。

首先，你要确定与某个级别合适的高管建立联系，找到你们双方都熟识的某个人，这人可能会为你亲自引荐。一旦你把希望向高管陈述的激发性观点成功地推销给了引荐人，你就可以要求他把你介绍给高管，并帮你安排一次会面。

个人引荐是每个优秀的销售人员所惯用的手段，尤其是在咨询业。但是在预算冻结期，再没有其他任何一种潜在客户开发方式值得这样花时间。反正，你不能让你的销售人员去追寻没什么质量的线索和追逐无法达成的交易。

接触高层购买者可通过为高管人员设计的研讨会，或是想方设法地寻找引荐人等途径。当然，你们公司也可以借助于一些社交网络工具，如 LinkedIn 和 Facebook 以类似方式利用你们所有的职业关系。有些公司将会发现，建立专有平台也是值得的。

你的销售团队能否适应？

当你的公司转为激发式销售时，销售周期的新节奏将令经验丰富的销售人员感到意外甚至挫败。过去，销售通常从潜在客户开发方式开始寻找线索，这些线索看上去很有前景。不幸的是，在销售团队与所有这些潜在客户会谈、寻找他们的"痛处"、证明其所提方案的技术可行性、并最终立项和拟订合同的这一过程中，销售流程很快就失去了前进的动力。整个销售周期特别会在中间阶段陷入僵局，因为一般在销售商进行很多证明之后，其商业提案才会被考虑。

激发式销售从一开始意图就更为明确。在找到机会后，销售和营销经理会深入研究目标客户的具体情况和其所在整个行业的总体状况，对要解决的关键问题提出假设，并计划如何与合适的高管建立联系。然而，一旦客户公司高管意识到存在这样一个问题和解决这一问题的必要性，销售过程就会加速。如果诊断性研究得出了预期的结果，而且销售商又能证明自己有能力解决问题，双方就可将重点放在实施工作上，评估所提方案的技术可行性、所需资源以及所要达到的结果。与大多数解决方案式销售形成鲜明对比的是，这一过程在每个阶段都会聚集新动力，而不是失去动力。

实际上，激发式销售方法正是很多公司对销售商最为看重的东西。在经济困难时期，预算削减已是基准，客户希望尽可能减少采购。当客户在担忧如何解决让他们最头疼的问题时，对有哪些可以利用的大好机会之类的各种信息，他们当然置若罔闻，而如果你给出一个激发式观点，你就能够让客户产生倾听的意愿，然后利用诊断性研究，将谈话转化为资金分配的重新排序。

从现在起，你们公司的每一次销售拜访是否都应该采用激发法？可能不必。激发式销售周期是资源密集型的，当某个重大商机很可能不保时，此种方法最有效。在经济繁荣期，激发式销售并不是获取订单最快或者最直接的方法。但是在经济低迷时期，面对最重要的现有和潜在客户，这种方法会让你的企业生存下来。

Exercises

Ⅰ. Answer the following questions.

1. Provocation-based selling is an approach to create room in a customer's budget for what you sell by developing a provocative point of view on a critical issue and lodging it with a line executive in your client's organization. To reach that senior buyer, scrap traditional lead generation methods and focus on referrals-based marketing.

2. **Solution Selling**：Competes for vendor preference within an existing budget；Aligns with the prevailing point of view；Addresses acknowledged pain points；Targets tactical problems；Begins with technical proof and then builds a business case；Starts as an IT or line-of-business dialogue；Asks questions to identify needs；Responds to issues described by the client.

   Provocation-Based Selling：Compels project investment outside an existing budget；Challenges the prevailing point of view；Addresses unacknowledged angst；Targets strategic problems；Begins with the business case and then provides technical proof；Starts as an executive-level dialogue；Uses an insightful hypothesis to provoke a response；Is proactive and leading, forcing issues out.

3. Developing a provocative point of view is not mysterious or reliant on serendipity. It can be approached methodically by following these steps：

   1. Identify a problem that has proved intractable to date.

   2. Use research and brainstorming to create a new lens for that problem. Your provocation will convey the message "You are thinking X, but you should be thinking Y."

   3. Articulate how this disruptive insight, and whatever novel approach you may have developed, will effectively solve the problem.

4. The value of the diagnostic study does not rest on the amount of money charged for it. The diagnostic study permits you access to important data with the customer's help and facts from people in the

trenches, which support your proposal with in-depth analysis. Meanwhile, it provides you opportunities to establish relationships with every major constituency, to discover their attitudes towards the issue you identify, and to uncover any competitors you must outshine. In brief, the diagnostic study is important for you to construct the sales proposal and win the follow-up business.

5. By abandoning traditional forms of lead generation, the provocation-based approach begins with a deliberately identified issue; then vendors develop a hypothesis about its solution and manage to gain access to customer's senior decision maker by referral-based marketing. Once the decision maker has acknowledged the problem and the need to fix it, the process speeds up. And at each phase the process gains momentum to proceed.

II. Paraphrase the difficult sentences or language points.

1. Because your customer's budget has been severely cut down, it is executives in higher positions in the client's organization who consider your sales proposals, and the managers you have dealt with in the past do not have the right any longer to make decisions on whether to buy your offerings or not.

2. This is the best way to conduct provocation-based selling.

3. Of course, it is difficult to come up with a challenging or disruptive point of view which your potential customer will consider as novel and helpful to their business.

4. When staff in your client's company are very worried about losing their jobs, they couldn't provide any novel ideas arousing deep thinking. In this case, your provocative point of view, like fresh air people need most, is easier to be understood and accepted.

5. …and present the provocative point of view to a senior executive who can make decisions to take actions you anticipate.

6. Analyze and evaluate any issue you consider by asking the following three groups of questions:

7. Would the issue you consider be critical and hard to handle so that the CEO of the company cannot fall asleep at night. Or does this problem seriously jeopardize the organization's ability to compete?

8. The aim is to break the executive's mental balance—and shake the ground for the present situation—without making him feel being attacked and defend against you.

9. Judging from the big money the meeting with the executive might bring to you, it is worth your efforts and time to rehearse and practice meetings like this before the real one comes.

10. If you have developed a provocative point of view, you can make the customer willing to listen to you. Then fully use your diagnostic study to realize the reallocation of budgets, thus change the provocation into a sale.

III. Choose the word or phrase that best explains the meaning of the underlined part from the text.

1. C   2. B   3. A   4. C   5. A   6. A   7. C   8. B   9. C   10. C

IV. Choose the best phrase or expression in the text from the following list to fit in each of the following blanks. Change the word form where necessary.

1. make waves   2. on the defensive   3. in a new light   4. on the part of   5. resign herself to   6. be equipped to   7. go around   8. setting the scene   9. committed to   10. put on the table

VI. Translate the following sentences into English.

1. A tiger team, including managers from each area of the enterprise, should be set up to address the issue.

2. The messages he pried out of the company's competitor fell on deaf ears.

3. The company encouraged its employees to make some proposals that would strike the board as original instead of aligning with their points of view.

4. Computer Network helps marketers develop messaging strategies and advertising programs that resonate

with their target customers.

5. We reserve the right to lodge a claim against you for damage in transit.

6. Developing a provocative point of view cannot solely depend on a flash of brilliance. In fact, it can be approached methodically by combing and analyzing the challenges the industry is facing.

7. In the downtown when it is tough to be selling to business customers, it is important to construct an outstanding sales proposal which is based on the facts provided by people in the trenches and underpinned by in-depth analyses.

8. Indeed, marketers have intuitively known for some time that certain customers outshine others in spreading promotional buzz about products and fads.

9. Friendly persuasion is the stock-in-trade of every salesman. However, many companies have defense mechanisms to shield them from sales pitches.

10. With limited budgets, senior executives in the company were sold on the solution plan with no strings attached and agreed to entertain it.

VI. Translate the following into Chinese.

1. 而且,他们也不会像客户公司的经理那样,身陷所在环境而难以对现状提出挑战。在经济普遍动荡时期,人们就更不愿招惹是非。当你的客户公司的职员因为过于担心自己的工作而不能提出任何有创见的或发人深省的想法时,销售商提供的新视角就像呼吸所需的新鲜空气一样更容易被理解和接受。

2. 如果你有这样的机会,抓住它;然后,你的支持者有能力会为你和高管的会谈作好安排——或者必要时为你做介绍。考虑到风险和收益,为这类会谈的演练投入时间和精力是非常值得的。在你争得的与高管会谈的有限时间里,你需要明确阐述你对问题的看法,了解高管对该问题的紧迫性的认识,解释这些和你公司业务的关系,并获准进行诊断性研究。

VII. Answer the following questions.

1. Four years ago Disney was in turmoil, but today it is enjoying a remarkable and profitable run of hit TV programmes and films with its strong creative momentum.

2. It is said by many that Mr Iger's management style has unlocked Disney's creativity and is better suited to the art of media synergy. But there is a different voice that more time is needed to make judgments on Bob Iger's cautious, centralized and consensual management style.

3. The Magic of Disney is the combination of creative momentum and media synergy in the new management style.

4. Despite the impact of the recession on the firm, Disney is optimistic about their future because of its creative momentum and proven ability to extract value from its hits.

Key to Unit Ten

课文参考译文

创始人的两难选择

每个准备创业的人都希望自己成为比尔·盖茨(Bill Gates)、菲尔·奈特(Phil Knight)或者安妮塔·罗迪克(Anita Roddick)。他们每个人都曾创建一家大公司并领导多年。不过,既是创始人又是CEO的成功者是凤毛麟角的。当我对20世纪90年代末和21世纪初涌现的212家美国新建企业进行分析研究时发现,到公司满四年时,只有40%的创业者还在CEO的位置上;我们记得在美国企业史上确实出了少数几个创业CEO,但他们都是例外。

然而,创始人并没有轻易放弃手中的权力。当投资者坚持要创始人交权时,大多数创始人都感到非常震惊。他们往往是以一种不愉快的方式被赶出办公室的,而且远远早于他们打算卸任的时间。事实上,创始人处理第一次权力交接的方式既能成就也能毁掉年轻的企业。

如果创始人一开始就能诚实面对自己创业的动机,那么权力交接就会相对顺畅。你也许会说,这还用问吗? 他们创业不就是为了赚钱吗? 是的,他们确实想赚钱。但是作为一个群体,创业者赚的钱和他们如果当员工赚的钱一样多。而且根据我的经验,创始人常常会做出一些同财富最大化原则相冲突的决定。

其中的原因不难推测,除了想赚钱,创业者肯定还有其他创业动机,那就是创建和领导一家企业的强烈欲望。令人惊讶的是,在赚钱和掌权之间,对其中一面的极度追求一定会妨碍另一方面的成就。创业者每走一步都面临挣钱和掌管企业之间的选择。没有搞清楚哪一个对他们来说更重要的创业者,最终常常是既无钱也无权。

创始人的内心世界

创始人通常相信只有他们自己才能带领新建企业走向成功。这种观点有些道理。最初企业只是创始人头脑中的一个想法。创始人洞悉市场机遇,知道如何用利用机遇打造新产品、服务以及商业模式,也清楚谁是潜在的客户。从一开始员工、客户和商业伙伴就把新建企业与创始人等同起来,而创始人也为自己的创始人加 CEO 身份倍感自豪。

新建企业的工作通常是创业者最爱的工作。他们把企业看成自己情感的附属,甚至不知不觉地使用"我的孩子"等父母的语言来称呼自己的企业。创业者给自己支付相对较低的薪水,就是这种情感的证明。即使在背景相当的情况下,创始人现金报酬也比类似岗位的非创业人员低20%。即使把每个人持有的股权价值考虑进去,情况也是如此。

许多创业者对公司的前途过于自信,而对他们未来可能面临的问题又非常天真。例如,1988年的一项研究中3 000名创业者对"您的公司成功的几率有多少?"这一问题的回答显示,有80%的受访者认定自己的成功率至少在70%,有三分之一的人称自己的成功率是100%。创始人的感情投入、超级自信和超级乐观也许是创造和管理新企业的必备条件,但这些情感因素日后会给企业造成问题。

成长的烦恼

创始人最终会认识到单凭自身财力、感染力和满腔激情还不能充分利用眼前的机遇。于是他们邀请亲戚朋友、天使投资人或风险投资公司来投资。为此,他们付出了沉重代价:通常他们不得不放弃对企业的总控制权。

一旦创始人不再掌控董事会,他们的 CEO 工作也就岌岌可危了。假若创始人当 CEO 的业绩不佳,董事会显然就要请他让位。当然,即使创始人做得很差,董事会要说服他们把自己的"孩子"送给他人抚养也是非常艰难的。奇怪的是,当创始人有业绩时,变更高层领导的需求却更加强烈。下面我来解释原因。

任何新企业的首要任务都是开发产品或服务。许多创始人认为,如果他们成功地领导公司完成了首项产品或服务的研发,那就充分证明自己拥有杰出的管理才能。他们觉得,投资者没有理由抱怨,并应该继续支持自己。

成功让创始人更难意识到,当他们在庆祝首批产品装船时,这其实是标志着一个时代的结束。从那一刻起,创业者将面临一系列不同以往的业务挑战。创始人必须建立企业大批量产品的营销和销售能力,并能为顾客提供售后服务。公司的财务会变得更加复杂,而 CEO 也要依靠财务高管和会计师来进行财务管理。公司的组织架构需要更加完善,CEO 必须创立正式的流程、形成专业化的职位,并组建管理层。在这个阶段,CEO 急需大幅度拓展自己的各种技能,而这些通常超出了创始人的能力范围。

因此,创业 CEO 越早领导公司发展到需要外部资金和新管理技能这个点,创始人就会越快失去管理控制权。成功之后,创始人不再那么适合领导公司,公司的权力结构也发生了变化,所以让他们更容易受到攻击。"

投资者在准备投资之前,会对创业者施加最大的影响,他们通常利用这个时机迫使创始人下台。《私募股权周刊》(Private Equity Week)最近的一篇报道清楚地说明了这一动态:"加州红杉市(Redwood City)的 Seven Networks Inc. 移动电子邮件公司已募集4 200万美元新的风险资金而其他有关 Seven 公司的新闻则称,该公司已任命 Onebox.com 前 CEO 洛斯·鲍特(Russ Bott)担任期新的 CEO。"

决定创始人是否继续掌权的时刻有时来得很快。譬如,一家硅谷的风险投资公司就坚持在首轮融资之后自己必须持任何其投资的新建企业至少 50% 的股权。另外一些投资者为了降低风险，会分期逐次少量出资，但每一轮融资都会改变董事会结构，逐渐威胁到创业者对公司的控制权。在这种情况下，因为创始人总要回来寻求更多的资金，所以投资者会让创业 CEO 领导企业的时日长些，但他们最终会在某个时刻取得对董事会的控制权。

无论是渐进的还是突然的权力变更，通常都会带来狂风暴雨。比如在 2001 年，位于加州的一家互联网电话公司完成了其第一代系统的开发，此时一位外部投资者要求任命新的 CEO，因为他认为公司需要的主管应该具有丰富的经验和知识来管理现有各部门高管、创建公司的未来部门，以及建立把公司各项活动紧密结合起来的新流程。这家公司的创始人最初拒绝接受这种变更，但在投资者花了五个月的时间进行说服，并在其间不断向他施加压力后，最终迫使他退位。

权力变更势不可避免，上面这位创始人也不是唯一与此抗争的人。我研究的创业 CEO 中有五分之四都抗拒这一点。如果变更对董事会而言清楚明白，为什么对创始人就不是如此呢？因为在这个阶段，创始人对公司深厚强烈的情感已经变成负累。已习惯作为公司核心和灵魂的他们，很难接受较为次要的角色，而他们的抵抗会使得年轻公司内的权力交接满是创伤。

抉择时刻

随着新建企业成长，创业者会面临一个两难选择，而很多人开始时并未意识到这一点。一方面，他们不得不募集资源以抓住眼前的机遇。如果他们选对了投资者，公司的财务收益将大幅飙升。另一方面，为了吸引投资者和高级管理人才，创业者不得不放弃大部分决策控制权。

这种基本矛盾造成了创始人对当"富翁"还是当"国王"的权衡。选择当"富翁"，可以让公司更有价值，但是创始人会靠边站，失去 CEO 职位和主要决策权；选择当"国王"，创始人可以保留决策控制权，继续做 CEO 和掌控董事会，但这往往会造成公司价值较低。对于创始人而言，选择当"富翁"不一定比选择当"国王"好，反之亦然。重要的是，他们的每个决策是否很好地符合开创公司的初衷。

以 Ockham 技术公司的共同创始人兼 CEO 吉姆·崔恩迪弗洛(Jim Triandiflou)为例，他在 2000 年意识到他必须吸引投资才能继续经营。他认为如果能引进一家知名的风险投资公司而并非一名没有经验的天使投资人，Ockham 会变得更强大。在多次深刻的自省之后，他决定冒次险，把部分股权出售给风险投资公司。最终他放弃了董事会的控制权，但作为回报，他获得了资源与专业技能，帮助公司价值成倍增长。

另一方面，也有些创始人选择自力更生以保持自己的控制权。Room & Board 的创始人约翰·加伯特(John Gabbert)是明尼阿波利斯一家成功的家具零售商，他已经开设了九家门店，曾多次拒绝能让公司快速发展的外部投资，因为他害怕那会让他失去控制权。只要自己能主宰公司，加伯特显然愿意维持他所做的选择。

大多数创业 CEO 开始时都既想要获得财富，又想要拥有权力。然而，一旦他们明白只能追求其中一项的最大化时，他们就需要弄清楚哪样对自己更重要。他们过去所做的关于共同创始人、员工和投资者的决策，往往能告诉他们哪一个自己真正在意。而一旦弄明白了这一点，他们就会发现权力交接的处理更加容易了。

假如创始人明白自己的创业动机是财富大于权力，他们就会自己引进新的 CEO。此类创始人可能还会与董事会一起探讨自己卸任之后的角色。相反，如果创始人认识到自己创业动机是权力，他们就可能做出决定，以放弃公司价值增长为代价，确保自己能够继续领导企业。他们可能更愿意做唯一的创始人，利用自身资金而不去吸收外来投资，拒绝任何影响自己管理控制权的交易，吸纳那些不会威胁自己对公司掌控权的高管人员。

对公司发展潜力的看法也是影响创始人选择的因素之一。当创始人认为他们的新建公司有潜力成长为极具价值的企业时，他们所做的决定往往不同于他们认为公司没那么大价值时所做的选择。譬如多次创业的埃文·威廉斯(Evan Williams)在 2003 年把自己的 Pyra Labs 出售给谷歌(Google)，但两年后对自己的 Odeo 播客公司他却引入了外部投资，因为他认为他有机会把 Odeo 做得更大。当初，威廉斯迅速交出公司控制权，是为了实现公司的巨大潜力，而他也已改变心意，于 2006 年买回公司，自己再次成为国王。

准备创业的人也可以运用上述思路判断自己应该实践哪种想法。那些渴望权力的人应当把目标限定在自己已经具备所需技能和关系的行业，或者是不需要大量资金的行业。而那些追求财富的创业者应该放开心态，投身需要大量资源的领域。由于他们不介意吸收外来投资，也不介意让高管来管理企业，因此他们能够更快地取得跳跃式发展。

钱与权的选择，让创业者真正理解成功对于他们的意义。对于想要管理自己企业王国的创业者而言，如果丧失了控制权，即便最后多富有，他也不会认为自己成功。相反，对于认识到自己创业的目的是积累财富的创业者而言，就算下台，他也不会觉得自己很失败。一旦创业者弄清了自己为什么创业，他们就必须如中国谚语所言，"在开始时决定好三件事：游戏规则、赌注和离场时间"。

Exercises

I. Answer the following questions.

1. The founder's dilemma is the rich-or-king choice founders have to face in leading their start-ups.
   Most entrepreneurs want to make a lot of money and to have absolute control over their companies, but it's tough to get both, for the maximization of one imperils the other. At every step, entrepreneurs have to make a choice between money and power. If they cannot make it clear which one is more important to them, then they often end up neither rich nor powerful.

2. Entrepreneurs need outside funds and new management skills in leading their start-ups to success, which results in their loss of management control. For both founders who well perform as CEO and those who underperform, leadership transitions are stormy and filled with pressure, and founders' resistance will cause traumas to young companies.

3. Choosing money means that a founder has to give up more equity to attract investors to fully capitalize on the opportunities before them, but s/he may build a more valuable company than one who parts with less equity, and ends up with a more valuable slice, too.
   Choosing power means that a founder is motivated by control rather than wealth and will make decisions that enable them to lead the business at the expense of increasing its value.

4. Founders need to know that they will face a rich-or-king dilemma as their start-ups grow and what each choice mean to them and their companies. There is no a definite better choice between money and power; what matters is how well each decision fits with their reasons for starting the company. If they don't know which is more important to them initially, their past decisions regarding cofounders, hires, and investors will tell them which they truly favor.

5. Success means that entrepreneurs' final achievements are the realization of their initial goals of or the demonstrations of their motivations for getting into business.

II. Paraphrase the difficult sentences or language points.

1. We know that there are a small number of founder-cum-CEOs in the history of American business, but these people are not included in the general statement that it is tough for entrepreneurs to have both power and money.

2. Entrepreneurs start and manage new companies usually out of enthusiasm or interest rather than pursuit for money.

3. It is hard for the board to persuade the founder to relinquish to another outside CEO control over the company s/he starts.

4. But, surprisingly, the need for a new CEO becomes even greater when a founder has successfully led the company's first new offering.

5. The new skills that the CEO needs at this stage are so much different and demanding that they are beyond most founders' abilities to acquire.

6. A recent report in *Private Equity Week* forcefully illustrates this point / the most influence investors wield over entrepreneurs just before they invest in their companies.

7. The moment deciding whether the founder can continue managing the venture sometimes comes very soon.

8. He is not the only one to have resisted and fought against the unavoidable leadership transition.

9. This essential paradox causes the rich-or-king dilemma.

10. Founders who want to make a lot of money should be willing to accept or go on with the kind of ideas or business where large amounts of capital are required.

Ⅲ. Choose the word or phrase that best explains the meaning of the underlined part from the text.

1. B 2. A 3. B 4. C 5. A 6. B 7. B 8. C 9. B 10. A

Ⅳ. Choose the best phrase or expression in the text from the following list to fit in each of the following blanks. Change the word form where necessary.

1. labors of love 2. step down 3. dole out 4. are open to 5. rope in 6. come to grips with

7. spring up 8. capitalize on 9. at the expense of 10. prone to

Ⅴ. Translate the following sentences into English.

1. When raising resources, an enterprise has to relinquish a share of its profits, or control over some decision making, or both.

2. If you are grateful for your job rather than complaining about it, you'll do a better job, be more productive, and probably end up getting a raise anyway.

3. Because of the economic downturn, annual pay increases have been pegged at five percent.

4. Through mutual respect, shared trust and equal opportunities, this company strives to empower each of its employees to stretch their abilities to the fullest in order to build an energetic and creative team.

5. Men in this job are usually related to the contractor, so that they wield virtual power of life and death.

6. In brief, users have to consider the tradeoff between usability and security of products.

7. After days of soul-searching, he had a change of heart and decided to take the risk of selling an equity stake to the venture firm.

8. Why bootstrap? There are a couple of good reasons for a company to consider bootstrapping its market entry.

9. "Online gaming isn't a core area for either AOL or RealNetworks, but neither wanted to cede it to Microsoft," says an analyst at Boston-based CIBC.

10. The founder of this company has delivered results: he has led the company to make the leap in 5 years.

Ⅵ. Translate the following into Chinese.

1. 无论是渐进的还是突然的权力变更,通常都会带来狂风骤雨。比如在 2001 年,位于加州的一家互联网电话公司完成了其第一代系统的开发,此时一位外部投资者要求任命新的 CEO,因为他认为公司需要的主管应该具有丰富的经验和知识来管理现有各部门高管、创建公司的未来部门,以及建立把公司各项活动紧密结合起来的新流程。这家公司的创始人最初拒绝接受这种变更,但在投资者花了五个月的时间进行说服,并在其间不断向他施加压力后,最终迫使他退位。

2. 这种基本矛盾造成了创始人对当"富翁"还是当"国王"的权衡。选择当"富翁",可以让公司更有价值,但是创始人会靠边站,失去 CEO 职位和主要决策权;选择当"国王",创始人可以保留决策控制权,继续做 CEO 和掌控董事会——但这往往会造成公司价值较低。对于创始人而言,选择当"富翁"不一定比选择当"国王"好,反之亦然。重要的是,他们的每个决策是否很好地符合开创公司的初衷。

Ⅶ. Answer the following questions.

1. The triumph of entrepreneurship is driven by profound technological developments—the personal

computer, the mobile phone and the internet. These developments have been reinforced by broad cultural changes that have brought entrepreneurialism into the mainstream.

2. The internet provides a cheap platform for entrepreneurs to build interactive businesses; the development of "cloud computing" is giving small outfits yet more opportunity to enjoy the advantages of big organizations with none of the sunk costs; the mobile phone has allowed entrepreneurs to break into telecoms that used to be one of the world's most regulated markets; and with the combination of touch-screen technology and ever faster wireless networks, the mobile phone is becoming the platform of choice for techno-entrepreneurs. All these have resulted in a cascade of entrepreneurship.

3. There are several reasons for entrepreneurship becoming mainstream. First, a growing number of respectable economists have converted to entrepreneurship and it is an important part of economics. Second, the social contract between big companies and their employees has been broken, so creating one's own business becomes a better choice. Third, so many institutions have given their support for entrepreneurship. Last, the media have also played a part in democratizing entrepreneurship.

4. In order to improve their position in the World Bank's business-friendliness rankings, the world's governments, by enforcing reforms and simplifying procedures of starting new business, are now competing fiercely to see who can create the most pro-business environment.